PUBLIC OPINION POLLING AND
POLITICS IN BRITAIN

DATE DUE

CONTEMPORARY POLITICAL STUDIES SERIES

Series Editor: John Benyon, *Director, Centre for the Study of Public Order, University of Leicester*

A series which provides authoritative yet concise introductory accounts of key topics in contemporary political studies.

PUBLIC OPINION POLLING AND POLITICS IN BRITAIN

DAVID BROUGHTON

School of European Studies,
University of Wales College of Cardiff

PRENTICE HALL
HARVESTER WHEATSHEAF

London New York Toronto Sydney Tokyo Singapore
Madrid Mexico City Munich

First published 1995 by
Harvester Wheatsheaf
Campus 400, Maylands Avenue
Hemel Hempstead
Hertfordshire, HP2 7EZ
A division of
Simon & Schuster International Group

Typeset in 10/12pt Times
by Dorwyn Ltd, Rowlands Castle, Hants.
Printed and bound in Great Britain by
Biddles Ltd, Guildford and King's Lynn

Library of Congress Cataloging in Publication Data

Broughton, David, 1957–
    Public opinion polling and politics in Britain/David Broughton.
    p.   cm. — (Contemporary political studies series)
    Includes bibliographical references and index.
    ISBN 0-13-433921-5(pbk.)
    1. Public opinion—Great Britain. 2. Great Britain—Politics and
government—1979—Public opinion. 3. Public opinion polls.
I. Title. II. Series.
HN400.P8B76 1995
303.3'8'0941—dc20   95-10435
                                                                      CIP

British Library Cataloguing in Publication Data

A catalogue record for this book is available from
the British Library

ISBN 0134 339215

1 2 3 4 5   99 98 97 96 95

CONTENTS

TABLES

PREFACE

A book on the theme of public opinion polling and politics in Britain seems particularly apposite in the wake of the general election of April 1992. Inevitably, the 'failure' of the polls to predict correctly an overall majority of twenty-one seats for the Conservative Party has engendered widespread criticism aimed at the use of polls in general as well as their specific value for observers and practitioners of politics alike.

This criticism derives at least in part from the apparently unstoppable growth in the number of polls commissioned and the obsessive poring over the results in the media to the virtual exclusion of alternative sources of information. Additionally, the increase in the number of polls throughout the 1980s was not accompanied by either a broader or a deeper understanding of what opinion polls can and do achieve and what challenges lie ahead for them in the future. The 'classic' textbook on polling in Britain remains Teer and Spence's *Political Opinion Polls*, published more than twenty years ago in 1973.

This lack of comprehension of the finer nuances of polling has not prevented many newspapers, even the tabloid press, from basing more and more stories on polling data. The range of 'poll stories' is enormous, covering topics such as who are the happiest people in the world (the inhabitants of Guernsey) and survey assessments of the impact of violence on television on the behaviour of ordinary people. A regular obsession of the tabloid press in particular is 'sex surveys', one of which produced the sober conclusion that 'lust is difficult to measure'.

The degree to which polls provide stories which newspapers will print can be exemplified by page 4 of the *Daily Telegraph* on 31 December 1987. On that day, three separate stories were drawn from polls. The first was based on a Gallup poll whose headline read '"Glasnost" failing to make impact on most Russians'. This poll was conducted in thirty-seven countries in all, and countries were classified by the degree to which their populations were 'optimistic' or 'pessimistic' about prospects for 1988 compared to the previous year. It included the first interviews by Gallup in the Soviet Union.

The second story on that day informed readers that 'women in the West are happier than men.' This conclusion was based on a comparative study of the quality of life experienced by people in the United States and the member states of the European Community. Cultural factors were deemed to influence the way that different people in different countries answer when asked about their personal happiness or unhappiness.

The third story told readers that Sir Francis Drake was believed by some children aged between 8 and 14 to be a well-known cricketer. This was part of a poll dealing with basic historical events and people which also examined familiarity with the Spanish Armada and the significance of the date 1066. In the poll, seven out of ten children knew that Guy Fawkes had attempted to blow up the Houses of Parliament. Touchingly, one individual child believed that Guy Fawkes had 'travelled the country organising firework displays'.

The purpose of this book is more specific: namely, to analyse the functions and use of opinion polling and its impact on politics in Britain. In particular, the criticisms of the role and performance of opinion polls during the 1992 general election will be considered.

The first chapter of the book briefly sets out the history of polling in Britain, including the roots of present polling practices and the latest developments in the conduct of polls since 1979. The second chapter discusses the assumptions and theories on which modern polling is based, in particular the dimensions of public opinion and the composition of the 'public' as well as the criticisms of polls as a means of establishing the contours of public opinion.

The methodology of polling is described in chapter 3, comprising the procedures and problems associated with questionnaire

design, sampling, interviewing and data collection, the interpretation of the data and the presentation of the final results. The next
two chapters are linked: chapter 4 looks at the use of polling by
those most closely involved in the conduct of national British politics, namely, the electorate, the government, political parties, the
mass media and pressure groups; chapter 5 looks at the use and
impact of polling both *below* and *above* national level, encompassing by-election polls, constituency polls, polls conducted in marginal seats and local and European election polls.

The ways in which the polls attempt to measure the importance
and impact of issues in British politics are analysed in chapter 6 by
means of considering five specific issues (the European Community, trade unions and industrial relations, immigration and race
relations, the environment and electoral reform). The concluding
chapter of the book brings together the various strands of the
previous chapters in an assessment of the importance of polling in
British politics and its likely role in the future.

The book mainly deals with opinion polls and the problems of
opinion polling in Britain, but in places it also touches on wider
questions of survey research in general. For much of the book, the
problems and challenges facing polls and surveys are similar and in
those sections, polls and surveys are taken together. Distinctions
between polls and surveys are often little more than matters of
greater detail and length in the latter although there is sometimes
more than a whiff of academic snobbery when survey specialists
are commenting upon and using poll data.

There are inevitably a large number of intellectual debts which
have to be acknowledged in a book of this sort. Particular encour-
agement throughout the extended process of writing was received
from John Benyon and David Denver as well as Clare Grist of
Harvester Wheatsheaf, who displayed great patience in the face of
a number of enforced delays in completing the book.

The book has benefited enormously from conversations with
pollsters, party officials and media representatives who often gave
freely of their time as well as providing much information. My
grateful thanks to the following must therefore be expressed:

Pollsters: Bob Wybrow (Gallup), Robert Waller and John
Hanvey (Harris), Nick Sparrow (ICM), Bob Worcester, Brian

Gosschalk and Simon Braunholtz (MORI), Nick Moon (NOP). Bob Wybrow was especially helpful in supplying Gallup data which forms the basis of much of chapter 6 and Bob Worcester allowed me to read and use the private MORI reports to the Labour Party.

Party officials: Rex Osborn (Labour Party), Keith Britto (Conservative Party) and Chris Rennard (Liberal Democrats).

Media: David Cowling (ITN) and David McKie (*Guardian*).

Others who provided help at various stages were Sir Thomas Arnold MP (Conservative), Geoffrey Hiscocks (Beaufort Research, Cardiff), Lesley Sopp (Consumers Association), Colin Francome, Denis Balsom and Ian McAllister.

Karen Owen typed much of the final manuscript with her usual unflappable calmness and care. Great support was received from Professor David Hanley as Head of the School of European Studies at the University of Wales in Cardiff as well as various colleagues in EUROS who either read draft chapters or encouraged me in other ways. In that context, particular thanks are due to Peter Dorey and Mark Donovan.

All of the above are of course absolved from any responsibility for the interpretation that follows. The errors that remain cannot honestly be ascribed to either sampling error or questionnaire design – they are, however, equally inevitable.

This book is dedicated to two people: firstly, to my late father, Jim Broughton, and secondly, to my niece, Ameenah. They have both influenced the writing of this book in very different but equally vital ways.

David Broughton
Cardiff, March 1995

1

The history of opinion polling in Britain

This opening chapter looks at the history of opinion polling in Britain, taking in the principal developments in polling from the 1930s onwards as well as considering the latest changes affecting polling practice, particularly the technological innovations during the 1980s. The chapter is relatively brief because more detailed histories are already easily available, specifically those of Worcester (1983: chapter 4; 1991: parts I and II) and Marsh (1982: chapter 2).

Given the amount of polling overall that is carried out in Britain today, it is perhaps surprising that political polling on a regular basis is only carried out by five main firms (see table 1.1). A very small proportion (3 per cent) of the membership of the Market Research Society of Britain (MRS) conducts political polling at all. Of the 416 members listed in the 1994 *MRS Yearbook*, only twelve firms list political polling as one of their specialisms.

There is a good deal of competition between these five firms for polling business: for example, *The Observer* changed its pollsters from Harris to International Communications and Marketing (ICM) after the 1992 general election. Some of the relationships are also not exclusive, with more than one polling firm being used by the same client: for example, both Gallup and Harris have conducted polls for the Conservative Party. Links between *Telegraph* newspapers and Gallup are the longest standing of the relationships noted in table 1.1.

Table 1.1   The five main political polling firms

Name	Founded	Main clients
Gallup	1937	Daily Telegraph Sunday Telegraph
Harris	1965	Daily Express ITN Conservative Party Financial Times
ICM	1989	The Guardian The Observer
MORI	1969	The Times Sunday Times
NOP	1958	The Independent Independent on Sunday Mail on Sunday Labour Party

All the above firms belong to the Market Research Society and they adhere to the Society's code of conduct. This code includes the need for poll results to be accompanied by a statement about sampling methods, sample size and dates of fieldwork. One of the more difficult parts of the code for pollsters to enforce is the clause dealing with distortion or misrepresentation of the data. The code also contains an agreement that additional information about the poll should be made available to journalists and interested parties in terms of more detail of the sample design, including clustering, response rate, the actual questionnaire used and the method of interview. These aspects of polling practice will be dealt with in more detail in chapter 3 and they are also included in the glossary of technical terms at the end of the book.

As can be seen from table 1.1, all of these firms have long experience of political polling in Britain. Although ICM was only established in 1989, this was a direct result of the closure of Marplan, which was first set up in 1959. Three directors from Marplan with substantial experience of polling were instrumental in founding ICM.

The oldest of the five firms is Gallup (originally the British Institute of Public Opinion), which was established in Britain in 1937 by Henry Durant after the pioneering American firm had been set up by George Gallup two years earlier. 'Modern' political polling in Britain therefore began in the late 1930s but its origins and roots can be traced back even further to the turn of the twentieth century.

The generally acknowledged 'fathers' of social surveys in Britain were philanthropists Charles Booth and Seebohm Rowntree (the 'chocolate sociologists', according to Marsh 1982: 16) with their 'poverty surveys' of London and York respectively. These surveys set out to collect a mass of information about social conditions and circumstances. As such, they were not opinion polls but the methods of social research which both Booth and Rowntree employed were instrumental in establishing the foundations on which polls have subsequently been built and developed.

Booth published the results of his survey in a massive seventeen-volume edition in 1902 in which he depicted the living standards of the working class in London and the character of the work from which they derived their livelihoods. He developed an eight-category classification, four categories above and four below the poverty line. Although the study was largely descriptive rather than analytical, its results drew attention to the extent and the severity of the poverty suffered by the London working class, and as such, it was a major contribution to the study of social conditions.

Rowntree's work on poverty in York began in 1902 and he set out to gather basic information about the earnings, housing and occupations of *all* families in York. He also used interviewers to gather the information directly from the families (Booth had collected his data from School Attendance Officers) and he gave much more thought than Booth to the concept of poverty, making a distinction between 'primary' and 'secondary' poverty. Rowntree's purpose was to define a minimum standard of living (the poverty line) and the distinction between types of poverty was a forerunner of much subsequent conceptual social research.

Further studies of working-class conditions were conducted by A. L. Bowley in Reading, Northampton, Stanley, Warrington and Bolton from 1912 onwards. Bowley used sampling for the first time for his surveys, where only a selection of the possible families were interviewed instead of every family. Bowley was aware of the potential bias in his results through the refusal of some people to take part and his inability to contact some of the families selected for interview (Moser and Kalton 1971: 6–11).

The focus of the early surveys therefore was on working-class life and conditions, specifically aspects such as housing, health, education, unemployment and general living standards. When British Gallup started questioning in 1937, the range of topics widened considerably. Many of the earliest questions and answers have been published (Gallup 1976) and they still make interesting reading. Whilst the potential responses were often limited to 'yes' and 'no', questions on the Spanish Civil War, satisfaction with Neville Chamberlain as prime minister and choosing between fascism and communism were clear antecedents of modern political polling research.

The question testing satisfaction with the prime minister was first asked in October 1938. Chamberlain received an approval rating of 57 per cent satisfaction, a figure calculated by subtracting those dissatisfied from those who were satisfied with his performance. The traditional voting intention question – 'If there were a general election tomorrow, which party would you support?' – was first asked in February 1939. Polls were conducted in six constituencies where by-elections were held during 1939. Gallup predicted the result correctly in five of the six seats. These polls were particularly helpful in establishing the credibility of polling as an alternative to party meetings and pub conversations, which were sometimes regarded as reliable sources of information about the likely outcome of elections.

During the Second World War, Gallup focused mostly on public morale and the acceptance of government schemes, although their political work was still published by the *News Chronicle* (a daily newspaper of the time) with whom they had an exclusive contract. This continued until the demise of the *News Chronicle* in 1960, when Gallup started to work for the *Daily Telegraph* and *Sunday Telegraph*.

The faith of the *News Chronicle* in the value of polling was tested when Gallup data suggested that the Labour Party under Clement Attlee was going to win the 1945 general election. Winston Churchill, after all, had led the country to victory in the Second World War and was a revered world statesman.

In the event, Gallup had *underestimated* the Labour lead by 3.5 per cent (6 per cent as opposed to 9.5 per cent). However, overall, the mean error was only +1.5 per cent. The mean error is the average of the deviations from the Gallup poll compared to the actual result for each party. This represented a very creditable result for the infant polling industry.

The front page of the *News Chronicle* on 4 July 1945 remains a model of how to report poll findings (reproduced in Worcester 1991: 7). The poll putting Labour 6 per cent ahead of the Conservatives is described as being 'interim' and the poll 'does not pretend to foretell the results of the election'. Additionally, it is stated that 'it must be emphasised that it is impossible to base upon these results any forecast as to the distribution of seats in the new House of Commons.'

After the 1945 election, Gallup continued to poll on topics such as attitudes to the National Health Service and independence for India, whilst the scope of the operation was widened even further to satisfy the requirements of journalism by including specific questions on the regular omnibus surveys. Omnibus surveys comprise questions paid for by a variety of different organisations at a cost of a few hundred pounds per question. The answers to each client's particular question or questions are supplied along with the basic demographic data of the sample covering social class, region, gender and age. These surveys soon became the mainstay of Gallup's business.

At the 1950 general election, Gallup correctly predicted a reduced Labour majority. The *Daily Express* poll made its first appearance but, along with a poll in the *Daily Mail*, it predicted the 'wrong' winner. Picking the winner of an election was as important then as it is today in terms of credibility for the polling firm involved. This was certainly the case in 1950 in the immediate wake of the polling fiasco at the 1948 American presidential election.[1]

The 1950s saw the political parties take polling seriously for the first time, although suspicions about its utility were to remain strong amongst senior Labour Party politicians such as Herbert Morrison and Aneurin Bevan. This scepticism was fuelled by technical problems over assessing the likely Liberal Party vote when it was not fighting all the seats and the tendency to complete the polling fieldwork some days before the election actually took place. The perennial problem of what to do with the 'don't knows', undecided voters and 'leaners' (those who incline towards a particular party but are not certain to vote for it) when publishing poll statistics also reared its head. A wider perception of the value of polling was not helped by the reluctance of the newspapers to publish the fieldwork dates or sample sizes of their polls. At the

1959 general election, National Opinion Polls (NOP) entered the fray for the first time with polling work for the *Daily Mail*. During the 1960s, several new polling organisations were founded and television began to take notice. Additionally, the parties began to commission private polling to supplement the data already available in the public domain. Opinion Research Centre (ORC, later Harris) was founded in 1965 and it won the contract to conduct private polling for the Conservative Party. Harris remain the main private pollsters for the Conservatives today. In 1968, Marplan began surveys for *The Times* and *The Guardian*. Another of the main polling firms, Market and Opinion Research International (MORI), was set up in 1969 and it soon became the Labour Party's private pollsters.

There were methodological developments as well. NOP introduced the idea of a panel survey comprising repeated interviews with the same electors. Experiments to assess the relative merits of random and quota sampling were conducted (see chapter 3).

Some hostility was directed at polls as a result of the Liberal victory at the Orpington by-election in March 1962. The publication of a NOP poll ten days before the by-election had indicated the likelihood that the Conservative candidate could be defeated if enough traditional Labour voters voted tactically for the Liberal candidate. After the debacle at Orpington, when the Liberal Eric Lubbock won the seat with 52.9 per cent of the vote, the Conservative Party commissioned NOP to conduct an investigation into what had gone wrong. Dissatisfaction with the Conservative government was seen as being important, more so than any widespread belief that the Liberals had the better policies. This finding and the conclusions of another survey of Conservative 'defectors' was fed into the publicity plans of the party in the period leading up to the next general election (Teer and Spence 1973: 159–61).

The use of polling data at by-elections to enable tactical voting to take place has occurred on a number of occasions since the Orpington by-election, usually to the benefit of the Liberal, Alliance or Liberal Democrat candidate. A more recent example of this phenomenon was the by-election held at Bermondsey in 1983.

The seriousness with which politicians now took poll evidence was also made clear during Prime Minister Harold Wilson's deliberations over when to call a general election in 1966. Alec Douglas-Home's decision to stand down from the Conservative

Party leadership in 1965 may also have been influenced by poll findings, although his electoral defeat in 1964 and his inability to project himself on television might well have been sufficiently serious drawbacks on their own to ensure that his leadership of the Conservative Party was increasingly questioned.

Poll stories came to dominate election campaign reporting and more people read about polls than in the past because the previous insistence on exclusive publication by the clients who had commissioned the poll was dropped. Polls had also received more and more attention because of the seemingly unstoppable growth in the unpopularity of the Labour government between 1966 and 1970 as evidenced by the polls. During this period, the party lost a series of by-elections, and its strength in local government was also savaged, culminating in the loss of control of the Greater London Council in 1967. This was followed by the loss of control in many major cities outside the capital.

In June 1967, the Speaker's Conference on Electoral Law recommended a 72-hour pre-election ban on the publication of poll findings by a nine to five margin. This recommendation was widely derided and not implemented on the grounds that this would deny the voters important information and would not in any event stop the commissioning of polls even if it prevented their publication. In addition, if polls were banned in the days immediately before an election, spurious and rogue polls would be leaked and accorded credibility in the absence of the counterweight of properly conducted polls. Rumours rather than hard evidence would prevail. The implication that voters could not be trusted with the information provided by polls could equally and logically be extended to the idea that they could not be trusted with the vote either.

Another key development was the drawing up by the pollsters of a code of practice which sought to regulate the relationship between the polling firms and their clients, particularly in terms of the publication of the results.

The growing use of polls and developments in the methodology they employed received a considerable setback through the record of the polls at the 1970 general election. Only one firm of the main five (ORC) adjusted its final calculation of the vote shares of the parties for differential turnout (supporters of one party being less inclined to turn out to vote than supporters of another party). This may have contributed to the outcome where ORC alone assessed that the Conservatives would win the election, although ORC also applied the idea of late swing to their figures based on last-minute interviews.

The pollsters needed therefore to explain what had gone wrong in 1970 as they were similarly forced to do after the 1992 election. Late shifts in opinion after fieldwork had stopped and inaccurate sampling were the main suspects but the direct evidence for these explanations was more suggestive than definitive. Other ideas included differential voting by people who refused to answer any questions, organised deception by Conservative voters and manipulation of the data by the polling organisations. In the end, most commentators agreed that a late movement of voters to the Conservatives was the major cause of the inaccuracy of the polls (Hodder-Williams 1970: introduction).

The lessons of the 1970 general election led to a change in the 1974 general election polls. Quota sampling gained the upper hand at the expense of random sampling (see chapter 3). This change was supported when polls using the latter method were the most inaccurate at the February 1974 election. The political parties continued to invest more resources in their own polling operations, with closer analyses of political issues and more detailed examinations of the preferences of 'target' groups of voters – those voters who needed to be won over to ensure electoral victory. Polling now became a permanent feature of the campaign strategies of the major parties. Computers also started to become significant for polling practice, especially in terms of the speed with which the results could be produced. Multivariate models of various voter types or groups which simultaneously took a number of different social characteristics into account could now be developed and tested empirically, then refined and tested again.

The last fifteen years have also been characterised by a number of key developments in political polling in Britain. We will come back to these in more detail in subsequent chapters but we can mention them here initially under two sub-headings: new developments since 1979 and long-standing concerns.

1.1   New developments since 1979

The first new development concerns telephone interviewing and sampling. This has become a more practical option for polling firms recently. It has been made possible by a rapid increase in the degree of 'telephone penetration' of the British electorate. The ability to contact respondents by telephone has been constantly improving. Some estimates suggest that about 90 per cent of the British electorate can now be contacted by telephone. This has made it easier to draw representative samples, but the major difficulty remains how exactly to 'weight' the responses so as to reflect adequately the electorate as a whole, including voters *without* telephones. Improvements have been achieved in this area in the last decade on the basis of 'compositional weighting' derived from measured social characteristics such as class, house tenure and car ownership (Miller 1987).

Telephone sampling can improve efficiency over other sampling methods because of the ability to spread respondents over the whole country without incurring heavy costs. Telephone interviewing allows greater central control of the interviewing process and easier callbacks when the respondents are not initially contacted as part of moves away from traditional PAPI methods (pencil and paper interviewing).

Two other technological developments are the increased use of CATI (computer-assisted telephone interviewing) and CAPI (computer-assisted personal interviewing). CATI enables interviewing to be centrally controlled and supervised, with interviewers entering the responses on a computer and then being given the next question on the screen automatically. This cuts down interviewer error, particularly on filter questions where particular responses to questions determine the next question to be asked, so that no irrelevant questions are put to respondents. Only logical combinations of questions are asked, thus avoiding irritating the respondent by putting questions which do not apply to them.

The latter method (CAPI) is still in its embryonic stage in Britain. It enables the interviewer to enter the responses directly onto a personal computer during the actual interview. This cuts out data entry as a separate stage, thus speeding up the task of processing the results. However, CAPI demands considerable capital costs which have to be recouped by the polling firms and, in addition, some doubts remain about the reliability of the required software. Both CATI and CAPI, however, may well become more viable in the future as and when the costs involved fall sufficiently. CAPI was used for some of the interviews for the 1993 British Social Attitudes

Survey (Lynn and Purdon 1994). It was concluded that the use of CAPI techniques improves the survey technique, its administration and the speed of data handling, editing and error checking. However, there may be some response effects in scale answers in particular, with a reduction in 'don't know' answers when using CAPI, producing an increase in middle category responses.

The second new development since 1979 concerns the increasing reliability of exit polls, which involve interviewing voters as they leave the polling stations on election day itself. These polls have become central parts of general election and by-election coverage since 1979, although they were also conducted at previous elections in the 1970s. Exit polls have been conducted at the last four general elections by Harris for ITN. The BBC commissioned NOP to do the same in 1992.

Exit or projection polls are explicitly predictive exercises which aim to provide figures for the likely distribution of seats in the House of Commons. As such, in 1992, they were conducted in marginal seats only since these are the seats where the election is decided. Projection polls should not be confused with analysis polls even though the latter are also conducted on election day and are sometimes called exit polls. Analysis polls aim, in contrast, to arrive at the national division of the party vote and to provide data on the reasons for the voting decisions of the electorate.

The results of both of these type of polls are only published after the polling booths close at 10 p.m. The methodology of exit polls was developed by means of a series of by-elections throughout the late 1980s and early 1990s, some of which were spectacularly accurate in their predicted outcomes. At the Mid-Staffordshire by-election of 22 March 1990, for example, the Labour vote was overestimated by only 1 per cent by the Harris/ITN poll and 'other' parties underestimated by 1 per cent. The exit poll exactly predicted the vote share of the Conservatives, Liberal Democrats, SDP and Greens.

At the same by-election, the NOP exit poll for the BBC overestimated the Labour vote by 2 per cent and underestimated both the Conservatives and Liberals by 1 per cent each. The average error for each of the three main parties over a total of eight by-elections between Kensington in July 1988 and Ribble Valley in March 1991 in exit polls conducted by NOP for the BBC was less than 1 per cent, which is well within the expected levels of sampling error. However, predicting the outcome of a general election is not as straightforward as a single by-election and the problems encountered by both Harris and NOP at the general election of 1992 reflect this.

The third development of note concerns an increase in the number of 'phone-in' polls which are often publicised and quoted, particularly by the tabloid press, despite their being inevitably unrepresentative and technically very dubious. They reflect a cavalier approach to polling which can nevertheless bring polling as a whole into disrepute when the dividing line between professional pollsters and the rest becomes blurred in the eyes of the audience.

In an ORACLE (ITV) teletext phone-in election poll conducted in October 1991, for example, Labour received 54 per cent of the vote, the Conservatives 33 per cent, the Liberal Democrats 8 per cent and the others 5 per cent. Needless to say, this was not the result at the actual general election six months later. In another television teletext poll published on Channel 4 in January 1993, the Labour Party was once more way ahead (61 per cent) of the Conservatives (22 per cent), with 12 per cent for the Liberal Democrats and 5 per cent for the other small parties. This result was based on 6,624 phone calls over a five-day period. These polls can only ever be representative of those who could be bothered to make the necessary phone call.

In addition, and allied to this, there are more 'bogus polls' than ever before. So-called 'poll findings' are reported, often on a regional or local level, without any attempt at giving the attendant technical details which the professional polling organisations automatically provide both as information and as a defence against criticism. To save money, the 'poll' will often employ students as interviewers, with little if any attention being paid to training or supervision of the fieldwork as it is carried out. Sometimes, even the long-understood fundamentals of polling are ignored to such an extent that it can only be wondered whether *anyone* is actually expected to take the results seriously. For example, a dispute over the siting of a memorial statue to Freddie Mercury, the former lead singer of Queen, was reported in *The Independent* on 23 November 1992. One favoured option was seemingly supported by a poll of 400 people in Kensington High Street in London, ranging from tourists to shop assistants. All of them apparently backed the proposal for a particular site. This example is one of many where no details whatsoever are given and where consequently the results cannot be genuinely assessed. The results are nevertheless described by the press as 'poll results'.

The fourth development, since the end of exclusive reporting of polls in 1970, concerns the secondary reporting of poll results. This involves the reporting of poll results by newspapers other than those who commissioned the poll. Whilst the polling firms themselves and those who commission the research welcome the publicity of secondary reporting, any control over the way in which the material is presented is effectively lost. Most of the quality press act responsibly in terms of secondary reporting but the danger remains ever present of a slanted news report which chooses to emphasise a single poll finding rather than a balanced appraisal of the poll data as a whole.

1.2   Long-standing concerns

In addition to the above new developments in polling, long-standing concerns also remain. Firstly, care always needs to be exercised over interpreting long-term 'projection' exercises in which various models of voting behaviour are used to assess the chances of a party some months before the election campaign actually starts. The main danger emanates from the use that parties make of these exercises in their propaganda as a means of establishing the 'likely' outcome of the election without explaining the purely hypothetical and conditional nature of the projection. This kind of exercise is often undertaken by smaller parties, to try to demonstrate that they are the main challengers to the incumbent party in a particular seat, as one means of establishing their credibility and gaining momentum before the campaign starts in earnest. This use of poll data also occurs during the campaign itself, when party leaflets claim that their candidate is in 'second place and closing fast' (or words to that effect) in an attempt to manipulate voters to their own particular party advantage.

Secondly, the tabloid press continues to adore snappy headlines which do scant justice to the poll story beneath. Not only do headlines dealing with poll results often mislead; they are often only tenuously related to the actual story. This is largely due to the lack of expertise of journalists (with a few honourable exceptions) and their lack of control over the headline given to their story by subeditors. Some interpretations of polls continue to ascribe to them a spurious accuracy, an accuracy even of one decimal place. This is a weight that polls cannot bear. All polls are always affected by sampling error to some degree; they should never be quoted as apparently definitive statistics.

Thirdly, a constant irritation for the pollsters is the hypocritical attitude of many politicians. Sceptics as to the value of polling are at least consistent in their doubts and occasionally grudging in their praise. Most politicians, however, accept poll findings when they bear out what they themselves think, yet criticise the polls when they do not, often dismissing the value of polls via a raft of threadbare clichés such as 'the only poll that matters takes place on election day.' The pollsters accept this situation as 'part of the territory' in which they have to operate, secure in the knowledge that this situation provides them with one of the best reasons for the very existence of polls.

The polls can at least credibly claim to be able to tell ordinary people what others are thinking, rather than people having to rely on what politicians *assert* about the public mood. The pollsters have no partisan axe to grind. Accuracy and the retention of credibility in the process inevitably remains the name of the game for the polling organisations, both for reasons of professional pride and for commercial survival in a highly competitive field.

The challenges that the polls have faced in the wake of the 1992 general election are largely based on the developments and concerns set out above. We will be dealing with many of these points in more detail in the subsequent chapters of this book.

Before those questions are considered, though, it is important to step back from such details and specifics and deal with the broader background and assumptions which underpin the theory of polling as a whole, in particular what exactly constitutes public opinion, how it can best be measured and the criticisms commonly voiced concerning the overall practice of public opinion polling in Britain.

Note

1. In 1948, Thomas Dewey was shown by the polls to be clearly and consistently in the lead over Harry Truman. However, Truman won narrowly on election day. The expectations created by the polls ensured that few people gave Truman much chance of winning. The pollsters

might have come in for less ridicule if only twelve years before the *Literary Digest* debacle had not taken place. The *Literary Digest* straw poll was based on 2 million responses drawn from telephone and car ownership directories. The presidential elections of 1928 and 1932 had roughly corresponded to the straw poll but in 1936, with only a minority of the American public owning either a telephone or a car, the inherent bias in the poll produced a prediction of a landslide for Landon, the Republican candidate. In the event, Roosevelt, the Democratic candidate won overwhelmingly. Shortly afterwards, the *Literary Digest* went out of business. See Squire (1988) for more details.

References

Gallup, G. (ed.) (1976) *The Gallup International Public Opinion Polls, Great Britain 1937–1975*, New York: Random House.

Hodder-Williams, R. (1970) *Public Opinion Polls and British Politics*, London: Routledge and Kegan Paul.

Lynn, P. and S. Purdon (1994) 'Time-series and lap-tops: the change to computer-assisted interviewing', in R. Jowell, J. Curtice, L. Brook and D. Ahrendt (eds) *British Social Attitudes 11th Report*, Aldershot: Dartmouth, pp. 141–55.

Marsh, C. (1982) *The Survey Method: The contribution of surveys to sociological explanation*, London: Allen and Unwin.

Miller, W. L. (1987), 'The British voter and the telephone at the 1983 election', *Journal of the Market Research Society* 29: 67–82.

Moser, C. A. and G. Kalton (1971) *Survey Methods in Social Investigation*, 2nd edn, London: Heinemann Educational.

Squire, P. (1988) 'Why the 1936 Literary Digest poll failed', *Public Opinion Quarterly* 52: 125–33.

Teer, F. and J. D. Spence (1973) *Political Opinion Polls*, London: Hutchinson.

Worcester, R. (ed.) (1983) *Political Opinion Polling: An international review*, London: Macmillan.

Worcester, R. (1991) *British Public Opinion: A guide to the history and methodology of political opinion polling*, Oxford: Blackwell.

Suggested further reading

The two books by Worcester (1983, 1991) and the one by Marsh (1982) cited above are good introductions to the topic of opinion polling. The edited volume by Worcester in 1983 contains chapters dealing with polling practice in countries other than Britain such as Australia, Germany, Japan and the United States. It makes interesting reading, therefore, in a comparative context.

Most introductions to survey methods also contain useful historical material regarding the development of surveys and polls. Some of the publications of the Market Research Society are also valuable, although some are rather expensive for non-members. (The Market Research Society, 15 Northburgh Street, London EC1V 0AH. Tel. 0171–490 4911; Fax 0171–490 0608.)

2

The assumptions and theory of public opinion polling

Whenever polling results are deemed to be 'wrong' or to have 'failed' to predict election outcomes accurately, doubts about the fundamental nature of the polling process are always raised. These doubts cover not only the specific *practice* of polling but also altogether broader questions about whether public opinion can truly be measured through polls and whether the impact of public opinion on politics can be adequately assessed by the same means.

In this chapter, the various dimensions and structure of 'public opinion' will be set out, along with the consequences for the role of public opinion in the political arena. The chapter ends with a consideration of the most common criticisms of polling as a method of delineating the state of current public opinion.

Defining 'public opinion' might seem to be a matter of straightforward common sense but 'public opinion' is in fact a multidimensional concept whose use is often subtly different in different situations. The entry on public opinion in the *Blackwell Encyclopedia of Political Science* begins, 'a freely used but far from precise or unambiguous concept' (Bogdanor 1991: 511). This will be seen to be a sound judgement as we move through this chapter. The concept of public opinion is blurred in particular by its use in a wide variety of separate if related disciplines such as political science, sociology, psychology and history and the fact that the two terms which it comprises have a number of distinct aspects and dimensions.

2.1   The concept of public opinion

The beginning of debates over the nature of public opinion is usually traced back to the period of the Enlightenment, beginning at the Reformation with the championing of secular as opposed to Papal authority, moving forward to Rousseau's idea of the General Will and then the development of liberal political philosophies by thinkers such as Locke and Bentham. Both envisaged public opinion playing a key role in arriving at the common good via reasoned and enlightened public debate.

Interest in the structure and impact of public opinion has been maintained in the twentieth century through the developmental work of Lippmann (1922), Blumer (1948) and Lazarsfeld *et al.* (1948) along with the founding of the quarterly academic journal *Public Opinion Quarterly* in 1937.

Lippmann's work centred on a re-appraisal of the role of public opinion within the democratic process. He particularly attacked any illusion that 'the public' could be regarded as being competent or knowledgeable enough to decide on public policy. The public were not interested in such matters, he argued, and in any case, the information available to them was inadequate and too incomplete for such a purpose.

Blumer's article in 1948 was important for its view that public opinion was a composite opinion formed out of several different opinions. Public opinion was the central tendency set by the competition between those different opinions. This highlighted the idea of a 'weighted average' which takes into account not just raw numbers of people holding a particular opinion but the strength of the opinion holders. In other words, who has what kind of opinion? This is of crucial significance in any assessment of the interaction between public opinion and the government.

Lazarsfeld's direct contribution to the study of public opinion was to develop a more technically complex idea of public opinion which encompassed attitudes, group identifications and the perceptions of events, all of which interact to produce an opinion. He was also instrumental in the development of modern quantitative sociology and in the early analyses of mass communications.

There have therefore been a number of different foci of debate concerning public opinion, but we can nevertheless identify a central theme which forms the background to most research on public opinion: to what extent is public opinion simply an aggregation of the views of individuals or can it be more justifiably regarded as the outcome of some form of collective debate which cannot be 'reduced' to the views of individuals? In other words, is public opinion essentially an individual or a collective phenomenon?

This long-standing debate is rendered more complex by the different understandings and usages of both 'public' and 'opinion'. Public is often equated with 'the people', derived historically from the usage of the term to mean a place open to ordinary people. However, public can also mean matters of common concern and general interest. In this sense, often seen in connection with matters of government or law, the opposite of public is not private but individual (Price 1992: 7).

Opinion at a fundamental level is used to distinguish judgements from facts. However, this is a crucial distinction which is rarely maintained by politicians, who wilfully mix the two, often claiming as facts what are undoubtedly their opinions. Additionally, opinion cannot be regarded as a neutral concept. It always contains a sense, even implicitly, of what is normal or traditional. These norms are derived from the customs, morals and values of particular societies. Such influences are important in that public opinion can act as a form of social pressure and control, psychologically directing people towards conformity with the traditions of a specific culture or community.

There is also a clear sense in which 'opinion' is blithely assumed to be based on knowledge and rationality. This 'opinion' is fashioned after the completion of a process derived from argument and debate. The main difficulty with this assumption, of course, is how exactly this process of debate is supposed to take place, who is involved and how the outcome of the debate is determined. These questions go to the very heart of the status of public opinion in democratic societies.

2.1.1 The dimensions of public opinion

The *characteristics* of public opinion can be seen in terms of a number of different dimensions: namely, the *intensity* of opinion, the *stability* of opinion, the *salience* of opinion and the *latency* of opinion.

Much psychological and sociological research has attempted to delineate these aspects of public opinion using a variety of empirical scales on which respondents are asked to locate themselves. The distribution of opinion along these scales measures public opinion on one or more issues at a time. Such scales can also be used to measure the properties of public opinion.

When looking at the *intensity* of opinion, it is clear that the location of a particular respondent on a scale may suggest an extreme point of view but it may simultaneously be the case that the person cares a great deal or very little about the issue in question. Opinions will therefore vary in the *intensity* with which they are held and this will be a very rough guide to the attention they receive from the government. The political impact of an intensely held viewpoint can be dramatic even if it is held by only a relatively small number of voters. Views on the topic of abortion are often intensely held by people.

Another important aspect of public opinion is its *stability*. Individuals may well have views on a wide variety of matters, but if those views are based on little or no information, they may well change easily on such questions as those involving electoral or constitutional reform. On the other hand, opinions may be firmly held and perhaps even unalterable. Highly stable and widely held views require a quite different approach from any government than matters on which opinion is unstable and uncertain. It has to be said, though, that on many issues of public policy, the general public is usually ignorant; it is often mainly a matter of the degree to which the public is ignorant.

A third aspect of public opinion is the *salience* of opinion and this is closely linked to *stability* of opinion. If an issue, such as unemployment, affects a person directly, its salience to them will be high and it is more likely that they will take an interest in the issue and be able to express a well-considered view on it. If the issue is not something which touches their everyday lives much, such as foreign policy, it is less likely that their views will be focused or detailed.

The final dimension is *latency* of opinion. This is an underlying opinion or attitude which is not expressed except in reaction to particular statements or actions. Latent opinions are derived from other more direct responses to questions. These responses form patterns of opinions from which the latent structure of the underlying attitudes can be inferred. An example would be demands for more policemen on the beat in the wake of a series of burglaries or car crime in a particular neighbourhood.

2.1.2 The composition of the public

Many analysts of public opinion make a distinction between *actors* and *spectators* in the composition of the public. Actors are those who are involved in the decision-making process, such as officials and concerned parties, those who are used to defining problems, proposing solutions and then persuading others of the correctness of their favoured solution. Spectators provide the audience for the actors, those who follow the decision-making process with a wide variety of interest and activity which depends on the nature of the precise issue of the moment. The issue which comes to the attention of the spectators largely depends on the process of issue definition performed by the actors. This is similar to the idea of activating specific divisions or cleavages in a particular society and ensuring that other potential cleavages do *not* become the objects of mass conflict and dispute.

The conflicts and disagreements that do arise depend on which specific problems are highlighted and publicised. This division between actors and spectators greatly complicates the identification of the *public* as a whole since the latter has both an active and a passive element which is shifting in size all the time, comprising groups which exist only temporarily and which then dissolve once their narrow and specific issue of concern has been resolved.

This distinction between actors and spectators is significant, nevertheless, because it is always important to be able to distinguish various groups within the public which can be identified and separated out from one another. For example, there are the active participants, the informed but non-active members of the population, the electorate as a whole and the population as a whole. Despite these distinctions, however, opinion polling mostly assumes the principle of 'one person, one vote' in its practice. This principle does not apply to polling conducted within particular groups only or enquiries which demand certain levels of activity for inclusion in the poll right at the start. However, most polls of the general public give equal weighting to all the people asked regardless of activity, knowledge or interest.

In this sense, the term 'public' is the same as the general public, even given the inchoate nature of mass opinions and the fact that they often appear to be based on little knowledge and interest. The main influences on the decision-making process are, however, those of 'effective' public opinion, which is not the same as mass public opinion. Following on from this, effective opinion is likely to be elite opinion, with the attentive but uninvolved public acting as go-betweens linking the mass and the elite. The attentive public group are those who take an interest in politics, are willing and able to discuss politics with friends and colleagues and who are interested in following politics in the media. The elite comprises politicians, various activists in the spheres of politics, bureaucracy, interest groups and mass communications – in other words, the talkers, the persuaders and the advocates, often referred to disparagingly as the 'chattering classes'.

There is a clear need for a *variety* of elites for this system of elite domination to appear legitimate and acceptable. Whether this is actually the case remains a point of considerable and heated debate, in particular over the extent to which elites are truly independent of one another in terms of educational background, assumptions, experience, knowledge and outlook. There does, however, remain a good deal of variability in terms of the issues that arise in the public arena and they involve different segments of society whose support or at least acquiescence is required for the problem or issue to be resolved.

It appears likely, nevertheless, that elite domination of public opinion is the reality of modern liberal democracies. Elite control of opinion formation is not essentially derived from its inherent legitimacy but more from the alternative of mass involvement. Many analysts of public opinion have long suggested that the evidence to justify mass involvement in decision making in public affairs is often lacking in terms of knowledge and interest in particular. The public world is too large and complex for ordinary people and their ideas are often filtered through a variety of haphazardly formulated prejudices and fears.

2.1.3 The structure of public opinion

In order to investigate the content of public opinion in more detail, we need to identify the key areas that can help to assess the ability of the general public to influence the government. These questions are mainly related to the four dimensions of public opinion identified above. Firstly, to what extent is the expressed opinion based on knowledge or experience? Secondly, are identifiable values or attitudes underlying the opinion? Thirdly, how firmly or strongly is the opinion held by the respondent? Fourthly, is the opinion rooted in a sense of group identity or belonging? Fifthly, how likely is the opinion to change and under what circumstances?

Above all, will the expressed opinion lead to action being taken? Will people with a particular opinion join protest groups or stage demonstrations? In this regard, we cannot ignore that what other people are thinking will also be taken into account. The perceptions of the balance of public opinion may be critical to the way in which opposite or different viewpoints are expressed. This forms the core of the theory of the 'spiral of silence', developed by Elisabeth Noelle-Neumann of the Allensbach Institute, whose research in Germany suggested that the willingness of people to express an opinion was affected by their perceptions of the opinions of others. If they felt that their opinion was not shared by others, the chances were that they would not venture their own view. This idea has been tested by Gallup in Britain but little evidence was found to support it (Webb and Wybrow 1986).

More recently, in January 1993, MORI tested the 'spiral of silence' hypothesis again in Britain by assessing the willingness of respondents to undertake various political activities for the party they supported, such as putting up posters, attending party meetings, giving money and canvassing. MORI concluded that the 'problem' in Britain was more related to a lack of commitment than any inhibitions about supporting unpopular views. Displaying posters in public was a more common activity than less public involvements necessitating more time and effort. Disillusionment and lack of enthusiasm were deemed to be more important among Conservatives than any 'shame factor' (Market Research Society 1994: appendix 6A, 125–6).

Nevertheless, the 'spiral of silence' idea does make two critical points about public opinion in general. Firstly, the process of opinion formation is not static but dynamic, comprising a series of stages of development and formation which overlap with one another and influence one another. Secondly, there is a crucial role played by the social context in which opinions are solicited or expressed and key roles are played by the perceptions of others and the expectations of others.

This is important in assessing public opinion because people implicitly make comparisons with other people and other things when responding to questions, even when they are not asked to do so explicitly by the question itself. We are therefore dealing with a large-scale political process which touches on both individual and collective concerns. The process encompasses a number of linked stages involving the recognition of a problem, the initial conflict about how to solve the problem, the weighing up of the alternative proposals for solving the problem, and the final stage is the resolution, the search for agreement and consensus for implementing the final decision.

Each of these stages overlaps, of course, although it is often analytically neater to divide the stages up into discrete segments. Does it make much sense in reality, though, to attempt to disaggregate 'public opinion' into its component parts? This depends on whether we are considering public opinion to be those decisions reached at the end of a process made up of an initiation stage, a debating stage and a decision stage. One might think this is indeed the best approach to adopt, given the regularity with which 'public opinion' as such a process is invoked and praised. The image that is conjured up by this is of a town meeting of knowledgeable and interested citizens at the end of which a collective decision is agreed by some mysterious process of mass deliberation.

Despite this lack of reality, we can nevertheless certainly assume that public opinion is a social process but one often conducted in a relatively unstructured way between individuals with only broad interests in common. This 'organic' view of public opinion assumes that concern and involvement over a particular issue are widespread and that the figures in authority are sufficiently receptive to such concerns to implement the eventual collective decision. More normally, and more realistically, however, most decisions are enacted after only partial consideration of public opinion or even only parts of public opinion.

The parts of public opinion that matter are the key to understanding public opinion and its impact on politics. Although the usage of the term 'public opinion' remains common, the reality of 'special publics' makes more sense. The questions on which *all* the public can genuinely be expected to have opinions are few and far between, whereas the reality of politics comprises the paying of attention to sub-groups of the public depending on the issue. This inevitably moves us away substantially from democratic ideals which envisage the public will as a whole prevailing; but it can be argued that smaller sub-groups of the public do in fact take account of other sub-groups and their views to produce a 'composite' viewpoint. This is easier to recognise if we limit public opinion to specific issues of public concern; after all, not all the opinions of the public on a variety of issues can reasonably be regarded as public opinion.

2.1.4 Public opinion and policy

The most common focus in this regard is that public opinion is concerned with substantive issues of public policy on the assumption that public opinion should determine policy choices. However, such a narrow focus excludes opinions about political parties and leaders, the performance of government as well as broader ideas about public affairs. For our purposes, all the above have to be included, but the definition based on public policy does draw a useful limit around the sphere of opinions we should regard as public.

At this point, we should also distinguish between public opinion on divisive issues and commonly held expectations. In other words, public opinion is mainly deemed to concern 'live' issues, those which do not touch upon settled community views or norms. However, it may be the case that these seemingly settled norms come 'alive' if the 'live' issues cause bitter, perhaps irreconcilable, disputes. As part of these norms, most conceptions of public opinion assume conditions of freedom of speech and discussion since this is central to the process whereby public opinion is actually formed.

The wide availability of information about public issues and questions is also a key requirement of the process of public opinion formation. A crucial consideration that is often taken for granted is basic agreement on fundamentals as to how opinion disagreements will be settled. The requirement of some degree of common ground lies at the root of debate and discussion; if this is not the case, the conduct of government is unlikely to be based on public opinion as such.

Whilst public opinion is never likely to reflect unanimity, it is always necessary to develop conditions under which minority opinion will accept the outcome of the deliberation process. The necessity for consensus is often recognised as providing the framework for public opinion. The process of public opinion formation implies the need to defer to majority opinion, however distasteful that opinion might be to the minority.

2.1.5 Summary

It is therefore always necessary to consider the concept of public opinion as a multidimensional concept, with subtly different usages and applications. Firstly, public opinion can be assessed in terms of its *distribution* in the creation of a broad social consensus, the patterns and regulations of opinion conflict and the concentration of opinion within certain groups within the electorate. Secondly, public opinion can be assessed in terms of its relationship to a selection of *social variables* such as gender, occupation and education. Equally, public opinion can be investigated by taking into account such influences as the family, education and the mass media. Finally, the links between *public opinion and politics* can be analysed, in particular the relationship between public opinion and political parties, elections, the government and pressure groups. It is this final area of investigation that will provide the focus for the chapters that follow.

Before we reach those substantive links, we need to consider whether polls can be justified as 'true' measures of public opinion by examining the various criticisms of polling and in particular, the claim that polls are the best method available to analyse the 'public mood'.

2.2   Criticisms of opinion polling

It is never difficult to criticise opinion polls on a number of counts – anyone can do it. Polls receive a lot of publicity and comment in the media; as a result, they are easy targets and allegations of 'failure' are rarely far away from the lips of disappointed politicians. It is an altogether harder task to assess in both depth and detail the validity of the more substantive criticisms of polling techniques which do indeed pose more serious questions for the polling firms.

De Vaus (1990: 7–9) groups the commonest criticisms of polls and surveys into three broad groups: (1) philosophical, (2) technical and (3) political. The largest of these three groups of criticisms is the first and we will therefore concentrate on that one.

We can state the main philosophical criticisms of polling as follows:

1. Polls cannot establish causal connections.
2. Polls are often meaningless because they cannot measure the memories, wills, goals and values of the respondents.
3. Polls ignore the context of people's beliefs and this leads to misunderstanding their behaviour.
4. Polls are essentially deterministic because they assume the importance of external forces, neglecting human consciousness in the process.
5. Polls are obsessed with testing hypotheses and statistical significance, omitting imaginative and creative thinking.
6. Polls merely assemble a mass of statistics and provide little of a theoretical nature.
7. Polls cannot measure complex sociological concepts such as power or alienation.

The criticism that polls cannot establish causality by proving that A causes B is one that is often made. This question goes to the heart of all empirical social research. It has to be admitted that polls can never be *absolutely* certain that every possible link between the various variables has been tested, that the 'correct' analysis has been performed and the 'correct' conclusions have been drawn. There will always be unmeasured (and indeed unmeasurable) influences which will produce errors in the analysis. Social research can only ever be conducted in a world of possibility and probability, never certainty, because of its subject matter rather than its techniques. The adage 'correlation is not causation' has been drummed into the heads of successive generations of social researchers, so that they always search for the 'missing link'. They are never satisfied with the assumption that merely observing change between two time points means that a causal relationship has been uncovered. Social scientists cannot create laboratory conditions and then intervene in the experimental process to see what changes on existing relationships are induced as a result. The ability to exclude extraneous factors by using control groups or randomised techniques is usually only available to natural scientists.

All social scientists can do, given this situation, is to examine the existing differences between groups of respondents and see if those differences are related to a variable for which data have been collected. The constant problem is the nagging possibility that another excluded variable is in fact causing the differences between the groups. We might conclude, for example, that there is a clear relationship between religion and voting behaviour but this might 'disappear' or at least be substantially weakened if we included occupation or gender in the analysis.

The best way to test for this possibility is to use *multivariate analysis*, which is designed to avoid faulty inferences being drawn from apparent links between the variables. This approach prevents too much reliance on simple correlations between two variables by substituting a more complex picture of the likely relationships between the variables. This approach allows a number of different variables to interact with one another and it also produces estimates of the size of the various effects so that the most important influences on the dependent variable (voting intention, for example) can be isolated and specified. The dependent variable is a measure of the behaviour or attitude we are trying to explain in the analysis.

A more complex picture will inevitably involve some consideration of human values, memories and goals as well as the context of the beliefs of ordinary people and the impact of 'external forces' on their behaviour and attitudes. Together, these points form the next three criticisms of polls cited above. Can polls measure such aspects of human consciousness properly or even at all?

It is sometimes argued that in-depth interviewing is the best approach to tackling these problems. Such qualitative techniques allow the respondents to structure their responses themselves by not being restricted to answering in terms of a narrow selection of response categories. Such an approach could not replace polls and surveys since qualitative interviews are often unrepresentative of the wider population. The depth of the interviews inevitably means that fewer are carried out and it is also much harder to generalise from a small number of such interviews. The ability to generalise about the wider group (often the electorate) is a main strength of polls and surveys. Nevertheless, qualitative interviews can be very useful in particular contexts by uncovering underlying feelings and attitudes, especially those dealing with very sensitive topics which might not be raised at all in interviews structured by the need to complete a standardised questionnaire.

The work of Fiona Devine in uncovering feelings about race and immigrants during her interviews with car workers in Luton shows that such interviews can be very useful indeed (Devine 1991, 1994). Quantitative and qualitative data and analytical methods are therefore complementary rather than competitors although it has to be admitted that quantitative studies continue to command the lion's share of polling interest as well as funded social research in Britain. Vital advantages, such as much greater publicity for their results and a much easier procedure for obtaining quantitative data for secondary analysis from the Economic and Social Research Council's Data Archive at the University of Essex, are also benefits almost entirely enjoyed by quantitative studies.

Some progress in quantitative studies could be made by developing more sensitive and more detailed questions so that the different dimensions of the various topics could be properly tested. Again, this is a problem for all kinds of social research, not just polls. Another possibility lies in the development of better statistical techniques which set particular variables within the broader context of the other measured variables. Analytical techniques such as multidimensional scaling can provide some of the context which surveys are often deemed to ignore. This was the broad thrust of Dunleavy's argument (1990), although, again, it can be argued that this simply makes the approach more technically sophisticated rather than more appropriate to tackling the problems of establishing different contexts and meanings.

The problem of establishing the context of people's beliefs and attitudes is one which polls will always struggle to solve. The danger that a broad and highly structured questionnaire will lead to a major misunderstanding of behaviour is clearly a serious one but it does not by itself invalidate polls as a technique of social research. Recognising this danger is the first step and reining back on the immodesty and certainty of the conclusions is the second. Finding ways of incorporating more qualitative work into essentially quantitative studies would also be helpful since this would reduce the 'aridity' of many polls which sometimes arrive at grandiose conclusions on thin evidential bases.

The alleged lack of imagination involved in poll design and conduct is also a criticism that is often voiced. Testing relationships for statistical significance is a central aspect of polling work which cannot be ignored but this does not mean that the overall procedure lacks creative thinking. This is always an essential element of designing questions for inclusion in polls and the fact that it is not emphasised much by the 'public' face of British polling does not mean that creativity is not valued.

Some of the polling firms have established units specifically to concentrate upon topic development and question design, with a view to testing a variety of different questions which can then be incorporated into future polls. As we will see in the next chapter, polls involve a long process comprising discrete but related stages and each stage plays its part in the overall utility of the poll. The fact that imaginative thinking is not particularly publicised is a recognition of this situation, where each stage is of value and importance in itself.

Given the small number of firms involved in regular political polling, any new experiments are rapidly disseminated to all of them and there are also regular conferences involving both academics and pollsters at which new developments are presented. In addition, there are foreign pollsters and academics whose ideas are also easily available to interested parties.

The presentation of poll results can be a tricky task since the raw data need to be set out in a way which is readily comprehensible to a non-specialist. The statistics derived from polls can often appear to be part of an attempt to mystify rather than simplify the results for the reader; the statistics are used more to impress than to illustrate. However, restrictions on space in newspapers usually mean that poll stories are largely based on one or two tables. Those two tables are often composites containing information drawn from tables which would normally be presented separately and this can lead to the charge that the statistics are indigestible. However, the presentation of the tables does not mean that the results are not based on sound theoretical underpinnings as set out in criticism 6 above.

The basis of many polls is intimately related to theoretical constructs and the included questions are often clearly aimed at eliciting responses designed to test various assumed relationships between variables. This is perhaps most obviously the case when questions are omitted from polls for reasons of space and criticism is engendered because of the consequent inability to track change over time. An example of this is a question on party identification which British pollsters have rarely asked in the past but which academics believe to be of direct relevance to their analyses of voting behaviour in Britain.

The desire to include such a question is predicated on a theoretical understanding of the likelihood that important links between the variables cannot be tested if such a question is omitted. The design of any poll or survey is rooted in a central research question which is usually derived from a desire to explore assumed linkages between variables. Theory in this sense drives the practice of polling since, without such ideas, the justification for including one question and not another would make little sense.

The final philosophical criticism of polls cited above suggests that polls cannot be used to measure complex sociological concepts such as power and alienation. This has not stopped many sociologists from trying to do so, of course, and some of the major sociological developments of the post-war period have resulted from these attempts. This criticism is related to the points discussed earlier about the context of the beliefs of ordinary people and it has to be admitted that it is difficult to be sure that these ideas can be measured adequately by means of the empirical techniques available to pollsters. However, this is once again a problem which all surveys have to face, not something which is unique to polls.

Whilst more detailed questions and longer questionnaires would help to map out the structure of beliefs, there can be no guarantee that more sophisticated techniques would help. Again, the use of more qualitative interviewing might be useful as a supplement to the responses elicited by the standardised questionnaire. There is ultimately no answer to the point of how best to measure particular concepts such as power. This does, however, tend to provide the focus for long-running academic debates rather than occupy the waking time of pollsters, who are more concerned with meeting the conditions laid down by their clients.

It is worth pointing out that credible explanations are never easy to put together but they can *only* be constructed by carefully collecting and analysing appropriate data. Polls can at least claim to be based on systematic approaches to data collection.

We have now considered the main philosophical criticisms of polls as set out by de Vaus. It is also worth mentioning briefly the other two categories of criticism, although we have touched on some of the central points they raise already.

The main *technical* criticism of polls is that they rely too much on highly structured questionnaires which only permit limited choices from which the respondent must choose. We have looked at this point in the context of the differences between quantitative and qualitative approaches to social research and have concluded that the two approaches could be more complementary, although, to date, they have been largely regarded as separate methods with little in common.

One way of dealing with this point is to develop better questions which allow for more respondent choice, although, as we will see in the next chapter, the presumed advantages of this depend to a great extent on the individual respondent. It is hard to see how the questioning of mass samples could be carried out without using a standardised questionnaire, particularly given the time and cost restrictions imposed on all polls. If being able to generalise to the population as a whole is the main aim of the research, the questionnaire administered to the whole sample will remain indispensable.

The main *political* criticism of polling puts the view that polls and surveys are manipulative in that they provide information to those in power who might then abuse their positions. A related point is that polling data do not reflect reality as such but are an ideologically based reflection which the public at large is taught to accept even though such an interpretation of 'reality' furthers specific and narrow interests rather than those of the mass public.

This is sometimes related to theories of power. Michel Foucault, for example, finds 'disciplinary power' in a number of linked developments which are all part of the polling process: namely, scientific methodology, systematic data gathering, quantification and calculation and the mass dissemination of knowledge. Observation, measurement and communication are necessary and sufficient for control to be exerted and this is backed up by processes of classification and categorisation.

In this sense, opinion polls, along with advertising and the media in general, together provide a particular way of looking at the world which is flexible and can change tack whenever 'resistance' is encountered to their institutionalisation of an approach to defining the public realm and the values and norms which underpin it.

The criticisms of polling outlined above do pose a number of thorny problems for polling organisations. Some can be overcome by adapting existing approaches; others have to be lived with and taken into account when drawing conclusions about the likeliest links between the main variables of interest. The final interpretation of these links essentially results from the knowledge and experience of the researcher involved and on that basis, as we noted in chapter 1, all the main polling firms in Britain have highly experienced practitioners working for them, some with twenty-five years of polling knowledge. From that experience, a great deal of reflection and insight can be derived, whilst simultaneously never forgetting that there is no single survey recipe, even though there are many survey cookbooks.

British polling firms have benefited in particular from the work performed in universities for the theoretical underpinning of poll questions. Without theories, polls can easily appear to be a mindless mess of statistics but this reflects a poor design rather than inherent faults with the polling method itself. Structured questionnaires are the easiest way of collecting large amounts of data quickly, but within them there are often open-ended questions to which the respondents reply with their own words which are recorded verbatim by the interviewer.

The likely responses to these open-ended questions can be assessed in advance by piloting the survey as a draft to be tested before the final version is decided. Whilst this does not happen all the time for reasons of time and cost, it is nevertheless a valuable exercise for ironing out question ambiguity and spotting accidentally omitted answer codes amongst other things.

The reporting of poll results could certainly be made clearer if some of the more mystifying statistical tools were dropped and more emphasis placed on setting out the logic of the polling operation involved.

Polls and surveys will always have weaknesses. These flaws are not, however, often inherent in the techniques themselves but in the way in which they are used. It is always important to remember that all the polling companies use different methods for different problems although the proliferation of polls in recent years has sometimes given the impression that polling samples of the British electorate is the *only* method of collecting information.

If we assume, however, that a poll is the best method of tackling a particular research question, there are a number of deliberate choices which have to be made as the research progresses. These choices range from questionnaire design to sampling technique to the method of interviewing to be employed.

The next chapter looks at these questions in some detail, specifically setting out the different aspects of the methodology of polling in Britain.

References

Blumer, H. (1948) 'Public opinion and public opinion polling', *American Sociological Review* 13: 542–54.

Bogdanor, V. (ed.) (1991) *The Blackwell Encyclopaedia of Political Science*, Oxford: Blackwell.

De Vaus, D. A. (1990) *Surveys in Social Research*, 2nd edn, London: Allen and Unwin.

Devine, F. (1991) 'Working class evaluations of the Labour Party', in I. Crewe, P. Norris, D. Denver and D. Broughton (eds) *British Elections and Parties Yearbook 1991*, Hemel Hempstead: Harvester Wheatsheaf, pp. 161–73.

Devine, F. (1994) 'Learning more about mass political behaviour: Beyond Dunleavy', in D. Broughton, D. M. Farrell, D. Denver and C. Rallings (eds) *British Elections and Parties Yearbook 1994*, London: Frank Cass, pp. 216–29.

Dunleavy, P. (1990) 'Mass political behaviour: Is there more to learn?', *Political Studies* 38: 453–69.

Lazarsfeld, P., B. Berelson and H. Gaudet (1948) *The People's Choice*, 2nd edn, New York: Columbia University Press.

Lippmann, W. (1922) *Public Opinion*, New York: Harcourt, Brace.

Market Research Society (1994) *The Opinion Polls and the 1992 General Election*, London: Market Research Society.

Price, V. (1992) *Public Opinion*, London: Sage.

Webb, N. and R. Wybrow (1986) 'The spiral of silence: A British perspective', in I. Crewe and M. Harrop (eds) *Political Communications: The general election campaign of 1983*, Cambridge: Cambridge University Press, pp. 265–79.

Suggested further reading

The book by Vincent Price (1992) cited above is a very clear and lucid introduction to the topic of public opinion. It covers a lot of ground in ninety-two pages. A special issue of *Public Opinion Quarterly* (volume 51, number 4, part 2, Winter 1987) provides a lot of very readable and widely applicable material on the subject of polling and public opinion, especially the article by Philip Converse on 'Changing conceptions of public opinion in the political process'.

3

The methodology of opinion polling

The art of opinion polling can best be seen as a complex process comprising a series of different yet inevitably related stages where decisions taken at the start steer the process towards certain options and away from others. Most public attention on the polling process is focused at the end when the results are actually published. Yet critical decisions about the research are taken all along the route and understanding the advantages and disadvantages of the available options at any one time is indispensable to a better comprehension of polling practice as a whole.

Although each stage inevitably overlaps with both the previous stage and the following stage, it is analytically easier to divide the various stages up into discrete units. There are six areas dealing with the approach to polling and the craft of polling methodology and practice which we will consider in this chapter, moving chronologically through the polling operation from the definition of the 'problem' to the final analysis and presentation of the results:

1. Defining the problem.
2. Questionnaire design.
3. Sampling procedures.
4. The interviewing process and data collection.
5. Analysis and interpretation.
6. Presenting the results.

These sections are further sub-divided, where necessary, to aid understanding of how the topics are related to one another and the choices which have to be made. Before we get onto the more technical aspects of polling the first task has to be a consideration of what exactly is the problem or topic to be investigated.

3.1 Defining the problem

The first area to be tackled is to assess what precisely the research question is and whether it is feasible to use a poll to investigate the topic of interest. De Vaus (1990: 27–44) sets out the critical details that need to be decided via a process of formulating and clarifying the research questions. It is not enough simply to state that 'I am interested in studying class conflict', for example. Decisions need to be made concerning what we want to achieve: what answers do we want to what questions derived from what problems in particular?

It is very easy to fall into the trap of going ahead and collecting data without properly defining the precise research topic beforehand. There is always the question of whether we are looking at a very narrow and particular topic or a more general topic and whether we are more interested in *describing* a particular phenomenon or attempting to *explain* it by collecting data appropriate to the establishment of causal linkages.

De Vaus suggests five specific questions which need to be asked and answered at this initial stage of the research:

1. What is the time period of our interest (pre-1945 or post-1945, for example)?
2. What is the geographical location of our interest (the whole country or a particular region or perhaps even comparing more than one country)?
3. Do we want to simply describe or are we more interested in comparing and specifying patterns for sub-groups (women, pensioners, trade unionists)?
4. What are the particular and specific aspects of our interest (class conflict in the factory and/or the office)?
5. How abstract is our interest (relating the topic of class conflict to other topics such as voting behaviour, social background or parental influence)?

De Vaus also suggests using previous research as a basis for further work, considering the 'facts' based on the detailed description of a topic, our own instincts about the topic and talking to those already involved in the field for their own insights and experiences.

Defining the research interest clearly and concisely is therefore a complex process of interaction between the definition of the topic and the data. It is particularly important to build in a degree of flexibility and to try and anticipate potential problems, since it is certain that the research will evolve and it will change in unexpected ways as the process of data collection continues.

Assuming that the above decisions are debated and made, with the conclusion that a poll would be an appropriate tool of investigation, we can now move to the first design stage of the polling process, namely, which questions do we want to ask our respondents?

3.2   Questionnaire design

It may seem a relatively straightforward task to design questions for people to answer. Whilst all questionnaires try to elicit full and accurate answers from respondents by making them feel at ease, a good questionnaire is a clearly structured set of questions which is not intended to resemble a conversation or to spark off a debate or argument between the interviewer and the respondent. The questions will reflect theoretical concerns and interests, with the view to establishing relationships between a range of different attitudes and actions. The questions as a whole provide a variety of measures which comprise the core of the research for which the questionnaire is the main instrument of investigation.

To this extent, the questions are both contrived and artificial and they are asked in an unusual and unnatural situation. The acid test of a good question is whether it enables researchers to measure the 'reality' in which they are particularly interested. The nature of this 'reality' is, of course, a matter of constant debate and the certainty of interpretation which is placed on some poll findings ignores the inevitable divergence between the answers given and 'reality'.

Much evidence suggests that most people try hard to answer questions as well as they can but there can never be a perfect relationship between responses and 'reality'. This discrepancy might well be due to some of the pitfalls related to questionnaire design which we will now examine in more detail.

3.2.1 The wording and language of questions

There are a number of important points which can be subsumed under this heading. Firstly, if we assume that a question is to be put to the general public, it obviously must be comprehensible to everyone. This necessitates the use of straightforward, everyday words and phrases since respondents will sometimes not admit that they do not understand a question but answer it anyway. This can apply particularly to political issues which might well have been in the news for some time but have still not been noticed by large sections of the general public. Asking people about their views on the siting of Cruise missiles in Britain in the early 1980s, for example, would come into this category as would views on the latest moves towards European integration as a result of the Maastricht Treaty.

Secondly, and leading on from the above point, there is always a need for questions to be clear and unambiguous. Ambiguous questions are often easy to spot since they do not allow a straightforward and clear answer to be given. If the poll focuses on different methods of getting to work, for example, it is critical to ask separate questions about each mode of transport. Putting a question such as 'Do you travel to work by train or bus?' is inherently ambiguous since answering 'yes' or 'no' is inevitably unclear. This need for care in question wording is crucial since the aim of asking the questions in the first place is to establish that differences between respondents do indeed exist and to try and account for that variation. This cannot be assumed simply by ensuring that all the respondents were asked *exactly* the same questions. Variations in response could be caused by variations in understanding the content of the question.

A particular difficulty in this regard is the use of terms or concepts with multiple meanings, even if the words themselves appear straightforward. For example, when asking someone if they had dinner yesterday, care has to be taken to ensure that dinner is not being confused with lunch by specifying what time of day is meant via a definition of the term 'dinner' immediately after the question. As a general rule, jargon and technical terms should be avoided in questions put to the general public, although they remain acceptable and are often necessary in polls of specialised groups.

Thirdly, the questions should be 'balanced' as far as possible. This means giving equal weight to all sides of a particular issue so that responses are not biased in one direction or another. The answers to such questions are then assumed to reflect the 'reality' of mass opinion on that issue. However, this makes the critical assumption that one single aspect of the issue at hand is a fair reflection of overall opinion on that issue as a whole. That may well not be the case on controversial and complex issues such as abortion or euthanasia, which have a number of different aspects to them.

This is a common criticism of polls: that they often only include one aspect of a multidimensional topic which reflects attitudes to that specific aspect but effectively ignores all the others. Examples of this would include looking at the health service in terms of waiting lists alone or taxation in terms of income tax only.

As a general principle, the structure of the question must not lead the respondent in a particular direction by its wording. If the respondent is being asked his or her opinion on an issue, it must be made clear that either agreeing or disagreeing is equally acceptable. This is not apparent if a statement on a particular topic is read out followed by the question 'Do you agree?' Leading questions are usually easy to spot in a questionnaire, such as 'Do you favour cutting money for the National Health Service even if this means that more old people die as a result?'

In addition, the use of 'probes' must be used with care by interviewers. Probes comprise additional information and detail provided by the interviewer to the respondent about the type of answer that *might* be given. Most commonly, probes are used when the respondent hesitates before answering. However, it is all too easy to load the question in favour of particular answers by giving loaded extra information regarding possible responses to help the respondent out.

It is best to give all the alternatives or none to ensure an unbiased response. For example, if a respondent is asked 'Do you read a daily newspaper?', a potential probe would be to provide a list of daily newspapers if the respondent appears uncertain; however, the list would of necessity be a long one and an incomplete list would risk a biased response. This would mean that the respondents were effectively answering different questions on the basis of the information provided by different individual interviewers, thus undermining the central principle of standardised interviewing.

Fourthly, it is always important that respondents understand the relevance of a question, either in terms of the stated aims of the poll or in terms of their ability to provide sensible answers. This can be vital in sustaining the interest of the respondent and their putting both thought and care into providing answers, particularly if the interview is long and occasionally complicated and demanding.

All the above four aspects of question wording and language can and should be fully tested with a pilot study of the draft questionnaire. This involves carrying out interviews with a small number of the respondent group, with the specific aim of testing the draft questions for problems of ambiguity and relevance. The particular value of such a small-scale study can be demonstrated by the number of wording ambiguities that always arise when the questions are tried out on a sample the same as or as similar as possible to that of the final sample of respondents.

The interviewers are instructed to carry out the interviews with a view to noting down and reporting back specific problems with particular questions. Problems can include questions lacking fluency when read out, a lack of comprehension on the part of the respondents and a tendency for inaccurate or incomplete answers to be provided by respondents. Of course, the actual 'accuracy' of the answer is often difficult to determine but the advantage of the pilot study is that the interviewers are systematically looking out for problems in this regard whilst conducting the interview normally. It is often possible, in addition, to record pilot interviews in order to be able to have a source of evidence independent of the reports of the interviewers.

Piloting a survey is always important but it is indispensable when the final questionnaire is to be filled in by the respondent on their own as part of a postal survey. A good method of piloting, which was used on the University of Sheffield survey of Labour Party members in 1989–90, for example, was to arrange pilot interviews and ask the respondents to complete the questionnaire in front of one of the survey team. At the end, the researcher went through the questionnaire with the respondent, asking the reasons for particular answers and querying why some questions had not been answered in much detail or indeed at all.

This produced some fascinating insights into how questionnaires are completed as well as specific problems with the content of that particular questionnaire. About fifty pilot interviews were conducted in Sheffield and Bristol for this purpose. The subsequent discussions with the pilot respondents centred mainly on the clarity of the instructions for completing the questionnaire, whether the questions themselves were comprehensible and whether the respondents had found any difficulty in answering particular questions in terms of the answer categories offered. In addition to problems of clarity and comprehension, these pilot tests also produced evidence of a potential problem with question order which suggested that a change might be desirable.

Question 5 of the Sheffield survey was open-ended (respondents answer in their own words rather than choosing from various categories on offer), asking the respondents for their most important reason for joining the Labour Party. This demanded some thought from the respondents. It was noticeable that two of the pilot respondents initially skipped that question and went on instead to the set of closed questions (for which they chose from a limited number of categories) which immediately followed. Unfortunately, they never returned to complete question 5. When this was pointed out after they had finished the whole questionnaire, they both admitted the mistake and duly completed it. This suggested that it might be wiser to move this open-ended question to later on in the questionnaire so that it came up when the respondents had 'warmed' to the questionnaire as a whole.

In the end, no change was made to the final version of the questionnaire because the open-ended question made intellectual sense in its original location as part of a block of background questions concerning Labour Party membership (for a full description of this survey, including the questionnaire and an analysis of the data, see Seyd and Whiteley 1992).

This example neatly illustrates the value of pre-testing questions in a pilot study. If there had not been the chance to examine the questionnaire immediately after completion but it had simply been received back through the post with the open-ended question left blank, there would have been no chance to discuss whether the location of that question was a potential problem or not and whether changes in question order were necessary as a result.

There would have been no direct evidence as to whether a problem existed or what should be done about it, if anything.

A useful summary of the aims of pre-testing a poll or survey is contained in Reynolds *et al.* (1993). The main categories of concern are 'double' questions, ambiguous questions, loaded questions or phrases, level of question difficulty, missing response categories, missing questions, non-response rates and degree of attention. Altogether, Reynolds *et al.* identify fourteen categories of concern and conclude that there is a good deal of normative literature already available on the topic of pre-testing which is largely based on common sense. What is lacking at present is much empirical evidence detailing the most effective method for pre-testing.

One invariable result of pre-testing a questionnaire is confirmation that the order in which the questions are placed creates a context which influences the way in which respondents approach the task of answering them. The second area of questionnaire design we need to consider, therefore, is that of question order.

3.2.2 Question order

A lot of research on questionnaire design has focused on the effects of question order on the answers of respondents. For example, in evaluating candidates or parties, the order in which the names are presented to the respondents can affect the answers given. One method of deciding the order is to present the names of the parties or leaders in alphabetical order, another with the government first followed by the opposition and yet another in terms of parties with the largest vote share, then those with the smallest. All of these criteria can affect the responses if the respondents infer that the order in which the parties or leaders are presented to them implies a continuum from 'best' to 'worst' or 'most important' to 'least important'.

It can also act to remind respondents of the very existence of politicians and parties, which may inflate their apparent support. In the British context, this is often thought to apply to the Liberals or Liberal Democrats, with their support appearing to change between polls as a result of the order in which the party names are read out to the respondents. It can therefore matter very much whether the party's name is included in a 'prompted' question or whether the respondents have to answer without such information being provided by the question.

One way of testing for these potential effects is to conduct two or more polls using different criteria for the ordering of the questions. Unfortunately, even such an experiment does not, by itself, establish which response is the most accurate; that still has to be decided ultimately in terms of judgements about the 'best' ordering for the questions based on past experience.

It always has to be remembered, nevertheless, that even apparently minor changes in question order can alter the responses, which are, after all, given after the stimulus provided by the question has been received by the respondent. These stimuli build up over the course of the interview by establishing a frame of reference in the minds of the respondents for answering questions which, in isolation, would appear to be unbiased and balanced. This 'perceptual environment' usually ensures that questions on political issues are *not* asked before the voting-intention question or evaluations of party leaders. This ordering is based on assumptions that by highlighting a particular issue associated with a particular party or politician, that issue might artificially increase in saliency by the very fact of its association. This could happen even if the question is not clearly biased or unbalanced in content.

This 'saliency problem' often involves the use of a particular politician's name in a question on policy. For example, the preamble to a question could state 'As you may know, Tony Blair's policy on the question of rail privatisation. . . . Do you think that this is an important issue for you personally?' There is the obvious implication that the issue is indeed important by the fact that the question states what Tony Blair thinks of it and the respondent is then pushed towards accepting that particular implication of importance in their own response. The answer of the respondents might also be guided by their overall attitude to Tony Blair rather than what they actually think of the issue of rail privatisation itself.

This is sometimes called the 'prestige problem' and is most commonly seen when the names of prime ministers, presidents or party leaders are linked to particular solutions to issues which are then often endorsed by the respondents, particularly those with little apparent interest or knowledge of the issue as judged by subsequent answers during the rest of the interview.

Most questionnaires are designed in such a way that 'blocks' of questions which tackle key themes in detail come immediately after one another. Such a structure is logical and consistent and this will also be apparent to the respondent. It would be very irritating for the respondent to answer a single question on unemployment, for example, early on in the interview and then be expected to return to the topic later on for no apparent reason. The use of 'blocks' of questions together makes it easier for respondents to answer because they are being asked to focus on one topic at a time. Nevertheless, the danger does exist that, since the questions are related, the wording of a particular question in the sequence will set a biased framework for answering the questions that follow.

To enable full answers to be given often requires a detailed preamble to a question in which information is provided to enable the respondents to answer within a particular framework. This can mean, however, highlighting particular actions, decisions or people which remind the respondents of things they had forgotten or indeed never knew and which can act to steer their answers in a particular direction. Attention is directed via the preamble to named actions or opinions, which heightens their saliency for the answering of the question, thus increasing the likelihood of narrowing the range of responses given.

In this sense, the very first question of the interview sets the tone and is therefore critical. There is an argument for allowing the respondents to 'warm' to the task of answering by beginning with an easy question to which everyone should have an answer rather than pitch in with a 'difficult' opinion question. British political polls usually begin with the voting intention question on the grounds that, although this catches the respondents 'cold', it gets a critical question out of the way early and, if asked first, it cannot, by definition, be influenced by the evaluations of party leaders or political issues that are asked later on in the interview.

It is therefore clear that not only is the exact wording of the question important to understanding the answers but it is equally vital to know the order in which the questions were asked. After all, opinions do not exist in a vacuum. The sequence in which the questions are asked creates an 'answering context' which can be manipulated both deliberately and accidentally to produce a bias towards favouring particular responses at the expense of others.

Another way of structuring an interview in a particular way involves the choice of the *type* of question which is asked and the categories which are offered from which respondents must choose. This is certainly one of the main criticisms of polls as a whole: that they do not allow enough choice for the respondents when answering. That is the subject of the next section.

3.2.3   Question type

Any study of poll questions over time would reveal a mixture of both continuity and change. Some questions drawn from research originally conducted in the 1930s could still be put to respondents today; others would be meaningless or at least form part of a very different frame of reference for contemporary respondents. As Smith points out (1987: 103), in 1954, Gallup asked which American city had the gayest night life. If that question were to be repeated today, presumably San Francisco would finish higher than fourth.

There are nevertheless strong continuities in the *type* of question asked even if the precise content is not directly comparable between different timepoints.

There are four main types of questions to be found in most polls. Firstly, there are *demographic* or social background questions about such things as the age, gender, occupation, religion, education and income of the respondents. These questions usually come in a block at the end of the questionnaire.

Secondly, there are *knowledge* questions which seek to establish the cognitive capabilities of the respondents, often in the form of filter questions which divide the respondents into those who might have opinions on a particular topic and those who cannot have opinions by definition because of a lack of knowledge. There has been a clear move away from putting pure knowledge questions into polls in recent years since, although they can be useful, more research interest is nowadays focused on the third type of question, questions tapping *attitudes and opinions*.

The range of attitudinal questions is enormous already and it is expanding all the time, covering topics in the news to timeless topics concerning personal income and religious views, for example. The main criticism of some attitudinal questions is that they are trying to be too up-to-date, asking respondents to give answers on topics about which they know little even if the topics have been discussed in the media recently. However, these are the topics that the media clients of the polling firms will want to be included. The challenge is therefore to design sensible and unbiased questions on a subject that has recently hit the headlines.

It can certainly be interesting to ascertain views on topics of immediate relevance in order to influence a continuing debate but it is also dangerous to be drawn into assuming that 'events' as such will clearly and quickly be reflected in the structure of public opinion. There is of course a need for polls to reflect the diversity of the times but news stories can disappear quickly, leaving few or no long-term traces. It is all too easy to believe that issues that flare up suddenly and provoke a heated debate must be influential in terms of their impact on public opinion. This is, however, to oversimplify to a great degree the nature of the links between public opinion and politics.

This point relates directly to the fourth and arguably most important type of poll question, that of measuring and assessing the *behaviour* of respondents. Behavioural questions are not asked in isolation from the other three types above but there does tend to be most interest in behavioural responses. In other words, in what way, if at all, do the attitudes or feelings of particular respondents cause them to take certain actions or to change their behaviour? In terms of this book, an obvious example would be why a respondent decided to vote Labour rather than Conservative at a general election.

There are of course problems associated with behavioural questions. Firstly, is the respondent telling the truth about what they actually did? Is it in fact the case that they thought about taking some action but ultimately decided against it? Most respondents try to tell the truth as they see it most of the time and it may well be the case that they are not actually lying. They might have genuinely forgotten what they actually did, particularly if the event was of little interest and took place some time ago. They might equally have 'projected' their current beliefs onto their ostensible past behaviour to make the two consistent, thus avoiding a sense of 'cognitive dissonance' which can make respondents feel uncomfortable when answering questions.

This can occur when a question is asked about past voting habits. If a respondent has voted for a small party in the past but currently favours one of the two main parties in Britain, it appears likely that they will 'forget' about this deviation and claim a consistent voting record. This also seems to apply to non-voting since voting is widely regarded as an important social norm and duty. Polls and surveys have long found considerably more people claiming to have voted at an election than is possible according to official turnout figures. This was most recently confirmed at the 1994 elections to the European Parliament, when ICM's poll produced a figure of 55 per cent claiming they were 'certain to vote'. Gallup's corresponding figure was 54 per cent and for MORI it was 45 per cent. The official turnout figure was 36 per cent (MRS 1994: 107).

Respondents might equally want to claim a particular course of action in terms of 'social acceptability' based on their perceptions of the current climate of opinion or their view of what the answer should be or even what they think the interviewer themselves would regard as the 'correct' answer.

Despite these necessary caveats, it remains the case that behavioural questions often form the chief focus and core interest of polling questions. It is the potential links between attitudes, opinions and behaviour that have provided the greatest insights into the motivations of ordinary people and it is the questions of action or inaction and explanations that try to account for them which will continue to be of concern on both theoretical and empirical grounds.

We have now briefly considered the different types of questions contained in most questionnaires. We now want to look at the various options offered to respondents for answering those questions.

3.2.4 Answer categories

Every questionnaire contains questions which permit a variety of response possibilities. The main distinction to be drawn is between *open* and *closed* answer formats. Open answers allow the respondents to compose their own replies without any help being given in terms of a list of responses from which they must choose. This is particularly useful when the likely responses cannot be predicted in advance: for example, 'What do you think are the three main problems facing Britain today?' is a question which could well elicit a very wide range of answers. Such an approach allows the respondents to use their own language and expressions to formulate their replies rather than being constrained to fitting those replies into an often narrow set of perhaps inadequate categories.

The disadvantage of open questions is that respondents often find them more difficult to answer and the actual answers take longer to code fully and accurately at the data preparation stage.

Closed answer formats give the respondents a list of replies from which they must choose: for example, 'Would you call yourself a feminist?', with the possible answers being yes, no or don't know. Depending on the type of question, there is sometimes an 'other' category to permit some flexibility in terms of unpredictable answers but pre-coded questions tend to be restricted to discrete categories from which the respondent can only choose one. This can cause problems if a person appears to fall into two or more categories on a particular question. This is another important reason for testing the questions in advance of the main survey by undertaking a pilot study. For example, when asking about crime and law and order and specifically whether the respondent had suffered personally from any crimes, the categories might be 'burglary', 'car theft', 'assault' and so on. However, what would the respondent reply if they had suffered both assault and car theft? Without a 'more than one' or 'both' category, that person's response would be only partly accurate through no fault of their own. The problem might not affect many people but the principle of designing mutually exclusive categories for closed answers remains a central requirement.

It is therefore a legitimate criticism of polls that without very careful vetting of question categories, information offered by the respondents might be artificially constrained into categories which do not reflect their own particular and individual 'reality'. This can also be a problem when considering whether the response categories should include a 'don't know' option. Most poll questions are designed to avoid a lot of 'don't know' responses since this makes any social research much less interesting when classifying the respondents into a variety of more or less coherent groups and comparing their answers to one another and to other questions. The 'don't know' group holds little interest for researchers on either theoretical or substantive grounds.

If the question concerns the respondents' own lives, feelings or experiences, an answer of some sort can reasonably be expected without allowing a 'don't know' response to be given or at least being given without being followed up with a probe and then usually a slightly modified follow-up question asking largely the same thing. However, if the focus of the question concerns an abstract idea or matters of which the respondents have no direct experience, then it is both plausible to expect and reasonable to allow some genuine 'don't know' responses based on inadequate knowledge and opinions.

When this does happen, a choice has to be made. All the respondents can either be asked all the questions and the respondents themselves are relied upon to state that they have no opinion on a particular topic. There is, however, evidence that some respondents will not do this, preferring to give some sort of answer rather than admit that they have never thought about a topic before. Alternatively, for the questions for which a 'don't know' might be expected, filter questions to screen out those who have not heard of the subject in advance can precede the main questions to try and ensure that the key substantive questions are only put to those respondents who have at least heard of the topic before the question is actually put to them.

In addition to testing the answer categories of a question in advance, it is also vital to retain the respondent's interest in an interview by varying the number of categories offered to choose from and the ways in which the respondents are expected to answer: for example, polls and surveys nowadays use a variety of different scales to tap the attitudes of respondents. These are often numeric, ranging from 1 to 10 or 1 to 100, for example. The two ends of the scales are defined in the question, by stating in the preamble to the question that, say, '1' means total agreement with a particular statement and '10' means total disagreement. The respondents are then asked to locate their response in numeric terms on the scale within those limits. This is a clear change for the better since it allows more differentiation to be made between the responses of different people. In the early days of polling, dichotomous responses of 'yes' and 'no' were the main responses allowed, even when answering broad questions on topics such as communism or capital punishment.

The move towards the greater use of scales was also linked to the development of multiple-item scales in statistical analysis, scales which were constructed from a set of responses to a number of related questions. Today, for example, scales are used to measure respondent self-placement on a left–right scale by defining 1 as left and 7 or perhaps 11 as right. This allows the respondent to place themselves on such a scale easily. It also appears that the vast majority of respondents in many countries are able and willing to do this. It remains, however, a moot point whether a 'centre' location should be marked on the scale on the grounds that this draws attention to such a 'moderate' position which some respondents might interpret as being the 'correct' answer. There does often appear to be a 'bunching' in the middle of such scales.

It is argued that if respondents want to place themselves at the centre, they can work it out for themselves if there is an odd number of categories, that is, 1–9 or 1–11. An exact centre cannot of course be found with an even number of categories. In addition to potential problems with defining the centre, there might also be a problem with defining 'right' even in a clearly political context since this term might still be taken to mean not the 'political right' but 'correct', thus producing a 'bunching' of responses at the far end of the scale.

Another example of a frequently used scale is a Likert scale ranging from 'strongly agree' to 'strongly disagree', with 'agree', 'neither agree nor disagree' and 'disagree' located in between. The respondent is invited to consider a series of statements and then give a response drawn from the scale options above. This kind of scale is in wide use in polling because it provides not only a sense of agreement or disagreement but also a strength for that feeling. In other words, not only does the respondent indicate the *direction* of their feelings but also the *strength* with which those feelings are held. In matters such as religion, for example, nominal adherence to a particular denomination is likely to be a much poorer guide to religious attitudes than the strength of underlying religious conviction on which those attitudes are built.

Another type of scale is a 'thermometer scale', designed to assess the feelings of 'warmth' or 'coldness' of respondents towards parties and politicians. The preamble used to introduce such scales usually defines '0' as disliking strongly, '100' as liking strongly and '50' as the neutral point, neither liking nor disliking. All numbers in between, though, are legitimate to express varying degrees of 'warmth' or 'coldness'. This kind of scale seems to be a familiar idea to most respondents who appear to be able to reply in such terms without problems.

Another variant of this type of numeric scale is to ask respondents to evaluate politicians and parties by awarding them marks out of ten. This has the same advantage as the thermometer scale in that it is an idea with which everyone who has been to school will be familiar and as a consequence they will be able to use easily. Both scales also have technical and statistical advantages in that, as genuine 'interval scales', they permit the assumptions of high-level multivariate analytical techniques to be met.

This part of the chapter has considered the main points regarding questionnaire construction. It should be stressed that these points are all significant in providing a solid basis for a well-designed polling instrument. Nevertheless, the best questions in the world will not ensure a credible poll if the sample to which the questions are put is faulty.

The next section of this chapter therefore is concerned with sampling procedures and the problems involved in contacting the respondents who provide the answers.

3.3   Sampling procedures

Sampling procedures remain one of the main mysteries of the practice of polling in Britain. The technical aspects of these procedures are admittedly complex at the level of statistical theory but the fundamental principles are nevertheless well established and capable of being explained to non-specialists. This is critical because an understanding of polls in Britain cannot be achieved without a grasp of why the details of sampling differ, quite legitimately, from poll to poll and indeed polling organisation to polling organisation.

In this section, I will therefore attempt to chart a course through the conventional practices of sampling, whilst not neglecting to mention the qualifications which are always necessary to arrive at an overall picture of sampling in the practice of polling.

The first question to be answered when deciding upon the approach to drawing a sample is straightforward: what is the target population? In other words, to whom are we interested in putting our questions? This might be the British population or the British electorate or perhaps more specialised groups such as doctors or teachers. Since the aim is normally to be able to *generalise* about the target population as a whole (doctors, teachers in Britain, etc.), it is crucial to know who was included or excluded. The answer to this question is normally obvious given the nature of the research questions which gave rise to commissioning the poll in the first place but it is also of critical importance to understanding the results since any sample can only be representative of those actually included in the sample frame. The most obvious sampling frame is the electoral register even though it is always somewhat out of date due to electors moving house or dying, for example.

It is also important to be able to estimate the chances of a particular individual being included in the sample. Without being able to calculate this chance of inclusion, the statistical basis for evaluating the extent to which the sample is representative of the group as a whole does not exist. For example, if the sample includes people who were easy to contact or who offered to take part on their own initiative, it is unlikely to represent the target population as a whole. Therefore the details of the sample design, specifically its size and the method employed to select the individuals within it, will influence directly the precision of estimates regarding how likely the sample is to approximate the characteristics of the target population.

We will return to these details later. The design of the sampling frame needs to be considered first because it sets the parameters for the whole sampling procedure.

3.3.1 The sampling frame

Any sample, by definition, will include some individuals and exclude others. Samples are usually drawn from a list of the individuals in the target population to be studied, such as electors drawn from the electoral register. This sample is defined in some way, such as they do the same job (social workers) or they take the same action (attended a protest meeting, for example). There may be a list of the members of the group available in advance or it may need to be drawn up later or, in the case of the protest meeting, at the same time. The sample may be drawn in more than one stage, with the first stage involving the drawing of some unit such as households. These primary units are sampled and then the individuals are selected from within those primary units. One example of this procedure would be to sample households and then draw a sample of individuals from those households using gender or age criteria, for example.

There are two main difficulties involved in drawing any sample. Firstly, how comprehensive is the sampling frame? Clearly, any sample can only be representative of the group who actually had a chance of being included in it. In reality, most samples leave out a few people from the target population. Choosing households and then individuals within them necessarily excludes the homeless, those in prison or in residential homes, amongst others.

It has to be recognised that, although most lists of the target population are good in coverage, they may be excluding parts of it with distinctive characteristics. Most obviously, telephone directories exclude those not on the telephone, those who are ex-directory and those who have moved house since the directory was published. This can be a serious problem in a large country like the United States, for example, where samples drawn in this way can sometimes only be representative of about half the target population because of the number of ex-directory telephone subscribers. It is therefore a crucial consideration to be able to determine the chances of any individual being selected for the sample and the extent to which those excluded are distinctive from those who are included.

On a practical level, there is often a choice for pollsters between saving money and time by accepting a sample frame which is known to omit some people and a more expensive and lengthier process of checking the comprehensiveness of the sample frame. If there is a list available, checks of some sort will always need to be made on how and when it was compiled, how up-to-date the list actually is, who has been omitted and in what ways might those omitted differ from those included on the list?

The second main difficulty in drawing a sample concerns a calculation of the probability of any particular individual actually being included. The idea of probability is not an easy one for most people to understand – look at the number of people willing to spend money every week on buying tickets for the National Lottery. Nevertheless, some grasp of the idea of probability is vital for sampling a target population because if it is not possible to calculate the probability of inclusion, it will equally not be possible to estimate the relationship between the sample statistics and the target population from which the sample was drawn. If the individuals are only entered on the list once (sometimes a big if!), this estimate can be calculated, but care has still to be taken if the sampling frame comprises a list on which individuals could legitimately appear more than once, such as visiting a shop over asix-month period, since this would increase the most frequent shoppers' chances of being selected. This problem can be overcome by adjusting the data at the analysis stage on the basis of other data regarding the number of visits made during the relevant period.

The main consideration at the sampling stage is the ability to calculate the different chances of selection in order to estimate the relationship between the sample as drawn and the target population that the sample is supposed to represent.

Once the nature of the sampling frame has been determined, the next decision is how to select the individuals to be included. There are a number of choices to be made at this point. The first choice is whether the sample will be drawn in a single stage or several stages. The latter will be necessary if no adequate list of individuals exists and there is no practical way as a result of getting at the relevant list directly. This involves linking the targeted individuals to some kind of group that can actually be sampled. Lists are then made of individual members of the selected group, with possibly a further selection from that list at an even later stage of sampling.

One example of this approach is telephone random digit dialling of households in a particular area in order to draw a sample of people living in those households. This can, of course, be both frustrating and time-consuming because of the large number of wasted contacts due to the numbers called not being households but businesses or their being disconnected or their being numbers not yet allocated to households.

For the vast majority of polls, however, single-stage sampling is possible because of the availability of lists of individuals such as the electoral register. It is nevertheless important to remember that samples will still differ for a variety of reasons depending on the research problem under investigation, even within the same polling organisation.

There are two main sorts of sampling employed in polls. Firstly, there is *random or probability sampling*, and secondly, *quota sampling*. *Random sampling* is dealt with in detail in the literature dealing with the statistical underpinning of sampling. Unfortunately, implementing the precepts of random sampling is usually impractical for polls. The normal metaphor for describing random sampling is to liken it to drawing raffle tickets out of a hat or coloured beads out of a tin. Individuals are drawn one at a time, independently of one another, and they cannot be replaced. To draw such a sample requires a numbered list of the population: for example, if we wanted a random sample of 100 people to be drawn from a list of 10,000 people, the individual names would be numbered and then random numbers could be used to produce 100 numbers in the same range. This would produce a random sample of the individuals on the list.

The speed of this operation is, of course, heavily dependent on the list being available on computer and the selection being performed by computer as well. Depending on the list of individuals involved, this might well not be the case. It is mainly for this reason that, although the logic of random samples is easy to grasp, they are rarely found in practice. Drawing a purely random sample would be very time-consuming indeed if the population is large, with prohibitive costs in terms of the time required.

There is therefore a variation of purely random sampling which can be used, called *systematic sampling*, which also produces a high degree of precision. The polling organisation firstly determines the number of individuals to be drawn from the list and then divides that figure into the group total, thus producing a fraction: that is, 100 out of 10,000 is $\frac{1}{100}$ of the list. To produce a systematic sample, a start point on the list is then determined between 1 and 100. By making the starting point random, the selection process is based on chance. The procedure is then to draw every 100th person from the list.

Care has, however, to be taken to ensure that the list is not ordered perhaps by age or gender or has a particular pattern to it which will defeat the objective of the random start. Most lists do not pose such problems but re-ordering the list or changing the selection interval will usually solve any such problem. Random samples are specifically drawn so that any individual selection is unaffected by any other. This may mean, however, that, by chance, the sample is unrepresentative since little is known of the group of interest *before* the data are actually collected. However, there are usually a few group characteristics which can be identified at the time of drawing the sample and these can be used to structure the sampling process to reduce the sample variation, producing a sample which is more likely to reflect the total group than a simple random sample. This is a process called *stratification*.

Samples are commonly stratified by region as well as urban or rural location. Most samples are stratified in this way because it is often easy to improve the quality of the sample by doing so and it does not affect the sample estimates providing that the probability of selection is the same across all the strata.

The second and most common type of sampling procedure is *quota sampling*. As with random sampling above, quota sampling is usually conducted within sampling units, normally constituencies. The constituencies are selected proportionally to their electorates after they have been ordered in a particular way, often the size of the Labour vote at the last election within a stratified structure of region and degree of urbanisation. This produces a list of between 100 and 200 sampling points, although some polls use fewer. The precise number of sampling points depends on the type of poll being conducted. If the poll is being conducted in one region only, then the number of sampling points will obviously be less, but care still has to be taken to avoid the problems of *clustering*.

Clustering occurs when interviews are concentrated in particular areas for reasons of time and cost in carrying out the fieldwork, with the danger of producing unrepresentative results. This can happen particularly when the sampling points below constituency level, that is, the ward or polling district, is selected, meaning that only individuals living in those small areas are actually interviewed.

Quota sampling involves giving interviewers the task of finding a specified number of people to interview who match a particular set of demographic characteristics. In other words, rather than seeking named individuals drawn from a list, the interviewers seek out 'types' of voters. The most common characteristics used are age, gender, social class and whether the respondents are working or not. The characteristics chosen are determined by evidence of the links to the key theme of the poll such as voting behaviour and/or political attitudes but the number of characteristics has to be limited because the more characteristics that are built into the quota design, the harder it will be to find individuals who satisfy the more unusual combinations of characteristics. Most polls work with about twelve cells for their quota designs, often two gender, four age, four class and two working status categories. The number of categories can increase rapidly if interlocking quotas are used whereby the different age categories are applied to each of the categories of social class, for example.

The overall intention of quota sampling is to produce a sample which is representative of the group of interest in terms of the quota factors employed. However, there will always be problems with incomplete quota fulfilment by interviewers, usually because of an inability to locate and interview particular individuals with the desired characteristics within an often tight period of time allocated for the completion of the fieldwork.

The value of quota sampling is reinforced by its speed in data collection but it remains the case that there is no theoretical basis for quota sampling. In the literature on sampling, there is next to nothing on quota sampling as a technique and yet it is the most widely used method of drawing samples. There is one 'classic' article by Moser and Stuart (1953) but in recent years few experimental tests of the effects of quota sampling have been conducted.

In one of the few tests of the various merits of random and quota sampling, Marsh and Scarbrough (1990) tested nine hypotheses about quota sampling and concluded that whilst random and quota samples were indeed different, they were not different entirely as expected on the basis of the available literature: for example, there was a bias towards the more accessible respondents but on the basis of friendship patterns rather than anything else. They concluded that the discretion given to interviewers was a major source of sample bias using a quota design and that it was consequently important to increase the debriefing of interviewers to stress the impact of clustering on the sample and to encourage interviewers to try harder to 'convert' those who initially refuse to participate.

The reasons for using quota sampling in polls are clear: they are based on feasibility, time and costs and the pollsters argue that the results produced over the years by using quota samples are at least as good as those using random samples. The debate over the use of random or quota samples has recently resurfaced once again in the aftermath of the 1992 general election when the use of quota samples was heavily criticised as one of the key reasons why the polls failed to assess correctly that the Conservatives would win the election.

The final MRS report pointed to evidence that the data on which the quotas had been set for the polls at the 1992 election were a source of error. In particular, the range of the quota targets for council house tenants lay between 17.5 per cent and 26 per cent although this figure should have been the same for all polls. This situation appears to have arisen because of some confusion over whether the percentage of council households as opposed to council tenants as individuals was the correct figure to set for the quota. There were also differences between the National Readership Survey (used to set the quotas) and the 1991 Census (which was not available at the time) in terms of the occupational structure, in particular the fact that the NRS had fewer professionals and managers than the Census and more manual workers. Given the strong correlation between occupation and voting behaviour, it seems likely therefore that the quotas actually used for the 1992 polls resulted in too many Labour voters being interviewed and too few Conservatives.

Changes in the NRS methods of classification have resulted in more respondents being classified in the top two categories of the social grade schema and fewer in the lower categories since the NRS started assigning its respondents in terms of the chief income earner rather than the head of the household (MRS 1994: 32–43).

This does not mean, however, that polls will suddenly start using random samples. As we pointed out earlier, random sampling, even as modified by a systematic and stratified approach, can be time-consuming and costly. It is therefore most often used when there is time available to collect the data over a longer period, something which is simply not available during a short election campaign.

The choice of any sampling strategy therefore turns on a number of choices, but the *quality* of the sample is always crucial. After all, the characteristics of the sample as such are of little interest but they are nevertheless vital to the extent that they enable the data to be used credibly to generalise from the sample to the target population. All design and sampling strategies have to be evaluated in this context: how confident can we be that the sample characteristics accurately reflect the target population as a whole?

Telephone sampling involves a different approach from both random and quota samples. In a way, telephone sampling is akin to simple random sampling beloved by statistical theory and it does offer the possibility of drawing an efficient sample, although only one comprised of people who can be contacted by telephone, of course. If the sample is efficiently drawn, the error estimates for a given sample size will be lower than for other sampling methods. This improved efficiency is derived from the fact that clustering in a small number of areas is not necessary to save time and money. Respondents can be reached anywhere and they can be spread out more evenly across the country or particular regions.

The main problem with telephone polls remains that of the bias in political matters based on the fact than not everyone can be reached by telephone, although this is increasing all the time, as we mentioned earlier. For national samples it is possible to correct for the shortfall of telephone subscribers more and more by adjusting the data to take account of the fact that telephone ownership is dependent on a variety of known social characteristics, such as social class, and the evidence suggesting that non-owners of telephones are more likely to be Labour voters than not.

Telephone sampling is increasingly being accepted in Britain, although there are still problems, particularly in local polls, where there is inadequate information on the characteristics of non-telephone owners with which the corrections for bias can be made.

We have now set out the three main forms of sampling used for polls in Britain. All samples are subject to both *error* and *bias*. The size of sample error can usually be calculated using straightforward assumptions on the basis that, over time, with a number of similar polls, errors will cancel one another out since they comprise both overestimates and underestimates of whatever is being measured. With repetition, therefore, the average result will approach the 'true' result. Errors will, however, inevitably cause a single poll to vary from the 'true' result. This is akin to tossing a coin and getting an estimate for heads and tails which is *not* 50:50.

Sample bias, in contrast, causes the survey estimates to vary *consistently* from the 'true' value. The sources of this bias can vary from poll to poll but it often involves problems of the nature of the sample, the location of interviews, question wording and question order effects. These effects can mostly be mitigated by adjusting the data at the analysis stage.

In an introductory book like this, there is no need to go into the details of calculating sampling errors since this is already easily available in any text dealing with sampling. These texts deal with standard errors and confidence levels which lie at the heart of such calculations. Another reason for not dealing with sampling error here is the fact that most calculations in the textbooks are based on random sampling, which, as we saw earlier, is not used much in political polls.

A further reason for not going into detail about sampling errors is that there is such variability in sample designs that to explain all the relevant factors would be likely to confuse the reader to little benefit. We can, however, make some final, general points relating to sampling which avoid technical justification.

Firstly, large samples are better than small samples for reducing sampling errors. Secondly, adding further interviews to a small sample reduces sampling error much more than adding a few more interviews to an already large sample. Thirdly, the appropriateness of any feature of sample design can only be evaluated in the context of the overall survey. Clustering the sample will save money and time but it holds dangers in terms of producing a representative sample.

The most critical point is to be aware of both the potential costs and benefits of the various options from which choices must be made within the context of the design and purpose of the whole survey. In the same way that respondents choose between answer categories, pollsters must choose in terms of their overall strategy and the purpose of the research. For example, the question often arises as to how big a sample should be. It is always important to remember that the size of the sample does not determine *by itself* the credibility of the poll. Including as large a percentage of the target population in the sample as possible does not automatically produce a representative sample. This is, however, normally not possible in any case because samples comprise only very small fractions of the total target population of interest.

At the 1992 election, the largest sample (more than 10,000 respondents interviewed by ICM for the Press Association) suggested a Labour lead of 2.5 per cent, slightly greater than the average estimate of the lead in other polls taken at the same time. A much bigger sample than normal therefore made no difference to the findings of which party was in the lead.

There are also problems in assuming that any particular sample size is better than another. Whilst most polls are based on samples of about 1,000 individuals, again much depends on the research problem and the overall design. Fewer respondents would be less costly for the budget without seriously impairing the ability to generalise from the sample to the target population if due care is taken with the other aspects of the sample design, particularly clustering.

The size of the sample might, however, be a major consideration if particular sub-groups of the sample are of special interest. The total sample size might not be worth increasing in order to produce better estimates overall but it could well be worthwhile to do so in order to increase the numbers of respondents in sub-groups such as regions. The significance of these sub-groups can be identified in advance from the theoretical concerns of the study and estimates can be made, often from past experience, about how many would be needed to provide an adequate sub-sample. This can certainly be an important factor in determining the sample size.

It is difficult to know in abstract terms whether 100 or 200 respondents for such a sub-sample would be sufficient. That depends on the type of analysis which is planned. Most researchers tend to believe, however, that fewer than 100 people dramatically reduces the utility of the data because of the severe restrictions on analysing the responses, particularly since there will always be missing data for some questions. Missing data result from questions not being answered by the respondent or from the accidental omission of the answer from the questionnaire by the interviewer. This can be a major concern in terms of the representativeness of the sample if there are lots of missing data related to key variables of interest.

In an important sense, though, there can be no definitive answer to the question of how big a sample should be since increasing sample size is only one way of improving the reliability of poll estimates. In particular, there are *non-sampling errors* and these are worthy of at least as much attention as sampling errors. There is also a tendency to assume that if sampling errors can be calculated (however inappropriately) the poll estimates will necessarily be more precise or accurate. This can be very misleading by implying an accuracy which is unwarranted.

A major source of non-sampling error is the problem of non-response and we will consider this next as part of the fourth section of this chapter, on the interviewing process and data collection. There is little doubt that interviewers can have a major impact on the quality of the data collected.

3.4   The interviewing process and data collection

Some polls are completed by respondents without an interviewer being present and this necessitates great care in all matters affecting question wording and question order as well as the precise instructions for completing the questionnaire and returning it.

Most polls, however, still involve the interaction of interviewers and respondents. The potential influence of an interviewer (good or bad) can therefore be a major variable in producing good quality data on which the subsequent analyses will depend. The task of interviewing can become particularly challenging if the poll includes a number of complex question structures and instructions, in addition to the job of getting the respondents to answer the questions.

The first task of an interviewer is to locate respondents and to get them to co-operate in answering the questions. The second task is to explain to the respondents the nature of the survey and the point of the questions in order that the initial co-operation is maintained throughout the interview. The third task is to ask the questions and to record the answers fully and accurately. In addition, interviewers must probe or follow up incomplete responses to ensure that the answers given provide the data required for the objectives of the poll to be met.

The initial task of getting respondents to co-operate can be problematic. Many people are prepared to be interviewed without much persuasion but it is always difficult to convince reluctant respondents to participate. The tone of the interviewer's presentation can be important in this, as can a convincing presentation of the study's value and relevance for the respondents, so that they are willing to give up their time to answer the questions.

The role of the interviewer is especially important when the approach to the respondent has not been notified in advance ('cold calling') or when the subject matter of the survey does not interest the respondent very much.

Whilst many respondents are flattered to be asked to answer questions, only a very few will have more than a vague idea about what they are supposed to do. To that extent, the interviewer plays a major educative and controlling role during the interview. The main problem arising from this is whether the interviewer is biasing the responses by means of their tone, speed, reactions or other aspects of their role in the interaction with the respondents. It is a fundamental assumption of all polling that the variation in answers is caused by variations in the respondents' views or experiences rather than differences in the stimulus provided by the interview experience in terms of the question format, the context in which the questions are asked or the way in which the questions are asked.

The relationship between the interviewer and the respondent can therefore be very important indeed, particularly in terms of respondent perceptions of the 'type' of interviewer. These perceptions can be influential for answering the questions, particularly in terms of age and gender, but any problems can be dealt with by not 'personalising' the situation, with the interviewer not giving their own opinion or reacting to particular answers or attitudes. To give such information, which would inevitably vary between interviewers, would undermine the striving for standardisation.

Interviewing is therefore critical to the collection of good quality data since bias will creep in very easily if interviewers do not gain respondent co-operation, if they are not consistent in the way in which they conduct the interviews and if they fail to maintain an atmosphere of respondent interest and motivation.

All polling firms are aware of the need for interviewer training and they are consequently committed to spending money on initial training and then regular refresher courses. The main difficulty for polling firms is that the nature and requirements of the work tend to produce interviewers of a particular sort, which does not reflect society as a whole. For example, interviewers need to have good reading and writing skills. The work is mainly part-time, not involving forty hours work each week, which restricts its attraction to those who are willing and able to take on such jobs. The pay is also not high. There must be flexibility in working hours, with many interviews of necessity being conducted in the evenings and at weekends. Mobility is often crucial for interviewers, demanding the use of a car to reach the respondents' homes. Some of these problems do not apply to telephone interviewing of course.

In face-to-face interviews, however, the above requirements mean that most interviewers are white, well-educated females with few family responsibilities. Special efforts are, however, made to recruit particular sorts of interviewers for specific tasks, such as black interviewers for asking racially sensitive questions to other blacks.

The evidence that suggests problems arising from this type of interviewer demographic profile is mixed. The most experienced interviewers are likely to be the best, regardless of their social characteristics, although race might be an issue for which the colour of the interviewer would be important. There is some evidence drawn from research in the United States that the race of the interviewer can be important in asking questions on the topic of race itself. However, matching interviewers and respondents on ethnic grounds might not be important in terms of data quality. It is, however, never easy to control interview allocation precisely to take account of such potential problems and the ethnic background of the respondent might well not be known in advance anyway.

A constant concern for polling firms with regard to their interviewers is the allegation that they complete their allotted tasks by 'making up' interviews. The possibility of this happening varies with the sample, the quality of the interviewers employed and the checking procedures used by the polling firms.

Such problems of 'self-completion' are most likely to occur with new interviewers, although checks are carried out on interviews regardless of who has conducted them. Two methods of validation are used by polling firms: firstly, they post a brief, follow-up questionnaire to the respondents asking for reactions to the interview; or secondly, they obtain a telephone number at the end of the interview, which is then called by a supervisor to check that the interview has actually been carried out. Such checks are likely to act as effective deterrents to interviewer cheating and they also act as reassurances to subsequent users of the data.

The main sign of problems with the interviewing process is a high refusal rate or non-response. This is a major source of error in any poll since the sample is designed to be representative of a particular target population. If, for some reason, particular individuals or types of individuals are not interviewed, the need for representativity is much more difficult to fulfil.

There will always be people who do not take part in polls and they fall into three main groups: firstly, those who are not contacted and who are therefore not given the chance to take part; secondly, those who are contacted but who refuse to take part; thirdly, those who are unable to do so for a variety of reasons such as illness or prolonged absence.

The response rate of a survey is a fundamental statistic relating to data collection. It is the number of people responding divided by the number of people sampled. The denominator includes all the people who were selected but did not actually take part, although this will not be the total sample if telephone sampling is used since not everyone is contactable by telephone.

The significance of the non-respondents in any poll is the extent to which they are different in some way from those who do respond, that is, the systematic differences between the groups of non-respondents and respondents. If the response rate is high (more than 70 per cent), it can be assumed that even if the non-respondents are distinctive in some way, the sample estimates are nevertheless likely to be good in terms of generalising about the target population as a whole. The lower the response rate, the more uncertain this must be until at a response rate of, say, 25 per cent, the final sample bears little relationship to the original sample, with a degree of self-selection and consequent bias which renders the results of little use when discussing the characteristics of the target population as a whole.

The vast majority of polls have response rates between these two extremes, based on ease of contact, the subject of the study, the interest it engenders in the respondents and the amount of effort which polling firms put into improving their response rates. There is no minimum response rate which is agreed to be acceptable for claims of representativeness, although a target figure of 75 per cent is sometimes quoted. In addition, response rates may vary dramatically in different areas. They may well be much lower in inner-city areas than rural areas or in polls which use random digit dialling for data collection.

The bias associated with non-response depends on the method of data collection. For a mail survey, there might be bias between those who respond quickly within a few days and those who need a reminder or more than one to do so. If this motivation is related to education and interest in the topic of the poll, this might well have a significant and biasing impact on the results.

Availability is a particular problem for telephone and face-to-face polls. Interviews carried out during the day using either method are certain to produce a distinctive sample, with a preponderance of housewives, the unemployed and the retired. Accessibility in cities can also be a problem because of respondent mobility, particularly amongst younger people, ensuring that particular individuals or types of respondents are hard to track down. In cities, direct access to respondents is also more difficult because of blocks of flats with security systems. Above all, interviewing at night in inner-city areas can be an uncomfortable experience for interviewers, resulting in certain groups of people being omitted from the sample.

At the 1992 general election, there were fears expressed that interviews carried out at the weekend were different from those carried out during weekdays for the reasons of 'availability bias' cited above. The precise significance of this for the poll results was a matter of dispute at the time but the final MRS report found that there had been no noticeable effect at the last general election (MRS 1994: 67–8).

Increasing response rates can be difficult within time and cost constraints and polling firms are finding it ever harder even to maintain present response rates in the face of social change involving an increase in single-person households, fewer families with children and more working women. Telephone interviewing can help overcome some of these problems since the effort required to contact people is greatly reduced. However, there is fragmentary evidence of resistance to all interviewing by older people, particularly those over sixty-five.

Overall, then, it is usually very difficult to know precisely just how biased a sample might be, but there is nevertheless little justification for assuming that non-response is unimportant. It is therefore a standard part of any poll to strive to increase response rates to a reasonable level and to avoid introducing bias which will produce major differences between respondents and non-respondents. There are several ways in which this problem can be tackled.

Much will depend on the time and money available to reduce non-response. A two-pronged approach, however, is often employed, initially to gain access to the respondents and then to enlist their co-operation.

There are a number of methods to gain access to the respondents. Firstly, if using telephone interviewing, many calls can be made at different times including evenings and weekends, when the respondents are more likely to be available for interview and when calls are also cheaper. Secondly, interviewers can be given flexible schedules which allow them to make appointments at times which are convenient for the respondents. Co-operation can be aided by sending a letter in advance. This reassures respondents and lets them know that they will be contacted soon and so they are expecting the call when it comes. This should increase their willingness to take part.

By introducing effectively the purpose of the poll by emphasising its importance and usefulness, co-operation is more likely. Allied to this are assurances of confidentiality and restrictions on access to the data. These are routine and normal in any poll. Striking a balance between persistence and responsiveness is important. Respondents often refuse to take part because they are asked to do so at the 'wrong' time but this is not necessarily a fundamental objection to being interviewed at all.

Increasing response rates to mail surveys is rather different from personal or telephone interviews because most people do come home to pick up their mail at some stage, assuming of course that the mailing list of addresses is accurate. For mail surveys, non-response is related more to persuading a respondent to complete a questionnaire without any personal persuasion from an interviewer. A mass-produced letter with a photocopied signature is unlikely to persuade many people to take part.

Research on this topic suggests than anything which makes a mail questionnaire look more personalised, professional and attractive will help to improve response rates. This can relate to the use of colours and contrasts in the questionnaire, offering money to complete and return the questionnaire, the use of stamps rather than anonymous business reply envelopes for the questionnaire to be returned and a signature at the bottom of the covering letter (original or photocopied) requesting participation.

Above all, the questionnaire for a mail survey should be straightforward to complete. In particular, it should be clear what exactly is expected of the respondent, with use of spaces to set the questions off from one another and easy response methods, for the most part only involving ticking a box or circling a number.

A critical point in achieving a high response rate in a mail survey will be repeated contacts via a reminder postcard, a second letter and another copy of the questionnaire, followed by attempts at telephone contact to 'sell' the survey by means of the personal touch not available via the post. Nevertheless, some non-response is inevitable. Three main methods can be used to correct for non-response: firstly, the final data set can be adjusted to take non-response into account; secondly, a sample of non-respondents can be surveyed using a much shorter questionnaire which forms the basis of the effort to persuade the previous non-respondents to take part; thirdly, proxy respondents can be employed.

Statistical adjustments to the final data can often be made on the basis of known statistics within the target population and the discrepancy between the known statistics and the actual sample. This does, however, make the assumption that respondents are the same as non-respondents in particular groups, such as older people, and this may not be true. Nevertheless, most polling firms do make adjustments along these lines in the belief that better estimates will usually be the result.

Contacting non-respondents may be an alternative if personal persuasion would be an effective means of improving the response rate. This could mean that original questions can be posed to the previous non-respondents and these answers can then be added to the main data set. However, it is more likely that this will only be limited since co-operation will only be agreed on the basis of a much shortened questionnaire. Contacting non-respondents is more useful therefore as a check on the bias in the main sample to aid the statistical adjustments mentioned above. The extent of this operation of contacting non-respondents will depend on time and money and only a small percentage of non-respondents will ever be contacted even if time is readily available.

Thirdly, proxy respondents or 'clones' can be used when non-response is encountered. This will usually be another member of the household or a similar person according to key social characteristics such as age and gender. It is unlikely that proxies will produce good data even given similar social characteristics if feelings, knowledge and beliefs are being questioned but they can be useful for reducing non-response in polls involving lots of factual questions. Nevertheless, reducing non-response in this way has to be handled carefully and openly, particularly when documenting the procedures employed to other users of the data.

We always need to remember, however, that calculating response rates assumes that the sampling design is based on probability. We have already noted that this is not the case in most polls in Britain which use quota samples comprising types of individuals rather than named individuals. Quota samples are often actually based on very low response rates but the response rates cannot in reality be calculated and the limitations of the data cannot therefore be usefully deduced. Unlike purely probabilistic sample designs, quota samples are affected by interviewer discretion and specific respondent characteristics, with no callbacks to trace the respondents who are initially unavailable. This can mean that particular houses or locations are favoured over others, with a preponderance of first-floor rather than fifth-floor flats being included as a result, for example.

If there are no callbacks required, the sample will be biased towards those who are at home such as women, the unemployed and the retired on the basis of availability. For this reason, the quotas are specified in terms of two or three separate social characteristics. The low response rate for quota samples might be related to the lack of need to persuade people to take part. The interviewers can move on to the next person who satisfies the quota controls when they come up against a refusal rather than make any sustained attempt to persuade the refuser to participate.

Non-response will always be a problem when collecting public opinion data but it is difficult to quantify how much of a problem it actually is because it is always problematic to find out about non-respondents. Attempting to increase response rates can have a significant impact on the overall credibility of a poll if, as a result, the response rate is increased significantly. The accent therefore must be on minimising the effects of non-response by giving a high priority in the overall survey design to increasing the response rate via the methods discussed above.

One decision which will certainly affect response rates is the method of data collection, and a discussion of the available options comprises the second part of this section.

3.4.1 Data collection

The choice of data collection method – mail, telephone or personal interview – depends on a number of related decisions encompassing the research topic, staff availability, costs and the wording of particular key questions. Most surveys use a single data collection method, although it is possible to combine them: for example, a combination of mainly a personal interview with some questions to be returned by post or non-respondents contacted by telephone rather than by an interviewer knocking at their door.

Choosing between the different data collection options rests on a variety of possibilities and strategies. Firstly, the quality of information for drawing the sample will be important. If the sample list contains full addresses and telephone numbers, personal or telephone interviews are possible. Personal contact might be made by telephone and then followed up by a personal interview to try and increase response rates. Telephone directories can be used to produce a random sample, although all addresses will not be included. If a particular individual is designated as a named respondent, different methods of data collection are feasible, although this may require an interviewer to complete the process if the mailing address is incomplete or inaccurate since the questionnaire may not arrive as a result. In addition, even if it is completed and returned, it remains possible that it has not actually been completed by the named individual to whom it was sent.

Secondly, the type of individual targeted will be significant. If there is reason to believe that the population of interest is not very well educated and will have difficulty in completing a self-administered questionnaire, a mail survey could be problematic. Such people are much more likely to complete an interview with an interviewer present. Mail procedures work best with a literate and above-average educated population who are more likely to be interested in the topic of the poll. If this is not the case, it is very likely that using interviewers to collect the data will be preferable.

Thirdly, the form of the questions will clearly be related to the data collection technique. Without an interviewer to clarify and probe, answer categories will have to be largely closed and simple. If open-ended questions are included, nevertheless, the responses will often tend to be difficult to code and compare since they will sometimes be incomplete and perhaps irrelevant, resulting from a misunderstanding of the question. They may nevertheless provide useful anecdotal and illustrative material which can be used in the final report.

The most noticeable difference in terms of data collection methods is with telephone questions, which have to be adapted to omit pictorial and visual cues. If such cues are indispensable, telephone interviewing cannot be used. Question content may also be affected by the data collection approach. This is particularly the case when dealing with sensitive topics. On the one hand, mail surveys might encourage respondents to admit negative beliefs or behaviour more easily since they do not have to admit such things to a stranger in their own front room. On the other hand, this might still happen, given an interviewer who realises the sensitivity of the questions but who nevertheless can establish and maintain the necessary trust and rapport which are required for respondents to disclose potentially sensitive information about themselves.

The likely rate of response is a key question in terms of deciding a data collection strategy. Mail surveys in particular are unlikely to produce a high response rate without a systematic procedure of follow-ups and reminders. Letters sent in advance of the actual questionnaire are useful in increasing the response rate, whereas telephone interviewing can achieve response rates similar to personal interviewing even if random digit dialling techniques are used. It must nevertheless be remembered that not everyone can be included in such telephone samples and there are certain to be refusals on the telephone as well as dead and unallocated numbers. These remain disadvantages in comparison with conducting personal interviews.

The great appeal of telephone interviewing (along with postal surveys) is the reduction in cost compared to personal interviews. The costs involved in paying an interviewer to call at someone's house, perhaps several times before just one interview is completed, is likely to be more than telephoning that person. This might not necessarily be the case, however, with polls requiring particular respondents, such as young people, who will still be difficult to reach even by telephone. However, cost is generally reckoned to be a big influence if opting for personal interviews. Even so, the objectives of the survey might make this the best approach despite the need to spend more in the process.

In addition to cost, the time available to conduct the interviews will be a vital consideration. Mail surveys usually take months to achieve an acceptable response rate given the need for reminders and second questionnaires to be dispatched, whereas telephone surveys can be completed in a few days. The length of time needed for a personal survey is hard to predict in advance because of differences in sample size and the number of interviewers employed.

The main advantages and disadvantages of each main data collection method are summarised in table 3.1.

In recent years, there has been a movement away from personal interviews to telephone interviews on the grounds of cost, more so

Table 3.1   The main advantages and disadvantages of different data collection methods

Data collection method	Advantages	Disadvantages
Personal interviews	Easier to elicit co-operation from respondents; ability to probe for more detail; instructions followed by the respondent; longer interviews possible; wide range of questions possible.	Clustering of interviews; lack of supervision of interviewers; higher costs; longer time period needed; inaccessibility to certain groups and areas such as inner-city areas, students and the young.
Telephone interviews	Lower costs; access to most social groups; shorter data collection periods; better central supervision and quality control of data; no need for clustering; better response rates.	Inevitably incomplete sampling frame; limited questions with no visual cues; harder to ask more sensitive questions.
Mail interviews	Lower costs; fewer staff employed; dispersed samples; long questions possible; no direct answers to interviewer required on sensitive questions.	Often lower response rates compared to other methods; need for complete clarity in terms of instructions and question wording; emphasis on closed rather than open questions; no interviewer present to ensure completion of questions; no checks on answer quality.

in the United States than in Britain because of the lower rate of telephone penetration in the latter. It remains clear as a result, therefore, that the data collection method depends critically on an understanding of the project's methodological goals and key decisions regarding cost and data quality.

It is always important to stress that the process of interviewing and data collection are centrally important components of polling designs. Interviewers affect response rates as well as measurement precision, although such effects are often hard to pin down and isolate. It is possible, however, to assess the extent to which interviewers are influencing the answers of respondents since it should be irrelevant who the interviewer was if standardised interviewing techniques are employed.

Another component of the data collection procedure which influences the quality of the data is the number of interviews which each interviewer has to conduct. The more interviews an interviewer has to carry out, the less reliable he or she will be in conducting them. By saving money by employing less interviewers, the polling organisation may be risking a decline in data reliability.

In summary, then, the role of the interviewer is often underestimated as part of the polling process because errors associated with interviewers are difficult to separate out from other types of error and they are always difficult to measure. Improving interviewer training and supervision might nevertheless be a very cost-effective method of improving data quality. Cost is, of course, a major influence when deciding on a data collection strategy and that decision steers the project onto a particular path regarding the content of the questionnaire and the administration of the poll. Both the interviewing process and the strategy for data collection need to be considered as leading naturally from the overall goals of the poll and the best means of fulfilling those goals.

The next section of this chapter on methodology considers the main approaches to analysing and interpreting the answers to the questions put to poll respondents.

3.5   Analysis and interpretation

When the completed questionnaires are returned, the next stage is to begin preparing the data derived from the answers for analysis and interpretation. This involves the creation of a structured data file which can be read by computer. Various operational decisions are taken regarding the structure of this data file, the allocation of numeric codes to the answers provided, entering these codes into a software program for analysis and then performing a process of 'data cleaning' which involves checks for accuracy, completeness and consistency before the actual analysis of the data begins.

Many of these procedures follow a set of long-standing and clear rules but errors can still occur by means of data entry mistakes or coding errors arising from misinterpreting particular answers. These errors will often be spotted through various means of quality control of the data entry process but it requires painstaking efforts to track down every error since they can take a variety of forms. Much will depend on the software package in use regarding the checks that are carried out. A number of such programs are easily available.

One particular source of potential error stems from the construction of the coding frame used to translate the answers to the questions into the numeric codes for analysis. Codes must be unambiguous and consistent: for example, if 'yes' to question 1 is code 1, then this must always be the case for every questionnaire. It is particularly important that missing data codes are consistently applied, that is, those codes for the questions which were not answered by *some* respondents. It is sometimes useful analytically to distinguish between different 'not answered' responses such as 'not ascertained', 'not applicable' and 'don't know'.

It is also a good idea to make the coding scheme fit the 'real' world as far as possible, for instance the age of a 45-year-old person should be coded as '45'. This makes it easier to perform checks on the data and errors are consequently easier to spot. Coding can be especially problematic when open-ended questions have been used since codes cannot be allocated in advance and printed on the questionnaire because the range of answers is not predictable. The main point here is to establish a set of codes which clearly distinguishes different answers from one another, whilst not creating a long list of separate codes, for some of which there might only be a few cases. This is largely a matter of experience and judgement but it is possible to reduce the number of categories to a smaller set without doing violence to the subtleties inherent in the data. In particular, the coding system must make analytical sense in the light of the objectives of asking the question and it should also provide categories which are useful when it comes to examining the relationships between the different variables.

Normally, a draft coding scheme is developed on the basis of a small number of questionnaires and then it is refined and expanded as more questionnaires are examined. This applies in particular to 'other' unpredictable answers that will need to be considered to see how they fit, if at all, into the existing code scheme. The overall idea is to produce an exhaustive coding scheme which ensures that each answer is only allocated a single code number and that a 'dump' of undifferentiated 'other' answers is avoided as far as possible. To check that this is actually happening, it is normal to check the coding process as it is performed, in particular to watch out for inconsistencies with coding open-ended answers between different coders.

Errors with data entry are sometimes discovered with a process of verification, where the raw data is entered once again and these data are then checked against the original entry. This might well be impractical, however, for a large data set comprising several thousand lengthy questionnaires and so attempts are also made to catch data errors by running software programs which can check up on errors such as excessive length in some of the lines of data (often meaning that some of the data have been entered more than once) and logical inconsistencies on some of the variables. The most obvious example of this concerns the gender variable, for which some respondents are coded as 'other' than male or female.

In the past, the data from polls were entered by punching holes in computer cards which were then entered into the computer. Nowadays, data entry involves direct input onto disks for storage and analysis and increasingly sophisticated software has been designed to permit the entry of only a pre-defined range of codes to check on the consistency of the data in the light of established criteria and to handle contingent questions in an appropriate manner. Many data errors will be 'caught' in this way, although simple transcription or typing errors which do not flout the established criteria obviously will not be.

As mentioned in chapter 1, technology is further speeding up the data entry process by means of computer-assisted telephone and personal interviewing, where answers are entered directly onto the computer. The biggest advantage of these systems is that the data file is created immediately and is instantly ready for analysis after the basic checking and 'cleaning' has been performed. This is in addition to further likely improvements in accuracy regarding data entry because of the software which will flag inconsistent and impossible entries. Such advantages will be offset, though, if the software is unreliable in any way. In addition, there can be no quality control over data entry because there is no completed questionnaire against which the entries can later be checked. This might be particularly problematic with open-ended responses although it does ease the pressure on the interviewers if they do not have to make decisions on the spot as to the appropriate code but can leave it to coders later on. However, computer-assisted systems require an answer of some sort to be entered before the interview can continue.

The final check on a data set is to ensure that it is complete and that only legal codes, as defined by the coding scheme, are present. The main way of checking this is to produce a frequency distribution for each variable.

Each variable has a number of different categories and there will be a different number of respondents in each category. It is common to show the frequency distribution of the variable by listing the category labels, the total number of respondents in each category and also the total number in each category expressed as a percentage. Sometimes, two columns of percentages are displayed, with the first column including all respondents and the second column producing different percentages by omitting those who failed to answer the question or who were not classified into any of the categories for some other reason. These points are illustrated in table 3.2.

This procedure of displaying the frequencies of the variables will show up 'impossible' codes but it is a time-consuming process with large data sets with lots of variables. The main survey error when

Table 3.2   A frequency distribution of strength of identification with the Labour Party by Labour Party members, 1989–90

Value label	Value (code)	Frequency (respondents)	Per cent	Valid per cent	Cumulative per cent
Very strong	1	2,762	54.5	54.9	54.9
Fairly strong	2	1,914	37.8	38.0	92.9
Not very strong	3	302	6.0	6.0	98.9
Not at all strong	4	56	1.1	1.1	100.0
Missing – not answered	9	36	0.7	Miss.	

Valid cases = 5035.   Missing cases = 36.

Source: A Study of the Labour Party Membership, 1989–90 (Q1), see Seyd and Whiteley (1992) for more details.

translating the answers into a data set for analysis involves the reliability and consistency of the open-ended coding. This will vary between projects on the basis of the quality of the coding frame and the initial training and degree of supervision of the coders. Special attention is often warranted when coding complex categories such as detailed occupations, specific crimes or diseases, for example, particularly when the relationship between such variables and others will be critical in the subsequent analysis.

These relationships will depend on the theoretical ideas underpinning the whole project and the richness of the data set will also depend on the way in which these ideas are operationalised and tested. When it comes to analysing the data after all the stages above have been completed, there are a number of levels of analysis which can be performed. A basic display of frequencies or marginals is usually the first step, followed by simple bivariate cross-tabulations involving two main variables (see table 3.3). Table 3.3 contains the absolute number of respondents in each

Table 3.3   **A cross-tabulation of occupation by trade union or staff association membership**

Occupation (recoded)	Yes, union member	Yes, staff association member	No, not a member	Missing – not answered	Row total
Salariat	1,599	62	565	56	2,282
	70.1	2.7	24.8	2.5	49.4
Routine non-manual	430	12	284	30	756
	56.9	1.6	37.6	4.0	16.4
Petit bourgeoisie	60	2	100	5	167
	35.7	1.2	60.1	3.0	3.6
Foremen and technicians	119	18	61	12	210
	56.7	8.6	29.0	5.7	4.6
Working class	809	36	330	31	1,206
	67.1	3.0	27.4	2.6	26.1
Column total	3,017	130	1,340	134	4,621
	65.3	2.8	29.0	2.9	100.0

Number of missing observations = 450.

Source: A Study of the Labour Party Membership, 1989–90, see Seyd and Whiteley (1992) for more details.

category of the cross-tabulation, followed by the row percentages. The totals for the columns and rows of the tables (absolute and percentages) are displayed at the bottom and the far right of the table, respectively.

These initial steps are always useful to illustrate the fundamental links between the variables and they act as the foundations on which more complex analyses can be built later. The complexity of the analysis will also be a major consideration for the way in which the results are presented and publicised. The outlet for publishing the results is clearly important since research must be published and disseminated to an interested audience to receive comments and criticisms if progress in social research is to be made. This point brings us to the final section of this chapter: presenting the results.

3.6 Presenting the results

At the end of the stages described above, the results of the poll must be presented in some way. There is usually no problem with finding an outlet for most results since the sponsors of the poll are often the media who will always want to publicise a story detailing the poll outcome and perhaps even a more in-depth commentary or leader comment as well. The presentation of the results can engender some tension between the polling firms and their clients since the latter are often only interested in the 'headline' figures which lead the report. This can mean an emphasis on a single finding which distorts the overall interpretation of the data. The polling firms sometimes do not have much say in the way in which the story is presented. There are exceptions to this, most notably concerning Gallup, who used to write their own reports. More recently, Gallup data for the *Telegraph* newspapers have been written up by Professor Anthony King of the University of Essex.

There are sometimes problems when polling firms are asked to conduct a poll for a pressure group which, by definition, is lined up on one side of a particular issue, such as abortion. The polling firms must ensure that the questions are as unbiased as possible for reasons of maintaining professional standards, and they always inform the client that the questions used must be published in full or at least be made available to other interested parties. The problem of interpreting what exactly constitutes 'full and fair' reporting of poll results is bound to be a sensitive issue.

One way of dealing with these tensions is for long-term relationships to be developed between the polling firms and their clients. Those that have done this generally have good and friendly links. An example is the relationship between Gallup and the *Daily Telegraph* and *Sunday Telegraph* over more than thirty years, during which time the presentation of the data has virtually always been both sober and reflective. This applies to the quality press in general but not so much to the tabloid press, which is much more interested in producing publicity for itself than an undistorted interpretation of the data.

This contrast can be seen most readily in the reports of poll results in the newspapers. The quality press are usually prepared to include at the end of a report containing poll results a paragraph which states the number of people interviewed for the poll, the type of sample (usually a quota design), the number of constituencies in which the interviews were conducted, how those constituencies were selected, whether those constituencies were nationally distributed, the dates of the fieldwork and the method of data collection employed.

For example, in *The Guardian* of 11 May 1994, data from an ICM poll are presented and the final paragraph reads 'ICM interviewed a tightly controlled quota sample of 1,438 adults aged 18-plus in 103 randomly selected constituencies country-wide. Interviewing was conducted face to face last Friday and Saturday.' This is very much in line with the code of conduct issued by the MRS, in which the polling firms routinely provide this type of information to accompany the presentation of the poll results. The main query relating to the above paragraph is what exactly 'tightly controlled' means, although the vast majority of readers would simply accept this statement at face value.

This kind of information regarding the conducting of the poll is, however, often omitted from the tabloid press whenever it publishes poll stories, leading to considerable suspicion that the poll has not been conducted properly. Despite this, stories based on the 'results' are still written up, sometimes in some detail, and prominently displayed in the paper.

The tabloid press would argue of course that they do not have the space to publish the details of the poll, although it would only ever occupy a single paragraph, or that their readers would not understand the details even if they were published.

The question of available space has to be a general consideration when the decision is made about how to present poll stories. Although polls provide stories for newspapers, they are rarely given a lot of space in any one issue.

One of the major accusations of the polls at the 1992 general election was that they wrongly assumed that the 'don't know' and 'refusal' groups could reasonably be distributed equally across the parties. It was reckoned then that these two groups were in fact disproportionately Conservative, and when the actual election took place that is how most of them voted. This meant that the polls inevitably underestimated the Conservative vote share.

In the ICM poll of May 1994, this problem was dealt with by adjusting the raw data to produce four different tables. The first table simply excluded the 'don't know' group, thus producing the 'headline' vote intention percentages; the second table re-allocated the 'don't know' group according to the reported past vote of the respondents; the third table adjusted the whole sample by reported past vote and the fourth table allocated the 'don't know' group and adjusted the whole sample by reported past vote at the same time.

The effect of all of these adjustments was to reduce the apparent lead of Labour over the Conservatives from 18 per cent to 10 per cent. The latter figure was regarded in the report as the likely difference between the two main parties if a general election were to be held immediately.

In addition, a further table was presented in the above report which was derived from a question about which party had the best policies for dealing with the economy. If this question was used, the Labour lead over the Conservatives dropped even more to only 7 per cent, although fully 40 per cent were categorised as believing that none of the parties had the best policies or they did not know. This figure for the 'don't know' group would be likely to diminish considerably in the context of an election campaign.

Overall, these developments are encouraging in that they show the pollsters to be experimenting with adjustments to the headline percentages and being prepared to give data for other questions that might be crucial for determining election outcomes. In terms of presentation of the results, this expansion of detail is certainly laudable although it is unlikely that even *The Guardian* will allow five tables to be used during an election campaign and so decisions as to which adjustment is likeliest to be most appropriate will have to be taken in advance of the next election. At the moment, all the polling firms are not giving this degree of detail in their reports and this can give the impression of widely different poll results conducted at the same time.

The normal way of presenting poll data is to use tables containing straightforward percentages as the basis of the story. Sometimes, the results from previous months are repeated, so that the picture of developments over time can be compared and contrasted, particularly if the same questions have been asked on a regular basis over an extended period. For example, the current percentage approving of the government's record is often given and then the corresponding figure for the previous month or the last election is then shown for contrast. There will often be a simple index of change added to the table to highlight any changes (either positive or negative).

Poll results in the media very rarely get beyond simple percentages and this can be misleading since it inevitably simplifies what is a complex phenomenon better portrayed by some awareness of the multifaceted influences which interact to produce the final result. This type of presentation and analytical approach is, however, the preserve of the academic monograph rather than a newspaper.

One reason why the media might now be reluctant to publicise poll results as prominently as in the past relates once more to the 1992 general election. Some members of the media felt very stung by the alleged inaccuracies of the polls which they had funded by spending many thousands of pounds. The 'return' for this expenditure in their eyes was not only meagre; worse still, it was wrong. The possibility that polls might be 'wrong' is ever present, of course, but this has always been the case. The media, however, appeared to have largely forgotten about this possibility and the problems associated with the 1970 election in the intervening five general elections and had assumed that appropriate changes had been made to polling practice. In that sense, the polls of 1992 were a considerable shock to them.

In order to try and avoid possible embarrassment by polls being 'wrong', the BBC opted not to lead their main evening news bulletin during the 1992 election campaign with a poll story. This appeared sensible and prudent because of the danger that a 'rogue poll' would appear at some stage during the campaign and that it would later turn out to be 'wrong'. It was therefore thought to be safer to risk not leading on a possibly great story for fear of ending up leading on a story based on a rogue poll.

This approach by the BBC came under particular pressure when the 'logjam' in the polls appeared to break on 1 April 1992, with a Harris poll reporting a Labour lead of 6 per cent over the Conservatives. This caused some confusion since Harris had also conducted another poll that showed the Conservatives to be in the lead by 1 per cent only the previous day. The Labour 'lead' was mentioned on *Channel 4 News* and ITN's *News at Ten* at the start of their respective programmes but it was still placed second on the BBC without any headline preceding it.

The question of how to present poll findings in the media remains delicate. This is never easy to do at the best of times, given the difficulty of presenting statistical material on television in particular, where graphics and tables appear momentarily before being consigned to oblivion and replaced by others. Poll results will always be newsworthy and they therefore cannot be ignored entirely. The 1992 election, however, reinforced previously latent fears that there were real and substantive dangers in going overboard on poll stories ('overdosing on data') whatever their source and whoever had conducted the poll.

This is unlikely to mean that polls will play any lesser role at the next general election in 1996 or 1997 but it does signal a wariness on the part of the media towards polls based on a very real concern that their money can buy a very good story or a very bad one. Allied to this is the realisation that the difference between the two is very slight and it simply cannot be predicted in advance.

One of the key dangers in presenting poll data is the placing of too much emphasis on change and leads. To talk of any party being 1 per cent 'in the lead' is fatuous, given the way in which the samples are drawn, as we saw earlier in this chapter. Sometimes, the figure of ±3 per cent either way for a quota sample is cited, without any realisation that this relates to each party, thus rendering the *range* for the difference between two parties considerably greater. Whilst the media are aware of this danger, it is largely ignored during election campaigns despite the issuing of routine 'health warnings' about the presentation of poll results.

The main difficulty for the media is that it is hard to write an interesting story which essentially concludes that there has not been any change in the polls since last month. The emphasis on continuity rather than change goes against the grain for the media, whose format and competitive edge mean that they need material which can be immediately absorbed in straightforward and broad ways. The inherent complexities of any polling data mean that polls in general are unlikely candidates for such treatment.

The two main concerns of the media are 'Is it understandable?' and 'Is it interesting?' Judgements on these questions tend to be ritualistic, based on common and past practice. The incestuous relationship between the different forms of the media in which television and the newspapers copy each other's ideas produces a consensus that emphasises presentation at the expense of content, with a constant search for the exceptional and an avoidance of the mundane. Unfortunately, the essential story told by many polls is that change is the exception and continuity with the past is very much the norm.

References

De Vaus, D. A. (1990) *Surveys in Social Research*, 2nd edn, London: Allen and Unwin.

Market Research Society (1994) *The Opinion Polls and the 1992 General Election*, London: Market Research Society.

Marsh, C. and E. Scarbrough (1990) 'Testing nine hypotheses about quota sampling', *Journal of the Market Research Society* 32: 485–506.

Moser, C. A. and A. Stuart (1953) 'An experimental study of quota sampling', *Journal of the Royal Statistical Society* (Series A) 116: 349–405.

Reynolds, N., A. Diamantopoulous and B. Schlegelmilch (1993) 'Pretesting in questionnaire design: A review of the literature and suggestions for further research', *Journal of the Market Research Society* 35: 171–82.

Seyd, P. and P. Whiteley (1992) *Labour's Grass Roots: The politics of party membership*, Oxford: Clarendon Press.

Smith, T. (1987) 'The art of asking questions, 1936–1985', *Public Opinion Quarterly* 51: S95-S108.

Suggested further reading

A very useful source of supplementary information for this chapter is the book by A. N. Oppenheim, *Questionnaire Design, Interviewing and Attitude*

Measurement (London: Pinter, 1992, new edition). It contains chapters on pilot work, questionnaire planning, question wording, attitude scaling and data processing, for example. In addition, the series of papers published by Sage in the series *Quantitative Applications in the Social Sciences* contains a number of very useful introductions to topics of relevance. There are now 102 papers in the series covering all the major analytical techniques of social science. In terms of this chapter, however, the three most useful papers are those by Converse and Presser entitled *Survey Questions* (no. 63), by Davis entitled *The Logic of Causal Order* (no. 55), and by Kalton entitled *Introduction to Survey Sampling* (no. 35).

4

The use and impact of national opinion polling

This chapter contains much of the material which comes most readily to mind when opinion polling is considered in terms of its national use and impact on British politics. The chapter is divided into five main headings, dealing in turn with polls and voting behaviour, the government, the political parties, the mass media and pressure groups.

Although these five topics can clearly be dealt with separately, there will inevitably be explicit linkages across the five sections and it is certainly not intended to argue that the material is of necessity confined to one heading or another. These 'cross-connections' are largely the result of opinion polling in Britain developing as a process that is dominated by different but linked groups of 'insiders', particularly those inhabiting the fields of politics and journalism who constantly feed off one another's ideas and gossip, especially during the frenzy of election campaigns. The 'conventional wisdom' about an election result that emerges from this process and the expectations it generates for the future are largely determined by these groups. The role of the general public is marginal at best in such deliberations.

This process of mutual dependence is strongly reinforced by straightforward self-interest on the part of such groups and it is often characterised by a peculiar atmosphere of simultaneous suspicion and respect. The commonest metaphor to describe this situation is one of a goldfish bowl, with the different participants swimming around, eyeing one another warily, waiting for someone else to make the first move. This process has been greatly strengthened by the advent of election campaigns dominated more and more by the requirements of television and the consequent demise of the public meeting as the main arena of political debate. Indeed, for many voters, it is now impossible to consider an election campaign without television naturally acting as its epicentre. Television is now the critical forum for determining what is said, how it is said and even the exact timing of *when* it is said to ensure coverage on the main news bulletins.

We will return to these themes in turn as we proceed through this chapter and we will end with a consideration of how polling influences and is influenced by the changing structure of British politics.

4.1   The polls and voting behaviour

The record of the polls in predicting the winner of an election correctly has long assumed considerable importance for British polling organisations. To that extent, the outcome of the 1992 general election could be regarded as disastrous since none of polls predicted an overall Conservative majority. Most had predicted either a hung Parliament, with either Labour or Conservative as the largest party or a small overall majority for Labour, although this latter idea had largely evaporated by polling day itself. This was reflected in many of the newspaper headlines on election day which suggested a late increase in support for the Conservatives. For example, the headline in the *Daily Telegraph* was 'Polls put parties neck and neck', whilst the front page of *The Guardian* read 'Tory hopes rise after late surge'.

The extent of this failure of the polls is most clearly demonstrated by a comparison of the performance of the polls at previous general elections dating back to 1970, the last occasion when most of the polls predicted the 'wrong' winner. Table 4.1 gives the vote shares of the main parties derived from the final polls and the actual election results between 1970 and 1992.

The assumption was that such a failure could only be a significant setback for the polling firms since what use were polls if they

Table 4.1   The final polls and actual election results, 1970–92

	Sample size	Conservative	Labour	Liberal	Other	Conservative lead
1970						
ORC	1,583	46.5	45.5	6.5	1.5	+1.0
Harris	2,661	46.0	48.0	5.0	1.0	–2.0
NOP	1,562	44.1	48.2	6.4	1.3	–4.1
Gallup	2,190	42.0	49.0	7.5	1.5	–7.0
Marplan	2,267	41.5	50.2	7.0	1.3	–8.7
Result		46.2	43.8	7.6	2.4	+2.4
February 1974						
Business decisions	1,056	36.0	37.5	23.0	3.5	–1.5
ORC	2,327	39.7	36.7	21.2	2.4	+3.0
Harris	3,193	40.2	35.2	22.0	2.6	+5.0
NOP	4,038	39.5	35.5	22.0	3.0	+4.0
Gallup	1,881	39.5	37.5	20.5	2.5	+2.0
Marplan	1,649	36.5	34.5	25.0	4.0	+2.0
Result		38.8	38.0	19.8	3.4	+0.8
October 1974						
Business decisions	2,071	35.5	40.0	20.0	4.5	–4.5
NOP	1,978	31.0	45.5	19.5	4.0	–14.5
ORC	1,071	34.4	41.8	19.4	4.4	–7.4
Harris	2,701	34.6	43.0	19.3	3.1	–8.4
Gallup	954	36.0	41.5	19.0	3.5	–5.5
Marplan	1,024	38.3	43.8	19.5	3.5	–10.5
Result		36.7	40.2	18.8	4.3	–3.5
1979						
Gallup	2,348	43.0	41.0	13.5	2.5	+2.0
MORI	974	44.4	38.8	13.5	3.3	+5.6
Marplan	1,973	45.0	38.5	13.5	3.0	+6.5
NOP	1,069	46.0	39.0	12.5	2.5	+7.0
MORI	1,089	45.0	37.0	15.0	3.0	+8.0
Result		44.9	37.7	14.1	3.3	+7.2
1983						
ASL	1,100	46	23	29	2	+23
Harris	567	47	25	26	2	+22
Gallup	2,003	45.5	26.5	26	2	+19
Marplan	1,335	46	26	26	2	+20

Table 4.1   *Continued*

	Sample size	*Conser-vative*	*Labour*	*Liberal*	*Other*	*Conser-vative lead*
NOP	1,040	46	28	24	2	+18
MORI	1,101	44	28	26	2	+16
Result		44	28	26	2	+16
1987						
ASL	1,702	43	34	21	2	+9
Harris	2,122	42	35	21	2	+7
Gallup	2,005	41	34	23.5	1.5	+7
Marplan	1,633	42	35	21	2	+7
NOP	1,668	42	35	21	2	+7
MORI	1,688	44	32	22	2	+12
Result		43	32	23	2	+11
1992						
NOP	1,746	39	42	17	2	−3
ICM	2,186	38	38	20	4	0
MORI	1,731	38	39	20	3	−1
Gallup	2,478	38.5	38	20	3.5	+0.5
Average		38.4	39.2	19.2	3.1	−0.8
Result		42.8	35.2	18.3	3.7	+7.6
Error		−4.4	+4.0	+0.9	−0.6	+8.4

Source: MRS (1994: 113–14 and 1).

could not even get the election outcome correct? The pollsters were duly contrite on the day after the election, aware of the apparently incontrovertible nature of the vitriolic criticism that was directed at them for such a 'failure'.

In this way, the pollsters were accepting the use of polls as predictors of election outcomes, something which they are always careful to deny at other times. Such 'health warnings' are routinely ignored by the commissioners of polls, and the pollsters themselves make the point lightly for fear of losing business if they point out too clearly that the data should not be used to predict. After all, the value of poll data will inevitably be seriously diminished if they cannot be used for the purposes of those who pay for such data to be collected.

Nevertheless, there is a clear sense in which most polls (with the exception of the predictive type of exit poll) should not be used to predict. The data always take some time to check and analyse and the situation the poll was assessing may well change in the time between the data being collected and the results being published. Polls are therefore best regarded as broad guides only to the political temperature of the country at a particular time, capable of delineating what many people are thinking but not generally capable of carrying great weight in terms of analysing the motivations of ordinary people or their likely behaviour.

The use of polls as 'oracles' to the exclusion of other political data and information is to ascribe to polls too great a significance. Whilst poll results are always likely to be a better guide to the political atmosphere at any particular time than canvass returns and the instincts of party agents, they remain instruments whose analytical value is greatly outweighed by the purely descriptive information they contain. The need to get the data collected and analysed quickly means that polls contain questions which cannot dig very deeply into the psyche of the ordinary voter and they are rarely detailed enough to untangle ideas of cause and effect. The emphasis of polls is much more focused upon 'what' rather than 'why', providing broad but inevitably shallow insights. Nevertheless, at election time in particular, the role of the polls in examining likely voting behaviour remains highly significant.

An obvious reason for this is the simple lack of alternatives. As an election campaign progresses, polls provide the main means of keeping up to date with developments. They play a critical role because they have no partisan axe to grind, something which cannot be realistically expected of any of the main participants in the campaign. Of course, the *interpretation* of the poll results will inevitably be a matter of debate and controversy amidst the jockeying for position by the competing parties but that is not the same as saying that polls are inherently of little use or are always biased.

One of the chief functions of polls is to track the campaign in terms of the issues that are of prominence and to check the effect of particular events and the reactions of the party leaders. This can be particularly important for party leaders as they attempt to wrest control of the campaign agenda from their opponents. In other words, whose message is getting across the best and what effect is the campaign having on the voting intentions of the electorate?

This last question is the one that is usually most avidly followed by the media as the swings between parties are totted up and explained or, indeed, the lack of movement between parties becomes a central focus. Conventional wisdom suggests that it will be the state of the economy which will form the main battleground, with the 'feel good' factor and questions of economic competence and management overriding other potential issues, such as the state of the environment. It is vital for politicians to grasp quickly these apparent shifts in public opinion in order to react, either by reinforcing the impact of an issue regarded as being favourable to them or attempting to downplay an issue which is likely to be favourable to their opponents. Naturally, politicians would ideally like *advance* intelligence to be able to plan their next move but the polls are the next best thing.

It inevitably remains the case, however, that polls are snapshots of the public mood taken at a particular time and in a particular way. The results of polls can never be taken as definitive since they are often attempting to measure movement and change which can occur extremely quickly or indeed not at all. Polls are also not particularly good or effective at getting to the bottom of the thought processes of most people since they are, by definition, transient in nature.

None of these points in defence of the polls made much difference in 1992, when the polls, in the context of the actual result on 9 April, were seen to be a long way out, particularly in comparison to previous general election outcomes (see table 4.1 again). Doubts were cast about the polls, even to the point where some were sceptical as to whether the Labour Party had *ever* been in the lead throughout the campaign. This led, in response, to a variety of explanations as to why the polls' prediction of a hung Parliament had failed to materialise. A prominent contribution to this debate was the initial report of the Market Research Society into the performance of the polls published two months after the election.

The MRS set up an inquiry team to analyse the failure of the polls. Its report was accompanied by a press release that spoke of 'fundamental problems', which implied that many polls at previous elections had also been inaccurate. This was an unfortunate phrase to use because the media fastened on to it quickly as yet another stick with which to beat the polling industry. Additionally, the phrase 'fundamental problems' was not actually in the report itself, only in the press release. This acted to irritate the polling firms, who, in any event, disputed the calculations used to arrive at this conclusion. The pollsters themselves concluded that there was no consistent bias favouring either main party over time. This dispute did, however, encourage the polling firms to investigate as far as possible whether the 1992 result could be attributed to changes in stated voting intention which had not been apparent at previous general elections.

Several of the polling firms went back to their respondents immediately after the election to try to ascertain why they had voted as they did and the likely effect of this on the overall outcome. As a result of these investigations, attention subsequently centred on a number of possible explanations. Many possibilities were canvassed, among them the non-registration of voters, differential refusers, respondents lying to interviewers, sampling error including too much clustering, interview procedures and locations and late swing.

The main problem in examining these possibilities was that they had not been concerns at the previous general election in 1987, when the polls were generally accurate, and none of the pollsters had made substantial changes to their procedures in the intervening five years. It therefore seemed unlikely that such procedures were suddenly the cause of such marked discrepancies. Other possibilities, such as non-registration due to the poll tax, might have been influential in certain seats where the number on the electoral register had declined steeply since 1987 but this was at best a minor factor when taken nationally. Eventually, most attention settled on two likely influences: namely, different actions taken in the polling booth compared to statements to interviewers, and the problems resulting from differential refusals.

The first possibility centred on the suggestion that many voters had indeed stated to interviewers that they would vote Labour and had intended to do so at the time of the interview. In the end, however, they had changed their minds and voted Conservative. This could not be construed as 'lying' since this had been the intention at the time of the interview. Once the real possibility of a Labour government came into view, according to this theory at least, that possibility acted to concentrate the minds of waverers sufficiently to entice them back into the Conservative camp. As the reality of a likely Labour government became more apparent to more people, enough voters took different action in the polling booths from their stated intentions to make the final polls inaccurate in terms of their final predictions.

In one sense, this possible explanation might be termed 'late swing' and could not have been picked up by the polls at all if it had occurred on election day itself after the polls had finished interviewing. However, it should still have been noticeable in the exit polls since they are *only* conducted on election day, and yet they too were inaccurate in terms of the final outcome, although not by as much as the pre-election polls. It was the case that, although the exit polls were inaccurate, they were not as far out as the other polls. Both the NOP/BBC and Harris/ITN exit polls overestimated the swing from Conservative to Labour in Conservative/Labour marginal seats by slightly under 2 per cent, less than half the error of the four pre-election polls conducted in the last two days before the election. This would suggest that although late swing may well have occurred, it is unlikely to have happened on the scale necessary to cause the noted discrepancies. There must have been other problems influencing the election outcome.

As a result of this, most post-election attention has centred on the sensitive question of differential refusers. These are the people who refuse to take part in poll interviews and who are known from previous research to be disproportionately female and elderly. Estimates vary as to how large this group might be within the electorate and the extent to which their decision to refuse to participate in polls could affect the assessment of the vote shares of the parties. It is known, however, that there is a substantial degree of refusing to take part in quota samples, of about one-third or even higher of all those approached to participate.

The political significance of this particular group of refusers is that they are likely to vote disproportionately Conservative when compared to other social groups. As such, differential refusal by this specific group of voters could have had an impact on poll outcomes given the context of the 1992 election, which appeared to be favouring the Labour Party, perhaps reinforcing the unwillingness of certain types of people to co-operate and to give 'unfashionable' views to interviewers.

This is sometimes termed the 'shame factor' and is akin to the idea of the 'spiral of silence' mentioned in chapter 3, whereby perceptions of the current climate of opinion have important effects on the willingness of people to speak out *against* what they perceive to be the current trend of opinion. Of course, this is very difficult to pin down empirically but it nevertheless does retain some intuitive plausibility as a possible cause of the failure of the polls.

One way around this potential problem is not to rely on the voting intention question alone but to widen the analysis to look at responses to questions on the economy and, specifically, the question of economic competence. With the always invaluable use of hindsight, responses to these particular questions would have contradicted the voting intention question in most polls since the Conservatives were well ahead throughout the campaign on this particular theme. This does suggest that the standard voting intention question may not be an accurate guide to behaviour for some voters and that a wider approach would pay better dividends for the polling firms.

The main difficulty with adopting this approach is that it will be impossible to tell its exact value until *after* the next general election, when it will become clearer whether the 1992 result was an aberration or the start of a new trend. Any changes made *now* on the basis of assumptions that a problem does actually exist might be defeated by a reversion to the situation prevailing before 1992, when no-one perceived differential refusers as a problem. This is the bane of the pollsters' life: always and inevitably being worried that changes introduced to solve one problem may cause another problem to emerge as a consequence. For that reason, the pollsters have been very reluctant to introduce changes in their practices and procedures overall, although there have been a number of experiments conducted since the election.

One experiment that did attract considerable attention after the 1992 election was the use by ICM of an actual ballot box to simulate the polling booth when asking people how they intended to vote. This meant that the respondents did not need to tell the interviewer how they intended to vote but would simply mark a mock ballot paper with their choice and then put it into the box. The thinking behind this was to try to test whether such a procedure for the voting intention question would reduce the number of refusals.

The initial results suggested that this experiment was worthwhile since the number of refusals did appear to drop. Other pollsters were more sceptical that this would have much effect overall on the basis that the total number of refusers had always been small. It is important to make a clear distinction here between those who refuse to be interviewed at all and those who agree to be interviewed but who refuse to answer the voting intention question (item refusal). The former group is both larger and a greater problem for the pollsters than the latter group.

If differential refusals had been a major cause of the discrepancies in 1992, what else might have been influential in addition? It is unlikely that any single cause could explain what happened; it appears much more likely that there were a number of separate but linked influences which interacted with one another to produce the discrepancy between the poll results and the election outcome. It was suggested, for example, that there might be a problem associated with interviewing people in the street rather than in their homes. People are easier to contact on the street as they walk by in a shopping arcade, for example; but did this bias the various samples too much in terms of representativeness? In other words, were the quota controls too broad, leading to interviewers talking to the 'wrong' people? Was there too much concentration upon urban areas to the exclusion of rural areas and small towns?

The MRS published its final report on the opinion polls and the 1992 general election in July 1994 based on the deliberations of a working party which it had established after the election, comprising both pollsters and academics. The report is a detailed and comprehensive document of 162 pages, containing 66 tables, which systematically sifts the evidence for what went wrong for the polls in 1992.

The conclusions of the working party attribute the 'blame' to three main factors, each of roughly equal importance. Firstly, there was some late swing, with the Conservatives gaining from some voters changing their minds after the end of poll interviewing. Secondly, some inadequacies of the quota system in operation were revealed. We have already mentioned this in the last chapter. It is important to set quotas on variables relevant for voting behaviour in political polls. There is little point in setting a quota for colour of eyes, for example, in a political poll: there is no reason to believe that such a quota would be of any relevance and some doubt must similarly be raised about the utility of age and gender in this context. Of much more significance for political polls would be occupation, housing tenure and trade union membership although it is some-times not easy to obtain accurate statistics for these variables. With-out accurate data on the most relevant variables, the polls are in danger of not arriving at an accurate picture of the distribution of political support throughout the country. Thirdly, Conservative sup-porters were less likely to reveal their loyalties to pollsters than their Labour counterparts, through both item refusal (refusing to answer the voting intention question) and refusing to be interviewed at all, although the latter was hard to quantify.

Minor factors that had some effect included the selection of sampling points within the constituencies by the polling firms, pro-ducing a slight bias to Labour, and interviewing people not actu-ally on the electoral register. Possible causes which were *ruled out* by the MRS report included deliberate lying by poll respondents, any impact by postal voters or voters living overseas, interviewing procedures and sample size.

The working party emphasised that methodological work should be carried out to verify the sources of the quotas and the targets set for adjusting the data by weighting to correct for bias in the sam-ples. The use of out-of-date and unreliable data for doing this had to be avoided. Further research into comparing quota and random sampling was also recommended. The working party also recom-mended that work should be conducted on encouraging people to state their voting intention and to consider different ways of re-allocating the 'don't knows' on the basis of reported vote in the past, although the infrequency of elections in Britain means that this might be hazardous in terms of the accuracy of that recall. The working party stated that the proportion of 'don't knows' should be published as part of the presentation of any poll. They believed too that attempts to increase response rates in general would also be worthwhile. The working party finally called for methodological pluralism and diversity in a broader effort to persuade the public of the value of polls (MRS 1994: x-xv).

The MRS report is also suggestive of the sheer complexity of public opinion and its relationship to voting behaviour. This may be considerably underestimated in terms of the questions put to re-spondents and the conclusions drawn about likely behaviour from the answers. Some of the questions used in polls do not dig deep enough or provide the detail required for a greater understanding of public opinion and how it is shaped and reshaped over time.

This is particularly the case at election time since the context of each separate election is inevitably unique. Whilst comparisons are always made statistically with previous elections in terms of the swing needed for a party to win an overall majority, for example, it is altogether more difficult to pin down the 'atmosphere' of an election and how its particular 'climate of opinion' differs from four or five years ago. Yet this climate might be critical to understanding the result of an election and how the outcome was influenced by aggregated, but nevertheless individual, voting decisions.

This point relates, of course, to the theory of the 'spiral of silence' which may or may not be operative and the 'shame factor' which may have diminished the Conservative vote in the polls in 1992 but did not act to reduce 'real' Conservative support in the polling booths. In this way, the apparent strength of the Labour vote may actually have been very 'soft' indeed, with a marked discrepancy between proclaimed intentions and actual voting habits. It has to be remembered above all that a stated vote intention is *not* a vote; it is simply an often vague preference given as a result of being asked a question by a stranger. There is nothing to lose by answering one way and then acting apparently in contradiction to the previously stated preference. The justification for this is that circumstances have changed and so has the intended action as a result.

Whilst there may have been a lot of sympathy for the Labour Party in 1992 and a lot of goodwill in general, this did not translate into votes for the party on 9 April. There remains a lot of difference between theory and practice in terms of voting behaviour. If the theory of 'instrumental' voting is correct, the result of the 1992 election should have been no surprise. This theory suggests that with the apparent decline of class loyalty amongst voters in recent years, the main question at elections is 'Which party will be best for me and my family?' This is usually translated into attitudes and perceptions focused upon the state of the economy.

One way of trying to confront the likelihood that instrumental concerns will be important predictors of voting behaviour is to ask more and detailed questions about the economy. This is difficult in a short interview of perhaps ten to twelve questions since there will always be other useful and interesting questions which are jostling for inclusion. Another way is to pay greater attention to what is happening in different regions of the country, particularly in the marginal seats, where the election is ultimately decided. Studying individual seats rather than focusing purely on national polls might well allow a more rounded interpretation to emerge. We will deal with this more in the next chapter.

Another way to achieve a greater balance and understanding is for the interpreters of polling data to reflect more and opine less. This is of course impossible to achieve during an election campaign, when the speed of events and reactions to them are almost instant. This applies to both politicians and journalists and, given this context, we should not be surprised when the conventional wisdom is seen to be inaccurate. More in-depth research is needed generally, particularly on the question of political values and attitudes and their impact on election outcomes, but the breathless nature of much polling in Britain and the obsession with catchy headlines and straightforward findings militate against this. It is rare to find a detailed exposition of the 'state of the nation', with the honourable exceptions of the poll commissioned by *The Guardian* every year or the reports of the annual British Social Attitudes Survey.

One particular role which the polls can play is to test the impact of the campaign on an election result. What was the 'swing issue' that finally decided the outcome? To date, the evidence on this question is mixed. Theoretically, with more floating voters and fewer loyal voters, campaigns should matter more in terms of mass political choice. As loyalty to a party becomes less predictable, the importance of issues and an instrumental approach to voting should become more important. However, campaigns might not actually affect anything if the agenda on which the campaign is fought is determined several months before the formal campaign actually starts. A distinction should be made, therefore, between the three-week official 'short campaign' and the 'long-term campaign' stretching back many months, if not years.

There is a strong case for saying that this distinction was important in 1992. The Conservatives started in January 1992 to emphasise the question of taxation via a nationwide poster campaign. Although the tone of this was essentially negative, in that it consisted of attacking the Labour Party, it did have the effect of setting the agenda and determining the issues to which the Labour Party had to respond. This is one of the advantages of being in government, since the issues which the government emphasises are usually put across much better than those chosen by the opposition parties. Some analyses of the 1992 election concluded that the question of tax was critical, whatever poll respondents said about its importance to them. By starting early, nearly three months before the campaign proper got off the ground, the Conservatives had a head start which they never lost in establishing in the public mind the 'dangers' of a Labour government in terms of the tax burden on ordinary people. The specific emphasis on the tax question was then linked to more general, long-term concerns about the competence of the Labour Party and its leadership.

The importance of agenda setting can be crucial to any election campaign. Arguably, of equal importance to Britain, was the question of European integration, given that the Maastricht Treaty had been signed only four months before polling day; however, the issue of Europe was barely mentioned during the campaign itself. This partly reflected the knowledge of the two main parties that they both had internal splits on the question, along with the belief that the issue failed to interest many voters anyway and would not be decisive in swinging votes either way.

Another potential issue in the longer term was the question of protecting the environment. Again, this received scant attention from any of the parties. The issue had exploded spectacularly into British politics in 1989 at the European Parliament election, when the Green Party won 15 per cent of the votes although no seats. Since then, whilst all the parties have made the right noises, little has happened to suggest that any of them would transform the issue of the state of the environment into a major concern on which they would actively campaign. As a result, concern for the environment has increasingly moved out of the party arena into the world of pressure groups such as Greenpeace and Friends of the Earth. The key point to remember is that the credibility of any proposed solution to a political problem depends on the *definition* of the aspect of the problem that matters the most and this is what all parties struggle to define in a way that favours them and weakens their opponents.

Critically, therefore, the outcome of the struggle for the agenda sets the tone for any election campaign, and the polls will follow this agenda in terms of the questions they put to respondents. The pollsters will not be able to ignore such concerns if they are trying to tap public opinion and its changes and vicissitudes.

What, then, is the empirical evidence to suggest that the polls do actually have an impact on voting behaviour? Do the polls do more than measure the state of, and changes in, public opinion and actually influence how people cast their votes? Two main possible effects have been identified over the years. Firstly, there is the *bandwagon effect*, which is the reinforcing of a party's leading position in the polls by the very fact that it is in the lead. In other words, voters want to climb aboard the bandwagon in order to be associated with the winning party. If the polls provide such information about majority opinion, this by itself will cause some people to adopt that majority view themselves. Secondly, the reverse of the bandwagon effect is the *underdog effect*, where the voters, when provided with information about the state of the polls, choose to adopt the minority or underdog view. These ideas are important because, if by the very fact that one party is predicted to win that becomes a self-fulfilling prophecy, the role of the polls in 'interfering' in the democratic process becomes a live issue of professional concern for the pollsters.

McAllister and Studlar (1991) using Gallup polls discovered evidence of a bandwagon effect amongst voters in three British general elections in 1979, 1983 and 1987. They found no evidence of an underdog effect and concluded that opinion polls are particularly useful in facilitating tactical voting in three-party competition. One possible caveat to this conclusion that no underdog effect could be found relates to the closing stages of the 1983 general election, when the lead of the Conservatives over the other parties narrowed slightly. This might have been partly due to the publicly expressed fears of Francis Pym about the Conservatives winning the election with a huge majority.

Whiteley (1986) found strong evidence of a significant bandwagon effect in operation which served to benefit the SDP/Liberal Alliance at the 1983 general election. This conclusion was based on a very small sample, however, drawn from Gallup data. The main problem is establishing a direct link between the polls and any influence they exert on voting behaviour is that so few people will admit to being influenced in this way. By doing so, they are tacitly admitting that they are unable to make up their own mind but rely on polls to do it for them. This means that direct questions produce only a small group for analysis even in large samples (the 1983 Gallup data comprised more than 4,000 respondents but only 124 individuals who admitted to being influenced in their voting decisions by what the polls were saying). Asking indirect questions about whether the respondents saw a poll and, if they did, who was in the lead are more tests of memory than a guide to behaviour even if the state of the polls is accurately recalled in response to such a question.

More experimental evidence of bandwagon effects was discovered by Marsh (1984) and Marsh and O'Brien (1989). The first article attempted to investigate a potential bandwagon effect on the topic of abortion. Marsh discovered that there was a powerful influence when people were told that the trend in opinion on abortion was in a permissive direction: they were then more likely to endorse permissive views. However, information about static current opinion had no effect. The second article attempted to establish the same thing on the topic of the EEC. Once again, by informing respondents of a moving bandwagon, this seemed to have a decisive influential effect on some of them since they subsequently changed their views in the direction of the bandwagon.

We can conclude this section, then, by saying that the evidence for the polls having a direct impact on voting behaviour has not been conclusive over time. Such a relationship is theoretically plausible but it is difficult to demonstrate its existence empirically given the small number of respondents who will admit to being influenced in this way.

4.2 The polls and the government

It may seem obvious that *any* government will need to take heed of public opinion. No government can survive for any length of time by brute force alone; there needs to be some form of two-way communication between the government and the governed for the maintenance of the legitimacy of the government and its acceptance by the people. This linkage and interaction is most obvious in liberal democratic societies at elections, when the choice of the electorate can determine who governs. In between elections, however, this process of communication is altogether more mysterious and complicated, particularly in terms of the actions and reaction of multiple, competing interest groups who are simultaneously attempting to influence government policy in specific ways.

The provision of information and attempts at persuasion characterise the actions of both the government and the interest groups. The government seeks acceptance for its actions and decisions, whilst the groups seek influence in decision making in return for granting their support for those actions. The decisions of the government might be rewarded with either approval or criticism, the latter sometimes blanket and virulent in nature. If the tide of criticism is greater and more persistent than the approval, the government may decide to change course or at least adapt the policy to take account of the reaction that the original decision provoked.

The likelihood of this happening will depend heavily on the size of the group offering the criticism and the group's strategic position, particularly if it is able to thwart the intention of the policy by appealing over the head of the government directly to wider public opinion.

The presentation of the costs and benefits of the policy when they touch upon the interests of key groups in society will inevitably be subject to distortion and deliberate misrepresentation. As such, the ideal of a reflective channel of communication between the rulers and the ruled comes up against an altogether messier reality, where many actions produce no reaction at all but where unforeseen and unpredictable responses can be provoked by a small but attentive and, above all, responsive sector of the public.

Any government has the resources under its control to command widespread attention from the general public. It can use the mass media to put across its point of view as it simultaneously attempts to both inform and shape public opinion. If the policy entails a radical departure from the status quo, the government may well choose to take a high-profile stance which *leads* public opinion in order to win the support of society. The authority of the government may be invoked as a means of pressuring backbench MPs to come into line on policies where disagreements exist within the governing party. By taking the lead on some issues the government is forcing others to stand up and be counted. It will assess the risks involved in doing this from a variety of sources, including letters and telephone calls as well as canvassing opinions from non-governmental sources such as the mass media and industry.

The commonest way of testing the water with a new policy proposal is to send up a 'trial balloon', which involves the public airing of options for a policy that are then debated and assessed in terms of the various reactions. This type of action is taken by every government, either officially via speeches or interviews or unofficially via leaks or from 'sources close to the Cabinet'. Responses to such a method of announcement may be expected from politicians, the media and the representatives for affected interest groups and other lobbyists. If the proposal appears to produce a firm and heavily weighted negative reaction from these groups, the policy may be dropped entirely or it may be adapted and changed in line with the views expressed when initially mooted in public.

Sometimes, it can be difficult to know even when the 'trial balloon' technique is being used by a government, since proposals and responses can appear in public before any firm decisions have been taken. A generally favourable response to a 'trial balloon' is likely to encourage the government to continue with the proposal and lead from the front in the implementation of the new policy.

The way in which this process of consultation is carried out and the options that are put forward can be critical in establishing the range of choices open to government. This 'context of opinion' acts to determine the limitations within which action may be taken but it does not ensure that action actually *will* be taken. Any storm of outrage whipped up in this way is often met with stalling and delaying tactics as the government attempts to deal with the reaction by letting the storm subside naturally without taking any substantive action. This is based on the assumption that immediate and effective opinion on most policy matters only comprises small groups of the public, specifically those who are alert, attentive, interested and informed. These are the people who regularly write to MPs, who organise campaigns to air their views and who comment in public on matters that particularly concern them. The mass public is rarely involved at this level.

The interaction between government and public opinion is not a process which lends itself easily to empirical testing. Almost by definition, hard-and-fast knowledge about what exactly goes on and who said what to whom is limited in scope. Instead, we are left with a great deal of surmising on the basis of a largely informal process of interactive links which involves both give and take as well as communication in two directions at the same time. The more formal channels of communication are more easily identifiable and assessable, particularly elections and the role of the media and pressure groups.

The polls play a role in this regard as well since they provide the basic information about reactions to a policy which do not bear the imprimatur of a disgruntled opposition or a disaffected interest group. In that sense, the data provided by polls are untainted and they are taken seriously by all sides as evidence of the 'reality' of public opinion on a specific topic.

The government is naturally interested in such information, whether it has been testing a potential policy change via 'trial balloon' or whether it has been gathering information regarding the effects of a policy in action and considering whether changes are needed as a result. Much of this work is carried out by the government itself through the Office of Population, Censuses and Surveys (OPCS) or by commissioning polling organisations to carry out work on selected themes such as health care and pensions.

The larger government ministries, such as the Departments of Health and Employment, regularly commission work of this nature, although little of it receives much publicity. Much of the work concerns the details of policies and how they are working on the ground rather than broader measures of government popularity. As such, these data attract little attention from the media beyond brief summary reports of the main conclusions culled from press releases. This use of polls may, however, be the most useful work carried out for government bodies by the polling organisations. Similar work is also regularly carried out for local government authorities and a whole host of quasi-official bodies and agencies.

Purely in terms of attracting the most publicity and comment, the main poll of interest to the government is usually the regular monthly poll carried out by most of the polling firms, dealing with government popularity and the popularity of the prime minister in particular. Such 'baseline' measures usually permit long-term comparisons across time. In this way, they can also produce headlines such as 'the most unpopular prime minister of all time' and 'Government hits rock bottom in whole post-war period – latest poll'.

The importance of these headlines is that they force the government to react to the latest data, thus producing another story for the newspaper which published the results of the original poll. The opposition will gleefully latch on to the latest results and feed them into their attacks on the government and there will usually be a wide range of media comment as well. Polling companies obviously like the publicity as well as the income derived from regular monthly polls.

Such poll evidence will also be important in terms of the actions the government takes to recover its popularity or to maintain it if the latest poll result was encouraging. In that sense, polling data provide evidence from *outside* the government about the current 'state of play' in politics which is often taken seriously in terms of current policy and personnel changes. If the latest poll, for example, suggests that a policy is unpopular, the government has a choice of whether to accept this 'public verdict' and change the policy or to attempt to lead public opinion towards accepting their view. Poll evidence, given its source, can be very important in this but it will never be the only source of information to be considered. In particular, if there are poll data apparently showing that certain members of the Cabinet are not popular, such a conclusion must be tempered with the knowledge that this might well be because they are largely unknown rather than not popular. Changing the personnel of the government on the basis of poll data is therefore fraught with danger and other factors, such as overall reputation in the party and 'unsackability' because of popularity on the backbenches, must also be taken into account.

In the same way, policy changes largely on the basis of poll evidence will attract the accusation that the government is at the beck and call of the pollsters, rather than firm in its resolve about the right policy to pursue. Other influences, such as backbench feelings and the views of the constituency parties throughout the country, will also need to be considered.

Polling data, therefore, provide one admittedly important source of information for the government, but it is only one source. There will always be alternative viewpoints available and they must also be included in the melting pot of government decision making. However, on one key question, it is widely believed that polls do have an enormous influence: namely, the decision when to dissolve Parliament and call a general election.

One pollster told me that on a scale running from 1 to 10 used to determine the date of the next general election, poll evidence should be ranked at 11! There is little doubt, therefore, that 'poll watching' is a crucial consideration for any prime minister when they are weighing up the advantages and disadvantages of potential election dates. The initial advantage is, of course, the very ability to pick and choose (something not open to leaders in many other countries) within the legal maximum period for the length of the current Parliament.

Various economic indicators are often believed to be crucial in deciding the date, although high summer is usually avoided because many voters will be on holiday and the winter months are avoided because this might mean a lower turnout if the weather is bad. This mostly restricts the likeliest date to spring, early summer or autumn. The last four general elections between 1979 and 1992 have been held in May, June, June and April, respectively.

Specifically political factors are also important, however, if the incumbent prime minister is to maximise the chances of re-election. The current state of popularity of the prime minister as shown by the regular monthly polls is likely to be a critical consideration, as is the popularity of the party in power more generally. There is always the temptation to delay as long as possible if the prevailing situation looks either bad or at least risky, in the hope that matters will improve. The danger of doing that is that the choice inevitably narrows with the passing of time, and things might even get worse, perhaps forcing the prime minister into calling an election when they have to rather than when they want to. Poll data will always be important in reaching this particular decision but, once more, poll data are used in alliance with other information taken from the constituencies and party workers, recent local election results and the 'instincts' of the prime minister. One factor influencing the final decision will be the type of campaign that has been planned, in particular its length and government commitments during the campaign, such as summit meetings and the publication of economic statistics.

This type of 'rounded' approach built on taking all relevant influences into consideration does not mean, however, that poll data do not play a critical role in the making of the final decision. Poll data are available widely and they influence more people as a result, with perceptions of political opportunity and advantage being adapted as new data are collected and analysed. In this way, poll evidence will have the upper hand over the impressionistic and partial views of even experienced party workers. The main danger is to put too much reliance on poll data to the effective exclusion of other opinions and information. However, it is unde-niable that poll data taken in marginal seats can be particularly valuable in this context (see the next chapter), although national samples are best used for 'headline' figures about the overall state of national government popularity.

In the end, there will always be *some* risk for any prime minister whatever the source of information used to calculate the best time to call a general election. Poll data do, however, provide a mostly reliable snapshot of the current public mood and the initial context within which the election campaign will be fought if a particular date is chosen.

The next section of this chapter considers the ways in which the British political parties use polls to measure their popularity as well as their policies in terms of content and presentation.

4.3   The polls and the political parties

In theory at least, the easy availability of public opinion polling data should be a considerable help to political parties. They can glean the latest views of the electorate on a wide range of issues simply by studying the newspapers and other published material. As a result of the development of more reliable sampling tech-niques and improved question wording by the polling firms, the degree of inevitable uncertainty regarding the preferences of the voters should be reduced, thus permitting the parties to adopt positions on particular issues, if they so choose, in line with the prevailing contours of mass public opinion.

The main questions that the parties have to confront centre not so much on the technical aspects of polling but, firstly, on the general use to which polling data should be put and, secondly, in particular, how crucial a role such information should play in deci-sion making and the development of party strategy. These ques-tions can still be sore points for sceptical politicians and party members who continue to criticise poll findings as being of little use in such matters. They argue that the low level of information amongst the electorate combined with hypothetical questions re-duces the value of such data, particularly if single questions only are used to tap complex, multidimensional issues and 'unpriced' questions are used to test attitudes.

There is the additional concern that the pollsters are too power-ful in British politics and the desire to win office means that polling evidence is adhered to slavishly, rather than as one source of infor-mation whose interpretation could be *either* accepted *or* rejected. The 'polling sceptics' believe that because a lot of money has been spent on getting this information, too many politicians assume as a matter of course that it must become a central plank of any cam-paign, even if this goes against past practice and the views of many others in the party. The argument in favour of adopting such a strategy is that the data do provide an unbiased source of informa-tion which simply cannot be ignored, even if it contradicts past certainties. Indeed, some would argue that polling data are of indispensable importance to a campaign if they do just that.

In response, pollsters deny that they are powerful figures in developing the strategy of any political party. They draw a clear distinction between powerful people and powerful polling evi-dence, on the basis that the 'personalisation' of the relationship between the pollsters and the party is misleading and is often used as a cover for the unpalatable nature of what the poll data are showing in terms of the party's popularity and its chances of re-election, for example.

Despite these internal concerns, the main British political par-ties remain very active in terms of analysing the published polls as well as commissioning private polls of their own to provide supple-mentary information concerning the views of the electorate. Some of this private polling meets the above criticisms by going into much greater depth on particular topics.

4.3.1   Published polls

What can the parties actually learn from the huge accumulation of information on the attitudes of the British electorate over the last fifty years? Firstly, there has never been a simple class–party align-ment amongst the voters. Any study of voting behaviour in Britain needs to confront the reality that the electorate can always be divided into at least three groups, one of which will not be Con-servative or Labour whatever its specific label, that is, Liberal, Nationalist or Other. Such analyses also need to consider the elec-tors who do not follow class cues in terms of supporting their 'natural' class party. As a result, the simplification of analyses to a single dimension of social structure will not provide an adequate guide to the behaviour of many voters.

Secondly, published polls provide data on the popularity of the party leaders, both in general terms about their performance (often relative to one another) and also in more detail in terms of a 'personality inventory' which allows the respondents to assess the leaders in terms of characteristics, such as decisiveness, a caring approach, toughness, ability to unite the nation and trustworthiness. A general conclusion over time has been that a popular leader can make a difference, although often only a marginal one, for the party's electoral appeal. In addition, all leaders enjoy a 'honeymoon period' when they first become leader but this soon dissipates as the political game is once more engaged with the party's opponents.

Thirdly, polls can be useful in establishing the importance of particular political issues and the priorities accorded by the electors to those issues. Polls can demonstrate the extent to which the voters are divided over the importance of an issue and the degree to which they care about that particular issue. It is, however, much rarer for polls to put different alternatives to their respondents about the best course of action to take on the issues specified. For example, on the issue of privatisation, it is uncommon for a poll to put explicitly, say, three or four alternatives about the future course of the government's policy in terms of alternatives such as 'A lot more industries currently in the private sector should be privatised', 'Only a few more industries such as the railways should be privatised' or 'Some currently privatised industries should be taken back into the public sector' or 'Leave the situation as it is.'

These questions are much more the preserve of an academic survey which is more interested in forcing the respondents to choose in terms of their policy preferences. Polls are more frequently used for measuring the distribution of opinion and its intensity rather than a more theoretical investigation into the support for hypothetical alternative policies or actions which the government might one day take. The main reason for this is the fact that the media who commission many of the polls are not interested in such hypothetical situations but really only want to know the current 'state of play' clearly expressed in concrete terms.

4.3.2 Private polls

The main parties also use private polling to supplement the publicly available information. They do this for a number of reasons. Firstly, by commissioning private polls, the parties can design the questionnaire to study in depth particular issues and topics of direct interest to them. The timing of the fieldwork is also under the party's control. Secondly, more detailed and specifically focused questions can often produce strategic information for the parties regarding the mood of the electorate which cannot be derived from a poll covering a wide range of issues. Thirdly, as a result of controlling the content and timing of the poll, the information sought can be clearly and specifically targeted, so that key social groups such as skilled workers or young married couples are selected for questioning. Finally, reactions to the latest party political broadcast, for example, can be sought in terms of instant feedback or the public images of the party leadership can be tested or a tentative advertising theme can be piloted before a final decision is taken. Additionally, contact can be maintained between the party and its membership, with the attitudes of members being fed into the communication channels of the party organisation.

Private polls began to be used by the major parties in Britain in the 1960s, following on from their extensive use in the United States for all types of election – gubernatorial, senatorial and congressional as well as presidential, most prominently in the campaign of John Kennedy in 1960, which included work on the strengths and weaknesses of Kennedy's opponents, the issues and images of the campaign and the opinions of the American public. This use of private polling is not surprising given the importance of the individual candidate rather than the party in American election campaigns (Teer and Spence 1973: 149–53).

In Britain, Kavanagh (1982) notes that private polls have long-term, medium-term and short-term uses for the parties. They are useful for collecting baseline data from which changes can be noted and further explored in the development of long-term party strategy. They can be used to cover the aftermath of a particular by-election result, or a set of advertising slogans or more general attempts to assess the ability of the party to communicate effectively in a non-election period. Private polls can also be useful for tracking particular issues or images in the short term, although here speed is of the essence since the information gathered might be out of date within the space of a day even.

The two main parties in Britain are both very reluctant to discuss exactly what extra substantive benefits they get from private polling that is not already available from published polls. The pollsters are equally guarded about discussing such matters but for different reasons related to confidentiality and long-term loyalty to highly valued clients.

However, at least in 1992, there seemed little reason for this coy approach by the parties. Butler and Kavanagh (1992: 149) concluded, after gaining access to the reports of the private polling conducted for the Conservatives largely by Harris that, 'it is hard to believe that [the private polls] contributed much to the party's strategic thinking.' They speculated that the main value of the private polls was as sources of reassurance that spectacular movements in opinion were not occurring beneath the surface being measured by the published polls.

Private polling costs the parties a lot of money (about three times more than for a published poll, amounting to between £20,000 and 30,000 a time) largely because of the depth of the topics explored. There may well be a feeling, therefore, within the hierarchies of the main parties that something extremely valuable must necessarily be the result of such exercises and that it must be withheld from being disseminated outside a small group of party officials. Holding that attitude is also vital in order to justify such expenditure to others in the party.

Even so, it is not particularly difficult to work out the broad results of the private polling if the campaigns of the parties are analysed. For example, at the 1992 general election, the question of taxation in general and the weakness of the Labour Party on the issue must have been a central finding from the Conservatives' private research in addition to the image of John Major as a man who could be trusted. The word 'trust' was used extensively in the campaigning of the Conservatives, tied specifically to the prime minister as a contrast to the Labour Party in general and Neil Kinnock in particular.

Private polling for the Labour Party has been controlled by the Shadow Communications Agency in recent years. The agency was established principally to modernise the party's campaigning methods and presentation after 1983. It also commissioned and analysed private polling data designed to assess both the strengths and the weaknesses of the Labour Party. Up until and including the 1987 election, this private polling was carried out by MORI and then the task was taken over by NOP in 1992.

The private reports by MORI to the Labour Party were made available to the author by Bob Worcester, and they make fascinating reading. Above all, no punches were pulled in spelling out to the Labour Party exactly what the data portend. For example, in a memo to the Labour Steering Committee dated 11 May 1983, Bob Worcester revealed that the Conservatives had a 5 per cent lead over Labour as being the party with 'the most concern for the interests of people like yourself'. Worcester comments that 'If you can't turn this around, you haven't a prayer.'

During the 1970s, MORI also devised a typology of the British electorate which included such characters as 'Old Fred' (a committed Labour voter), 'Enoch' (those with authoritarian tendencies), as well as categories of voters such as 'Labour what's in it for me?', 'Conservative who governs?', 'disillusioned', ' apathetic but would vote'. Two other groups were the 'floating Left' and the 'floating Right'.

This typology was derived from a complex analytical technique called cluster analysis but its usefulness for the Labour Party mainly derived from the data on the size of these groups in the electorate and what the party should stress to either win or retain the loyalty of each group in turn. By summer 1986 this typology had become a 'political triangle' depicting the strength of party support but also concentrating upon party and leader images along with an assessment of the most important issues of the time.

There is specific advice in one report of 1986 regarding the image of Neil Kinnock, suggesting that the party needed to stress more often that he was capable, could be trusted to act in the interests of all British people and that he would make a good prime minister. Overall, it is stated that to use such phrases in speeches would have improved Kinnock's image as well as helping to dampen the view that the Labour Party was divided.

In the reports throughout the 1970s, there are arguments put forward by MORI in favour of using panel studies (repeated interviews with the same people at different times), small-scale studies, the investigation of voting motivations and the role of political semantics such as the impact of using alternative words in questions, such as coalition or a government of national unity.

All of the above suggestions came up against scepticism from inside the Labour Party at regular intervals since they inevitably require considerable funds to be spent if the research is to be carried out properly. As a result, at the 1979 election, for example, the number of polls conducted declined compared to 1974, with only two polls being carried out in the first ten days of the campaign. Reports were produced only every three days rather than every day as before. MORI attempted to meet this problem by costing their proposed research programme in detail, but their argument that the best value for money would be achieved by deciding as early as possible what was needed and then sticking to it was thwarted in 1979 by the 'scramble' to agree a campaign budget at the last minute. In 1983, the private polling budget was only agreed four months before the actual campaign started.

The lack of funds also afflicts the Liberal Democrats, who mainly rely on the published polls, although in the run-up to the 1992 election they did commission a direct-mail company to conduct a series of telephone polls in ten specific target seats, such as Bath, Cheltenham, Richmond and Hazel Grove. Only about 400 people were interviewed in each constituency and so the data could not be used for predicting the outcome of the elections in those constituencies. Instead, the data were utilised inside the Liberal Democratic campaign team to work out the best way of presenting their argument to specific groups of voters, in particular the proposal to put a penny on income tax to pay for more education spending. The questions focused on local issues as well, such as possible hospital opt-outs in the constituency and the local situation in terms of the poll tax, for example, so that the local candidate could be informed of the strengths and weaknesses of the Liberal Democrats' case.

In general, it is not cost-effective for the Liberal Democrats to commission polling of their own, particularly when there is so much data already in the public domain. Such data can be very useful in terms of establishing whether and how the Liberal Democrats can become identified with particular issues, whether they can 'own' a specific issue in the minds of the voters. This is a perennial problem for the Liberal Democrats, who tend to be 'squeezed' between the two main parties at general elections and who find it difficult to excite the wider electorate about constitutional reform, even when it is expressed in terms of 'fair votes' rather than 'proportional representation' and 'coalition government' rather than 'hung Parliaments'.

All of this type of polling provides evidence of attitudes drawn from *outside* the national party machine and it also produces an independent measure of issue salience in terms of the current public agenda. In this way, particular policies which appear to be supported by the public can be promoted within the party's propaganda and campaigning, whilst others will no longer receive such emphasis if it appears that they are not supported by the wider electorate.

4.3.3 Qualitative research

In addition to testing the attitudes of specific groups of target voters within the electorate, both main parties also pursue further research by means of qualitative questioning of small groups of voters, perhaps eight to ten people at a time, who are brought together to discuss a range of topics without being asked to complete a structured questionnaire. The main use of this information for the parties is to pre-test specific ideas and concepts without having to rely on purely quantitative interpretations of majority opinion. This kind of research is analogous to the prototype of a new product being tested before being marketed fully. Some of the Labour Party's policy changes which finally appeared in the 1989 Policy Review were initially tested in this way.

It has been argued that this type of research is not polling as such, but the division between strictly quantitative and qualitative studies has been diminishing for some time and, as we mentioned in chapter 2, the two approaches are now being seen more and more as complementary rather than contradictory, particularly in the search for the meaning of the actions and reactions of the ordinary voter. The research for both is conducted by pollsters and both approaches will inevitably be in competition for party funds.

The focus of the qualitative research in group discussions is often the 'core' themes for promoting a party and/or attacking their opponents. Specifics rather than general claims are tested and the tone and type of language that should be used are also examined. The stress is often on themes such as looking to the future, improving standards and on new but practical ideas. This research can eventually produce an overall theme into which particular policies are slotted, with key words and phrases being repeated to produce the overall image and effect. Negative language, looking to the past and worsening standards are all to be avoided. Instead, the party will claim that it is in touch, it is looking to the future, its policies are popular with the wider electorate and their opponents have failed to keep their promises on a range of issues.

The Conservative Party from the early 1980s experimented with in-depth interviews with small groups, helped by Richard Wirthlin, one of President Reagan's pollsters, who had dealt in detail with the psychology of voters, in particular the questions of values, core beliefs and emotions. The party wanted to get below the surface to explore the deeper structure of how the voters looked at politics, and Wirthlin gave a number of seminars on these themes. However, this engagement proved to be very expensive and it was stopped on grounds of cost after Chris Patten became party chairman.

Nevertheless, the idea of using in-depth interviewing of small groups has not gone out of fashion; indeed, some would argue that the insights provided by such groups are more important than the raw quantitative data from national samples, particularly in terms of the human context of politics and delineating the underlying value patterns which underpin political attitudes. Whilst such work cannot be used for purposes of prediction, it can certainly be used to analyse particular issues and to monitor changes in perceptions of party and leader images.

We can see therefore that there is a great deal of information available to the parties regarding the preferences of the electorate, derived from published and private polling as well as qualitative research results from the discussions of smaller groups of voters. How then do the parties specifically use this information in the development of their electoral strategies and the constant struggle to influence the framework and content of the political agenda?

4.3.4 The development of electoral strategies

If we assume that political parties are interested in maximising their vote share at an election, the theory of Downs (1957) suggests that parties should not have sharp disagreements with their rivals on issues of the greatest importance to the electorate. 'Rational' parties should converge near to the centre of the distribution of public opinion by not staking out radically different positions from one another in their appeal to the voters. By not polarising on salient issues, partisan change within the electorate should not lead to a radical restructuring of political forces; instead, change should be more gradual and consequently easier for the parties to shape and control.

Of course, the actions of parties may well not be 'rational' in this sense since the opposition may need to engender conflict on a salient issue in their attempt to attract enough votes to win the election. Without a polarised party system in which the choice offered to the voters on key issues is clearly laid out, there might not be a good enough reason for enough voters to switch parties at the election.

With access to information derived from opinion poll data, parties should be much better informed about the attitudes of the electorate than in the past, when they had to rely on the views of politicians, party workers, the contents of their post and newspaper editorials. Parties will not take up exactly the same position on the salient issues but they will adopt broadly similar ones in order to control the potential for partisan change. They can always simultaneously stake out radically different positions on issues of less immediate relevance to the electorate in the hope that these issues may slowly help to undermine the loyalties of their opponents' voters. What does this theory mean for the ways in which the parties approach the task of deciding their electoral strategy?

If we once more assume that the primary task of a party at an election is to maximise its vote share, it is of course possible for a party to devise a strategy based *entirely* on poll findings. On that basis, the party would target uncommitted voters in marginal seats by means of propaganda aimed at meeting their particular concerns. Since this could well lead to a fragmented and incoherent appeal, it would also be necessary to formulate a supplementary but wide-ranging appeal which dispensed with specifics as far as possible and substituted emphasis on issues such as leadership competence and experience in positive terms for themselves and negative terms for their opponents.

In a sense, it can be argued that this effectively deprives the voters of an actual choice if the main argument of the campaign centres on 'valence issues', where the aims of the policy are agreed between the parties but the means of achieving them are framed in terms of such aspects of politics as personality, image and perceptions of competence and ability. Whilst those active in politics within the parties and associated groups will understand the *content* of the differences between the parties, the voters are very likely to be uninterested in the substance of partisan conflict.

Naturally enough, no party starts any campaign with a completely blank page in front of it. There are too many debts from the past to repay, too many relationships and links to maintain for any party or its leader to have a completely free hand in deciding the party's electoral strategy. In an important sense, therefore, no party will be entirely at the mercy of public opinion as expressed through the polls since if the polls appear to be stacked against the party, the most obvious option available would be to promote the party with renewed vigour rather than to introduce wholesale changes in line with the polls.

Much will depend on what the party is trying to achieve. If it is in government, maintaining support will be enough to retain office. In that way, the campaign will probably concentrate upon the party's known strengths as borne out by the polls and also upon the main weaknesses of their opponents. A long-term perspective is needed to assess properly the development of the campaign strategies of parties. They will begin the campaign early, if not literally the day after the previous election. They will always be aware of the impact of particular policies, always keeping track of the popularity of the party as those policies are implemented.

In this way, the strategy of the government will be different from that of the opposition. Firstly, the government might well expect to gain from any 'incumbency bonus' achieved by delivering economic benefits to most voters. This bonus can be protected over the lifetime of a Parliament by stressing continuity, the need to maintain the present course of the country, the general risk of changing over to other parties and the specific weaknesses of those parties. The effectiveness of this approach depends to some extent on the length of the voters' memories, generally reckoned to be short and fallible. If the government can deliver an economic upturn which provides tangible evidence of success from which individual electors feel the benefit, the reasons for switching their votes to the opposition are reduced in importance. If the reality cannot be changed for the better in time for the election, at least the presentation of the government's record can be refurbished and given a new slant. Poll evidence can also be used as the basis for such a campaign.

For the opposition, the approach has to be different from that of the government. If the opposition is to succeed in displacing the incumbent party, agreeing with the government is an unlikely recipe for success. An aggressive campaign might be more productive but that does risk incurring the dislike of potential supporters who reject the mud-slinging and the explicit personalisation likely to play a major part in such a strategy. The opposition might also have to overcome a general cynicism regarding the promises of politicians and even whether the government can reasonably be expected to tackle effectively problems deemed to be outside their direct control. In the battle concerning which party has the best policies, polling data might be significant in that the expectations of the electorate can be clearly delineated in terms of issues favouring one party or the other.

In an idealised political world, election campaigns would be the fulcrum of enlightening debates about policies and issues. The reality is that the values and principles which give rise to policy stands change very slowly and the derived policies become clearly associated with particular parties over time. As a result, the room for policy changes and the ability to bring them about quickly is usually very limited.

Whilst public perceptions about policies may well change, substantive policy changes are difficult to push through without causing severe internal party conflict, something which is too risky as an election campaign approaches. As such, any genuine debate over issues takes place well before the campaign formally gets under way.

4.3.5   Policy developments

In line with Downs' theory outlined above, polling data should push parties towards policy positions which accord with public opinion if the aim of the campaign is vote maximisation. This might mean considerable policy change particularly after an election defeat, on the grounds that the voters had explicitly rejected the platform on which the party had sought their support.

However, this is very likely to cause internal conflict within the party, as mentioned above, since to the activists and party members the agreed policies are more than a means of gaining votes: they symbolise the general ideological orientation of the party towards central questions of political conflict.

If parties move towards the centre of the distribution of public opinion, this may lead to the development of a heterogeneous party profile in which different groups vie for supremacy at any one time. The more open and differentiated the party organisation, the less binding will be the membership of that party, which will leave the party vulnerable to changes in the political environment. Whilst this might well give the party leader a considerably greater manoeuvrability in terms of making policy changes and getting them through the party organisation since the ability of the membership to resist will not be very strong, such actions will also weaken the integrative role long played by parties in terms of bringing likeminded and committed individuals together to mobilise the electorate in support of 'their' party.

There are therefore obvious dangers for parties in simply following the evidence of polling data in terms of policy formulation. Whilst this might prove to be a good move electorally, the price to be paid could be very high in terms of party organisation and internal conflict, particularly if the achievements of the government in office are accompanied by the onset of disenchantment amongst the ordinary party members.

4.3.6 Polling data and internal party structures

We mentioned earlier the existence of sceptics who doubt the value of polling for divining the mood of the electorate. These people have mainly belonged to the Labour Party, dating back at least to Nye Bevan, who complained that polling 'took the poetry out of politics'. Others believed that polling was alien to democracy and that it would lead to a betrayal of the party's traditional doctrines since the results of polling would certainly conflict with the long-established principles of the party. The whole question of representation is related to this point in terms of the roles of MPs and parties as well as the way in which public opinion is assessed and the way in which political decisions are taken.

The 'anecdotal approach' to politics, based on party meetings and contacts with the voters whilst campaigning, long provided sufficient evidence to those in the Labour Party who argued that they knew what was good for the people and that polls were superficial and transient. Additionally, as mentioned above, conflicts over policy were all too common, with poll results being bandied about in support of one side of an issue or another. This helps to explain the Labour Party's late entry into taking political polling seriously, long after the Conservatives had been gathering and using such information. The fear that internal conflict would be reinforced by poll findings meant that little was commissioned on the grounds that factional disagreements would inevitably resurface when the results were known (Teer and Spence: 165–72).

In addition, there was the simple problem of a lack of money. The funding given to commissioning polls could always be used in a number of other ways, and to be effective in testing the impact of, say, television broadcasts or an advertising campaign, a long-term commitment to spending money on polls was required. The Conservatives had more resources for this purpose and they also quickly perceived the uses to which polling data could be put in terms of party propaganda through a streamlined and coherent party organisation. Conservative Central Office also made sure that the potential benefits of polling data were widely understood within the party and that they had the resources to pursue such research on a regular and long-term basis (Teer and Spence 1973: 155–65).

The increased use of polling data by parties also tends to change the relative importance of the different units of the party structure in favour of the party leadership. If we assume that an image of party disunity damages the party in the eyes of the electorate, then loyalty to the incumbent leader becomes a virtue. The leader and his or her close supporters have much more freedom to redefine the goals of the party and the means of achieving them, with the lower levels of the party having few serious sanctions they can impose. It would require a leader of remarkable self-restraint not to exploit this situation for his or her own benefit.

Freedom of manoeuvre for the leader also permits any party to get to grips with changing the party organisation to get the best from recent technological developments in running an election campaign. The use of direct mail will often require a centralisation of campaign effort, as will accurate party membership records, in order to organise a coherent election campaign. These developments have also changed the previous and long-standing relationships between the different levels of the party structure, with intermediate groups increasingly being by-passed as more and more power and control are centralised at the top. The role of the party members in terms of voter mobilisation remains but it is often superseded by direct appeals over their heads to the voter via the mass media, especially television.

This brings us on to the next section of this chapter, which deals with the role of the mass media and how opinion polls have played a part in the recent changes affecting the fighting of a modern election campaign.

4.4   The polls and the mass media

The principal way in which the general public sees the results of polls is via the mass media. Both national and regional newspapers regularly publish the results of a variety of polls, such as a 'poll of polls', regular monthly polls and one-off polls devoted to testing public reactions to particular themes. Television and radio similarly commission polls on a wide range of topics of current interest to their viewers and listeners. In addition, both the newspapers and the electronic media routinely report the results of polls commissioned and published by their competitors and rivals. Indeed, the sheer number of polls published may have the result of dulling the impact of any individual poll, particularly at election time.

For the mass media, the value of polls is clear. Firstly, they provide a source of material which is often a major tool of political reporting. They provide a yardstick against which political developments can be measured and they come untainted by any fear of party political distortion. Secondly, leading on from the above, they enable the media to comment on the current political situation by relying on empirical evidence rather than insider gossip and rumour about what is going on. Thirdly, they are a useful means of publicity. If the poll is widely reported, as is usually the case these days, the paper or channel will also always be mentioned in the report. For newspapers, this might mean extra sales; for television and radio, this will mean that they are seen by the public to be carrying out such work as part of their duties to report the political scene.

There is little doubt, however, that these advantages for the mass media were seriously called into question by the outcome of the 1992 general election. The chief question for the future could be simply stated: could the considerable expenditure on polls be justified when the money bought such poor results? Several newspapers, including *The Guardian* and *The Independent* actively considered cutting back on their poll expenditure although this was more part of a general cost-cutting exercise in a recession than solely because of the outcome of the polls at the election. In addition, such cuts in poll spending could only have ever been temporary, particularly in the run-up to the next general election, because of the lack of alternatives.

Clearly, some repair work had to be done by the polling organisations, although none of them have suffered as a result of the 1992 election in terms of their business from either political or non-political clients, something which suggests a greater understanding of both the value and the limitations of polls among those who are most actively involved in commissioning and conducting them.

Most of the media are willing to insert 'health warnings' into their use of poll data but not to the point of spoiling a good story or undermining a snappy headline. Many poll stories would not receive the publicity they do if they started with a paragraph such as this: 'According to the best available poll projection, the Conservatives were ahead of Labour by 5 per cent two days ago. Given inevitable sampling error, the result of the general election could be anything between a hung Parliament and a Conservative landslide. In any event, there could be a last-minute swing either way.'

This is the kind of sober and, above all, *tentative* prose which characterises a sound grasp of the nuances and complexities of polling data. The detail of the story following on from the above opening paragraph would be similarly subtle and shaded. The problem for the polling firms is that the tabloid press in particular will always want to dramatise and simplify the story that the data are suggesting. Few, if any, would be interested in publishing the qualified and sceptical appraisal that comes naturally to experienced pollsters.

Other specific problems in this regard stem from the headline introducing the story, over which even the journalist writing the story often has little or no control. Problems also arise from secondary reporting by other outlets which summarise and consequently distort the main thrust of the poll evidence to suit themselves editorially or simply for reasons of lack of space. By doing this, the resulting story can be rendered difficult for the reader to understand because the cuts were performed by a sub-editor with no knowledge of the poll material.

Another potential source of conflict between the polling organisations and the media lies in the design and content of the questions. The polling firms will always want to devise questions which they think will best assess the topic of interest. There might, however, be little interest or understanding within the media for this caution, leading to arguments over the wording of questions and the length of the fieldwork. What is minimally necessary to a pollster might seem extravagant and superfluous to a journalist. For example, many of the tabloid papers are interested in conducting surveys on sexual matters, particularly in recent years the impact of AIDS on the behaviour of people and how many sexual partners they have had in recent years. This is obviously a very sensitive subject to investigate, with the real possibility of a high degree of refusals to answer such questions as well as real doubts about the accuracy of many of the answers that are actually given. Pollsters, however, can find ways around these problems technically by using showcards, for example, so that the answers do not have to be given to the interviewer verbally. Pollsters will certainly draw the line at being asked to put questions such as 'How many times a week do you do it?' or indeed any of the 'unpriced' variety of question we mentioned earlier. Many of the pollsters have gained through experience a gut instinct about poll results which, when allied to a healthy scepticism rather than blind faith, can enable them to look at results and say 'Do I believe this?'

Another complaint which the pollsters have regarding the presentation of their poll data in the media lies in the concentration on one or two questions, usually the voting intention question and perhaps one other if space or time allows. This is particularly the case when comparisons over a longer period are made, but this material is presented without the necessary emphasis or attention being given to the possible reasons for any change. Pollsters would, however, immediately admit that their perspective is quite different from that of a journalist in that they are not necessarily looking for a news story from the poll and they tend instinctively to place poll results in a context which is based more on the long-term and trends than on the immediate present and the possible future.

There is also a clear element of competition between the media and the parties, with the pollsters in the middle in terms of setting the agenda for discussion and debate. Before the advent of mass media communication, some of the functions of parties were to spread information to the public via party members, shape policy stands and register the opinion of activists. The growth in the dominance of electronic means of communication has largely usurped the traditional party role in these respects.

These changes are sometimes said to have contributed to an 'Americanisation' of British politics, particularly the changes in campaigning introduced after 1970. There are three areas where changes in campaigning are particularly noticeable: firstly, there is the growth in the centralised control of the party campaign strategy; secondly, there are the moves towards the promotion of campaign uniformity, with the same message being disseminated regardless of location; thirdly, there is an increasing emphasis on concentrating resources on publicising the campaign message via television, important parts of which are the findings of opinion polls and taking the advice of professional consultants and advertising experts.

In the 1980s, the parties considerably increased the significance they ascribed to the role and influence of the media and this brought the treatment of the parties and political reporting into the spotlight. This makes the role of polling data even more sensitive since it will be used and perhaps abused by both sides in the struggle to control the contours and events of an election campaign.

The media clearly play crucial roles in how the voters perceive the agenda on which campaigns and elections are fought, in particular which issues are seen as important and which are not. This is often based on opinion poll findings. The priority in terms of the coverage of issues inevitably implies to readers and viewers that this is what is important and what people should be caring about. Additionally, the criteria for the evaluation of parties and their leaders are also set by the media, based on past experience as well as present conventional wisdom.

The overall relationship between the media and the polling firms is crucial because the former provide the main outlets for the latter's work. In such an interdependent relationship, there are bound to be tensions and disagreements, particularly about presentation and timing and the media's habit of wilfully mixing news and comment together to produce a powerful brew of both the possible and the desirable. There is no reason to expect this to change in the near future, despite the massive changes which the media have undergone in the last five years, with the development of satellite channels and changes in ownership and control.

In this way, the 'information superhighway' of the future will still transmit poll data and its interpretation as now although most probably considerably faster and with even less cumulative reflection and genuine insight. For that reason, the polling firms will have to continue to accept that the reach of their main clients will remain considerably more secure than their grasp.

4.5   The polls and pressure groups

Polls are used by pressure groups for some of the same reasons as the media. Above all, pressure groups are interested in getting publicity for their cause as one means of influencing the media to be sympathetic to their views. In addition, the poll data can be used as a focus for campaigns and for lobbying MPs and the government.

There is a long history of pressure groups using polls to lobby the government against particular policies, stretching back to the campaign of the Aims of Industry against nationalisation in the 1950s (Teer and Spence 1973: 175–6).

It is of course difficult to tell how effective poll data can be in this context, given the plethora of other available information, but many pressure groups clearly regard it as money well spent. If the data collection is carried out by a reputable national polling organisation, the credibility of the results will be enhanced. This means that 'serious' money will have to be spent rather than relying on group members to conduct the fieldwork since using the latter leaves the group wide open to the charge that the sample could not be representative and consequently it should not be taken seriously.

Polling data can become a central element in the activity of a pressure group when they are attempting to mount a new campaign or are trying to rebut the claims of their opponents. One of the most spectacular and long-running struggles in this regard has been between the two sides of the abortion debate, with SPUC (Society for the Protection of the Unborn Child) confronting a variety of groups on the 'pro-choice' side of the issue over the years, such as the National Abortion Campaign.

Both sides have competed vigorously with one another for public attention and credibility since the 1967 Abortion Act and both have used polls extensively to reinforce their own particular views on the subject. One of the main battle fronts has been the wording of the questions put to respondents, on the grounds that the questions were biased or only allowed a limited and constrained response choice in order that the 'correct' answer would emerge to suit the group which had commissioned the poll in the first place.

Both sides have paid for questions on the omnibus surveys of the main polling organisations. Gallup, in particular, has conducted much of this work but their questions have been criticised by the 'pro-choice' side for being biased. For example, Gallup have put the following question to gynaecologists: 'Talking specifically about abortion on demand, are you in favour of it in all circumstances, in some circumstances or not in favour at all?' The accusation levelled by the 'pro-choice' side centred on the view that those who believed in abortion on request could not in effect say yes to any category. The most obvious choice would be for them to choose the 'in all circumstances' option but this might be construed to mean abortions being forced onto women. Abortion on demand was also believed to be an old-fashioned phrase, best replaced by abortion on request (quoted by Mildred Gordon MP, report of Standing Committee C on the Abortion (Amendment) Bill, 30 March 1988, pp. 248–9).

Of course, it is unlikely that on such an emotive topic as abortion both sides will agree on the content and appropriateness of the questions being put. This issue does clearly demonstrate the difficulty involved in formulating neutral and balanced questions on certain topics. It is very easy to design questions which subtly lead in one direction or another, even if the extremes of the debate are avoided, such as framing questions in terms of a women's right to choose or killing babies.

The heat of this debate on abortion has flared up on a number of occasions since 1967, most recently during the deliberations over David Alton's Abortion Amendment Bill in 1988. This dispute has continued since then with the current 'score' appearing to be a bitter, ill-tempered draw, with neither side able to produce a knock-out blow in terms of their arguments. This is hardly surprising, given the type of debate involved, but the nature of the issue will certainly mean that this struggle will not disappear since it continues to touch many people's intensely held personal feelings.

In recent years, a number of other pressure groups have used polling data as part of their attempts to further their particular cause. This is especially apparent with groups, such as Greenpeace, who conduct research into public perceptions of environmental issues and problems, the results of which are then fed into the group's communication strategy. They also conduct assessments of public opinion regarding the priority given to environmental questions and occasionally, the perceptions of Greenpeace itself and its image in relation to other organisations.

The normal method of publishing the results of the polls that Greenpeace commission is by means of a press release in which the view of the group is set out. Letters are also sent to the relevant government department. The press releases are also sometimes targeted on the local press as a means of putting pressure on the local MP. In 1991, for example, Greenpeace commissioned a telephone poll in the Copeland constituency of Jack Cunningham (then the Labour Party Campaign Co-ordinator) to test feelings about a proposed underground dump for waste which Cunningham had supported. Cunningham complained that the poll had been used selectively, with only an initial partial release since the poll had shown that he would still retain the seat at the next election. Greenpeace claimed that, according to the poll, 40 per cent of Labour voters in Copeland would be less likely to vote for a candidate who supported such a dump. There were, however, doubts expressed over the balance of questions such as 'If the candidate that you supported were an adviser to a company found guilty of polluting the Irish Sea with toxic waste, would you still support this candidate or not?' Of the sample, 54 per cent said they would not support the candidate, 19 per cent said they still would support him or her, 18 per cent said 'it depends' and 9 per cent did not know.

Another example of pressure groups using polls as an independent means of gaining publicity was a poll conducted by MORI for the International Fund for Animal Welfare published in February 1992 as part of a campaign to end fox and stag hunting in the United Kingdom. The results appeared to show that the Conservatives could lose the election if anti-hunting voters switched to Labour. The conclusion of the group was that 'after years of being ignored by politicians, animal welfare in general and fox and stag hunting in particular are on the political agenda.' This demonstrates clearly the intention of the group to use the poll data to put *their* issue on the agenda and to try and force the parties to take the issue seriously.

The report contained a description of the methodology used for the poll, and the results are broken down by gender, age, class, work status, trade union membership and type of housing. The results are given in percentage terms and are accompanied by illustrative pie charts. This kind of poll has more technical credibility because of the detail provided in the report, although the hard work still needed to get the issue of animal welfare on the political agenda is demonstrated by the result that only 1 per cent of the sample taken in Labour/Conservative marginals spontaneously cited animal welfare as the most important issue for them when it came to deciding how to vote at the election. Additionally, more than half of the sample had no view as to which party had the best policy on animal welfare.

4.6   Conclusion

Polls do not simply measure the current state of public opinion. They also provide the voters with information which they can use to make decisions and to form attitudes and opinions. It is therefore vital that polls and their impact are understood better and more widely than at present, particularly by the media, which continue to be obsessed by the idea of 'horse race' political competition. This leads to misleading headlines on poll stories on a regular basis.

The state of the polls can also have internal consequences for parties. A persistently poor showing in the polls can have a negative impact on party morale, with pressure for change increasing as poll evidence mounts and the options come to be defined in terms of a 'consensus interpretation' of the story they are telling. This can turn very quickly into a self-fulfilling prophecy which makes change inevitable even if not immediate.

The question remains, however, whether opinion polls actually have much effect on the electorate. Are polls accurate guides to behaviour? Are polls capable single-handedly of changing voting decisions as opposed to reinforcing attitudes already in place as a result of other influences? Considerable caution in attributing such power to polls should certainly be maintained, particularly when the evidence available to date on this specific point remains so uncertain and ambiguous. It is of course tempting to assume that political polling must have an impact of some sort if only because such a belief is widespread amongst politicians and the media. This is important in itself because such beliefs will mean that sophisticated media techniques and poll watching will continue to be a major tool of political reporting and interpretation regardless of any consistent and demonstrable empirical impact.

We need to remember in this context that election campaigns can be largely matters of elite persuasion, involving efforts by some elites to persuade other elites of the credibility of particular parties and candidates. The role of the 'spin doctors' is crucial in this. In this sense, the ordinary voters are merely intermediaries who keep the exchange going but who are not the principal actors involved. The potential power of incumbency and the ability to raise considerable funds to prevent rather than induce political change should not be underestimated. The incumbent party can try to prevent change by running campaigns based on the 'benefits' of continuity, which provide a self-reinforcing logic to those already in office. In this sense, the central choice for the voters is greatly simplified down to a single question: whether they want to change the government badly enough. The reasons for 'risking' a change need to be simultaneously both salient and compelling. Very often, they are not compelling enough to enough voters.

In this light, opinion poll data can certainly throw light on the strengths and weaknesses in the perception of parties but such perceptions may or may not matter. Even if a party leads its opponents on the 'caring' issues, it might not convert enough voters to its cause if its general credibility is in doubt. Both major parties in Britain are constantly engaged in a struggle to mould public opinion to their agenda of concerns which polling data have shown will favour them electorally. Unfortunately, for the parties, it is not that simple to convince a sceptical and often uninterested electorate that one party is clearly better than the other.

Polls are undeniably important pieces in the political jigsaw puzzle but they are only a part which will never produce the completed picture alone. As guides to public opinion, they are indisputably useful but the inevitable differences in interpretation of what they are telling the parties at any one time will mean that they should be used as one source of evidence amongst others. It should not be assumed that they can or should be employed as infallible guides to the often fickle and unfocused public mood to the exclusion of other means of party persuasion and campaigning.

References

Butler, D. and D. Kavanagh (1992) *The British General Election of 1992*, Basingstoke: Macmillan.
Downs, A. (1957) *An Economic Theory of Democracy*, New York: Harper and Row.
Kavanagh, D. (1982) 'Political parties and private polls', in R. Worcester and M. Harrop (eds) *Political Communications: The general election campaign of 1979*, London: Allen and Unwin, pp. 141–51.
Market Research Society (1994) *The Opinion Polls and the 1992 General Election*, London: Market Research Society.
Marsh, C. (1984) 'Back on the bandwagon: The effect of opinion polls on public opinion', *British Journal of Political Science* 15: 51–74.
Marsh, C. and J. O'Brien (1989) 'Opinion bandwagons in attitudes towards the Common Market', *Journal of the Market Research Society* 31: 295–305.
McAllister, I. and D. Studlar (1991) 'Bandwagon, underdog or projection? Opinion polls and electoral choice in Britain, 1979–1987', *Journal of Politics* 53: 720–41.
Teer, F. and J. D. Spence (1973) *Political Opinion Polls*, London: Hutchinson.
Whiteley, P. (1986) 'The accuracy and influence of the polls in the 1983 general election', in I. Crewe and M. Harrop (eds) *Political Communications: The general election campaign of 1983*, Cambridge: Cambridge University Press, pp. 312–24.

Suggested further reading

The most accessible source of further reading for this chapter is the Nuffield series written by David Butler and different collaborators after each modern general election, in particular the chapter on the polls. There are usually also related chapters on television and the press.

5

The use and impact of sub- and supra-national opinion polling

In the last chapter, we considered the evidence that polls at national level have some impact on voting behaviour and the outcome of elections. We concluded that the evidence for this was mixed at best, with differing interpretations of the likely impact of polls. The empirical evidence for the conclusion that polls *did* play a role in influencing the vote choice of the electorate appeared inconclusive.

In this chapter, we are going to consider the use and impact of polls both *below* and *above* national level, and the chapter will be divided into four main sections: polls at by-elections, constituency polling in general, polls in marginal seats and the role of polls at local and European elections.

5.1 Polls at by-elections

By-elections in Britain nowadays attract a lot of media attention. They are usually pored over and analysed, not only in terms of the likely winner but with reference to the political impact on the national government of the day if it should lose the seat or perform badly. In this sense, by-elections can be regarded as tests of current government popularity.

In the past, there have been 'spectacular' by-elections, such as Orpington in 1962, when the Liberals won the seat from the Conservatives, and Bermondsey in 1983, when the Liberal/SDP Alliance won the seat from Labour. However, the impact of even wild swings against the government is often muted by strong evidence that voting habits return to 'normal' at the subsequent general election, when the task of electing a government rather than a constituency MP is uppermost in the minds of the voters. During the 1987–92 Parliament, for example, the Conservative government lost a total of seven seats at by-elections; they won them all back at the 1992 general election.

For this reason, although by-elections provide excitement and drama, it is often of a very temporary and synthetic nature which is largely unrelated to the questions dominating national politics. Of course, the government will not want to lose *any* seat to its opponents but the government candidate at a by-election provides a very easy target for disgruntled supporters who want to demonstrate their dissatisfaction without giving any commitment to other parties.

When they lose a by-election, the government will say that they are disappointed but hear what is being said, whilst the opposition parties will latch on to the result as further evidence that they are 'on a roll'. By-elections provide an often irresistible opportunity for 'natural' supporters of the government to protest and vote tactically in a totally harmless way, often by choosing the Liberal Democrats (or the SNP in Scotland or Plaid Cymru in Wales).

It has to be remembered in addition that purely local issues might be influential in a by-election as well as national issues. Drawing national conclusions from such a by-election outcome is therefore often dubious, particularly if predictions of a general election result are also extrapolated on that basis. There is little long-term danger in this, however, if Peter Snow's defence that 'it is only a bit of fun' is noted and accepted.

It remains the case, above all, that the interpretation of any by-election result is heavily influenced by media expectations of the outcome. Of course, all the parties will claim they are going to win *every* by-election, even in the face of evidence that they will do well instead to save their deposit. These claims, however, are important not only in keeping up morale during the by-election campaign to encourage the efforts of the party workers but also in trying to guide the behaviour of the constituency electorate and to mould the final result as far as possible.

How do by-elections and the context set out above affect the task of polling? Polls taken at by-elections are clearly different from polls taken at national elections. When the poll has only been taken in a single seat, the information it provides can be used by voters to vote tactically, usually to defeat the incumbent party, often the government. This can only be realised at a by-election since the aggregate information of a national poll does not provide a sufficiently reliable picture of what is happening in each seat for decisions on tactical voting to be taken sensibly.

There are a number of examples in the past where tactical voting appears to have taken place and determined the outcome of the by-election, where the Liberals or Liberal Democrats in particular have been the beneficiaries of an effective squeeze on the Labour vote sufficient to displace the Conservative candidate. At the Ribble Valley by-election of 7 March 1991, for example, the Liberal Democrats took the seat from the Conservatives by increasing their vote by 27 percentage points compared to the 1987 general election. The Conservatives lost 22 per cent compared to 1987 and, crucially, the Labour vote share went down by 8 per cent. The Liberal Democrats thus appeared to benefit from a large amount of protest voting from 'natural' Conservative voters. They also ensured that enough Labour voters saw voting Liberal Democrat as the only way of bringing about the defeat of the Conservative candidate.

A by-election can be used in this way by voters to send a clear 'protest' signal to the government of the day regarding a particular policy such as the imposition of VAT on domestic fuel. The problem for the opposition parties is how to take this protest beyond the constituency and use it as the focus for a wider campaign of opposition. The government of the day rarely appears to be worried by the loss of by-elections unless such a loss threatens their overall majority in the House of Commons. There is a widespread expectation that the protest, which appeared so potent at the time of the by-election, will soon peter out.

The struggle, therefore, for the opposition parties is to try to articulate that originally local and specific protest at national level and to use the issues highlighted as a means of pressurising the government into changing policy or personnel or both. The context of a particular by-election and the opportunities presented are therefore often straightforward to both the parties and the electorate.

By-election polls present special challenges and problems for the polling organisations. Given the media interest likely to be generated by most by-elections, the main pollsters are often commissioned to carry out polls in the constituency concerned. The same pressure as at national level to get the result right exists but this is made more difficult if tactical voting is a real possibility. Given the swings in by-elections in recent years, few seats in Britain can be regarded as safe at a by-election, even if the incumbent party had a massive majority at the previous general election. At the two by-elections held in 1993, for example, the Conservative government lost seats at Newbury and Christchurch, with losses of 29 percentage points and 32 percentage points, respectively, compared to the 1992 general election result, both to the Liberal Democrats. At the 1992 general election, Christchurch had returned the Conservative candidate (Robert Adley) with a majority of 23,015, making it the party's seventeenth-safest seat in the country.

The main difficulty for the polling organisations is the fact that poll results published during a by-election campaign are likely to play an influential role in determining whether tactical voting does actually take place. If it does, there might well be substantial changes in voter preferences very quickly and any poll taken *before* this happens could be a long way out in terms of its assessment of the vote shares of the parties. Predicting the outcome of a by-election can therefore represent very dangerous territory for a polling organisation unless an exit poll is used. Such polls, as we mentioned in chapter 1, have an excellent recent record of getting very close to the actual final result of by-elections. This is apparent from table 5.1, in which a selection of recent by-election results and the exit poll predictions are compared.

Table 5.1 does, however, contain figures for two by-elections where the exit polls were relatively 'wrong', namely, the by-elections at Mid-Staffordshire and Langbaurgh. The first might be explained by the widespread feeling that Sylvia Heal, the Labour candidate, was strongly favoured to win the seat, thus making Conservative supporters less willing to declare their actual preference, which was seen to go against the tide. However, it might

Table 5.1   **A comparison of exit poll and actual by-election results in selected constituencies**

By-election	Party	Exit poll	Actual result	Difference
Mid-Staffordshire	Labour	53	49	4
(22 March 1990)	Conservative	30	32	–2
	Liberal Democrat	10	11	–1
	SDP	2	3	–1
	Green	3	2	1
	Other	2	3	–1
Eastbourne	Liberal Democrat	52	51	1
(18 October 1990)	Conservative	40	41	–1
	Labour	5	5	0
	Other	3	3	0
Bradford North	Labour	51	52	–1
(8 November 1990)	Liberal Democrat	26	25	1
	Conservative	17	17	0
	Other	6	6	0
Ribble Valley	Liberal Democrat	49	49	0
(7 March 1991)	Conservative	38	39	–1
	Labour	10	9	1
	Other	3	4	–1
Langbaurgh	Labour	46	43	–3
(7 November 1991)	Conservative	35	39	–4
	Liberal Democrat	18	16	2
	Other	1	2	–1

equally be chance, since another exit poll at the time overestimated the Labour vote by only 1 per cent (as opposed to 4 per cent) and it got the other parties' vote shares exactly correct (with the exception of 'Other').

The second by-election at Langbaurgh overestimated the Labour vote by 3 per cent and most commentators put this down to the fact that the Labour candidate was Asian, suggesting that, while some people publicly declared their support for him, this support was not realised in the privacy of the ballot box. Subsequent by-election exit polls also have a good record.

In addition, at the Christchurch by-election of July 1993, NOP and ICM were both able to predict from voting intention polls taken roughly a week before the by-election that the Liberal Democrats would win the seat with a majority of about 18,000 and a vote share of about 62 per cent. In fact, the actual majority turned out to be 16,427 and the Liberal Democrat vote share was 62.2 per cent. There will always be dangers in aiming for this type of precision in advance in a single constituency, however. In the other by-election of 1993 (Newbury), the vote share of the Liberal Democrats was considerably underestimated, perhaps as a result of a late surge which a poll taken a week before the by-election could not expect to detect.

If by-election polls are taken during the campaign and particularly towards the end, the risk is clearly one of the polls being seen to play an influential role in terms of providing information on which the voters can base tactical decisions. In addition, depending on when the data were collected, the polls might be inaccurate in their assessment of the likely outcome. It should be remembered, however, that the very existence of by-election polls could not have been the cause of massive swings at by-elections in the past. For example, when no polls were publicised, the Conservatives still overturned a huge Labour majority of 23,000 at the Ashfield by-election in 1977.

In the 1980s, most by-elections were polled. The ones that were not tended to be in the safe seats where it was assumed that the incumbent party, usually one of the opposition parties, would still cling on to the seat, even given the expectation of a much reduced turnout. As a result, there is rarely much interest. A recent example would be the Rotherham by-election, held on the same day as the local elections in May 1994, which attracted very little coverage in the media because of the certainty that Labour would hold such a safe seat. The Labour candidate had had a majority of more than 17,000 at the 1992 general election.

In addition, polling interest tends to be weak in seats where the government could not possibly win whatever its overall popular standing, because there tends to be more interest in the performance of the government's candidate than that of any of the opposition parties.

The information culled from by-election polls has sometimes made clear the nature of the options if the voters want to vote tactically. For example, in Bermondsey in 1983, it was evident that to defeat Peter Tatchell, the controversial Labour candidate, a voter would have to choose Simon Hughes, the Liberal/SDP Alliance candidate rather than the Conservative candidate. Many chose to do this and Hughes won with a landslide, taking nearly 58 per cent of the votes cast.

We should nevertheless remember that such poll information will not *necessarily* have much effect. It is usually assumed that the likeliest effect of such information being made public will be to precipitate a collapse in the vote of the party least likely to unseat the incumbent. This might not happen, of course; in which case the outcome of the election will remain in doubt, particularly if the poll does not provide clear information regarding the best way to vote tactically, say, in a tight three-way (or perhaps four-way in Scotland and Wales) marginal seat where the result could be very close indeed.

These by-election polls should not be expected to have a predictive capacity, as the pollsters continually remind us; however, these 'health warnings' are habitually ignored by politicians and commentators. The real danger for the pollsters is that the size of the swing at the by-election will mean that not only do they get the actual winner wrong but the shares of the vote are also inaccurate. It is a genuine but usually decried explanation that the poll was probably right at the time the data were actually collected.

A good example of these problems occurred at the Brecon and Radnor by-election in July 1985. NOP, MORI and Beaufort (the Welsh pollsters) all polled during the campaign. In the end, Beaufort, who only conducted one poll, were the nearest to the final result, although their poll was taken nearly a week before the by-election took place. Beaufort also predicted that Labour would just win the seat. MORI and NOP thought Labour would win easily, with a vote share of more than 40 per cent. In fact, Labour gained 34 per cent and the Liberal Democrat candidate obtained 36 per cent and the seat. The Conservative candidate received 28 per cent of the votes.

This example demonstrates very well how things can go wrong in a seat with three parties all credibly in the hunt for victory. Amongst the reasons given for these poll outcomes was that sampling was conducted with too few sampling points in a large, sprawling, geographically heterogeneous seat. The seat was the ninth-largest in the country in terms of area and it was ranked fifth in terms of the number of its constituents who were employed in agriculture, fishing and forestry (17 per cent, according to the 1981 Census).

In addition, the way in which the samples were drawn was questioned (using census enumeration districts or local government wards) as well as the method and location of interviewing (face to face or by telephone; at home or in the street). These potential problems probably did have some effect since the exit poll conducted on the day of the by-election was also inaccurate, although it did predict a narrow Liberal Democrat victory.

In addition to these problems, it is very likely that the turnout at a by-election will be substantially lower than at the preceding general election. In the twenty-four by-elections held between June 1987 and December 1991, turnout compared to the previous general election dropped in every one. There were, however, wide disparities between the different by-elections, with turnout declining by only 1.9 per cent at the Mid-Staffordshire by-election compared to a full 40.5 per cent decline in Knowsley South. The average decline over the period was 16.7 per cent. Other spectacular declines in turnout occurred at the by-elections held at Epping Forest (27.2 per cent), Bootle (33.1 per cent) and Hemsworth (32.9 per cent).

This almost inevitable decline in turnout, often steep when compared to the previous general election, can also have a marked effect on any poll carried out, particularly if it is assumed that all or most of those who state a party preference will actually vote. The polling firm has to assess the relative propensity to vote of each party's supporters and also to estimate the likely turnout and the effect this will have on the respective vote shares of the parties. A by-election turnout of, say, 40 per cent might well put a radically different slant on the question of differential party abstention than a general election turnout of roughly 75 per cent.

Greater use of 'certainty to vote' questions helps in this regard by providing information about those who are the unlikeliest to turn out and vote. These respondents can then be excluded from the calculations used to assess the vote shares of the parties if it appears from the answers that they are unlikely to vote.

The turnout at by-elections appears to follow no particular pattern (other than that it is likely to decline compared to the previous general election). Certain factors are likely to be influential, nevertheless, including the marginality of the seat in question, the popularity of the government of the day, the role and effectiveness of minor parties, even the weather. All these influences make the task of predicting the turnout difficult. If the seat is marginal, the turnout should hold up reasonably well since the contest will be close. In contrast, the drop in turnout could well be precipitous in safe seats, where votes simply increase the in-built majority for one party rather than decide the result.

By-elections and the polls taken during them are special for the reasons given above; however, some of the problems that have to be faced at by-elections are common to constituency polls taken at other times and we will now turn to these questions and their possible answers.

5.2   Constituency polling in general

One of main attractions for the polling firms of polling in specific constituencies is that they can usually attract local clients in those seats who are more interested in those particular seats than the overall national picture. For the local media, for example, polls in identifiable, nearby seats can focus attention on what their readers will regard as important local news and analysis. On the basis of the poll evidence, the local newspaper can follow any campaign in more detail than would otherwise be the case and in such a way that the interest of its readership is maintained for an extended period.

This interest can of course be enhanced by the presence of a particularly well-known or controversial candidate or equally if a close contest is in prospect. Media speculation can also provide the sense that this or that particular constituency will tell us how the campaign is going nationally and who will be in Downing Street on the day after the election. During the 1992 general election, this 'bellwether' importance was most often ascribed to the constituency of Basildon in Essex, with many commentators claiming that they knew Labour had not done enough to win power again when it failed to regain Basildon from the Conservatives.

Analysing constituency polls goes right back to the first Gallup polls in the late 1930s, as we mentioned in chapter 1. Although such polls have a long history, they continue to pose particular problems for polling firms. A key problem relates to drawing the constituency sample. National samples can be constructed on the basis of consistently applied quotas, with the same sampling points being employed on a regular basis. The information for devising quotas and the spread of sampling points necessary to sample a *single* constituency is much harder to obtain. The information may not be easily available for a start and it may well be out of date as well, with no alternative data to supplement it. Information on key social distributions such as housing tenure may have changed considerably over a relatively short period of time but accurate data on this are nevertheless critical to obtaining a representative local sample.

Considerable care also has to be taken that the sampling points chosen do actually represent the constituency *as a whole* and not just its urban areas, for example. If this is not achieved, there must be a real risk that the poll will be inaccurate. Local knowledge and insights can be very useful for this purpose, with the relevant information being garnered from the local media and local interviewers, although even they might not be able to provide the data in an easily usable form. This local knowledge was arguably one of the advantages which Beaufort possessed in comparison with both NOP and MORI when conducting the Brecon and Radnor by-election poll mentioned above.

In addition to these technical problems, there will always be financial pressure from local clients for the size of the sample to be reduced to save money despite the potential problem of insufficiently representative sampling points mentioned above. This argument suggests that if the opinions of roughly 1,000 people can be used to generalise concerning the *national* political mood, surely about 100 will be enough to analyse the situation in a single constituency? This kind of expectation is very hard to dispel and local clients, who are often erratic commissioners of polls and who are consequently unused to major expenditure on them, are often unwilling to pay for what they regard as extravagant sample sizes. In fact, for constituency polls, obtaining large samples of roughly 1,000 respondents is as important as ever. Samples that slip to fewer than 500 respondents in size and are limited in terms of the sampling points used might be very inaccurate indeed. The expectations of the local clients regarding the accuracy of the poll will not change, however, even when these caveats and warnings are brought to their attention.

There is also a largely logistic matter of actually organising the polling to be conducted. Since constituency polls are commissioned for a particular purpose with a deadline such as a by-election, it can be problematic to arrange everything quickly and accurately when the pressure of work stemming from inevitably tight deadlines is at its most intense and unyielding. All polling firms will simultaneously be conducting a variety of polls (not just 'politicals') and this might lead to cutting corners regarding the number of interviewers employed for a particular task and/or the number of interviews conducted during a specific fieldwork period.

These pressures can mean that most of the interviewing is carried out in the street rather than by visiting the respondents at home. This might produce a very strange sample because of the ease with which certain categories of respondents, such as housewives and pensioners, are available. Such moves towards a higher degree of self-selection is unlikely to produce a reasonable spread of residential locations. For example, in rural seats, if there is pressure on to complete the interviews by a tight deadline, it is unlikely that the full constituency will be covered to get the interviews. This might well result in neglect of the more outlying and inaccessible parts of the constituency. Once again, this might have happened during the Brecon and Radnor by-election in 1985.

In an ideal world, the above problems could be dealt with to a large degree, even though they would need money to be spent and more time given to reflect and think things through. In the real world, however, they have to be coped with as effectively as possible.

One possible change could be to return to random sampling from the electoral register. Whilst even this register is never completely accurate or up to date, this might be the best approach to circumventing the problems caused by the lack of availability of local data which is necessary to set sample quotas. Another possibility is to go over more to telephone polling since this would overcome any problems with excessive clustering in terms of sampling points and there would be no need to visit all parts of the seat to get a reliable snapshot of the mood of the voters. Care would always still have to be taken to deal with the inherent bias in telephone interviewing (see chapter 3 again).

The main problem of constituency polling remains, though. There is a clear mismatch between the desires of the polling organisations to conduct reliable polls and their clients who want 'quickie' polls done cheaply without realising the inevitable trade-off in terms of accuracy. The interest in constituency polls is

unlikely to diminish but it has to be hoped that a greater understanding of what can and cannot be achieved and at what cost will
be spread more widely to potential clients before such polls are
commissioned. The interest in such polls might well be fanned
even more by the advent of an even greater degree of tactical
voting in certain key seats or when a close result in particular
constituencies seems likely.

5.3   Polls in marginal seats

Polls taken in marginal seats are potentially very interesting but
also difficult to explain to a wider audience. They are interesting
because they represent the seats where the election will be decided
rather than the 'safe' seats which will not change hands this side of
Armageddon. Consequently, polling in a selection of marginal
seats is undertaken by exit polls to predict the partisan composition of the House of Commons and to contrast the parties' perfor-
mances in marginal seats with the national polls conducted in all
types of constituency.

Polls taken in marginal seats are often problematic because the
distinction between a poll of marginals and a poll of national seats
is hard to get across to an audience, even to those who have
commissioned the poll, and the interpretation of the data drawn
from a poll of marginals can go wrong as a result.

Interest in what was happening in marginal seats really took off
at the 1987 general election, with about twenty polls being conducted in such seats during the campaign (Norris 1989). This
interest had been increased by the widespread belief that the
national polls could not be used, as in the past, to produce accurate projections of seats which each party would win. If the
national polls alone had been consulted, a clear Conservative
victory in 1987 was the only possible outcome based on a very
steady pattern of support for all the main parties. However, the
national polls might not have picked up any changes taking place
in particular seats since they do not have big enough samples in a
national poll to sub-divide the samples below national level. As
such, regional analysis rather than national analysis might tell a
different story if different parts of Britain were moving in different partisan directions. This might well be crucial in regions

with a high concentration of marginal seats, such as London, the West and East Midlands and the North West, since this would play havoc with seat projections derived from assumptions of a monolithic national picture. Polling in marginal seats would enable these projections to be refined and changed.

In addition to the possibility of regional differences, there was the possibility of tactical voting taking place in marginal seats, in particular with the opponents of the Conservative government voting for whichever party stood the best chance of ousting the incumbent Conservative. This has been a regular and repeated occurrence at by-elections, as we saw above, but no-one was sure how or if it could be organised at a general election (Fishman and Shaw 1989). Nevertheless, the possibility that it would happen gave a spark of interest to the campaign since it would also undermine the basis of normal seat projections. If tactical voting took off in the marginal seats, this could reduce a comfortable working majority for a government to no majority at all, depending where it happened and to what degree. In addition, the possibility of tactical voting taking place produced nervousness on the part of campaign managers, whose plans were liable to be seriously upset by such 'novel' voting habits.

Polls in marginal seats should produce a better indication of which seats will change hands than national polls. However, the methodology of conducting marginal polls has a number of associated problems. The first question in this regard must be what exactly is a 'marginal' seat? There are no established criteria to answer this question, which means that each polling company will have a different list of marginals to choose from when conducting a marginal poll. As a rule of thumb, a marginal seat is one which might change hands from one party to another at the election, based on the small majority of the winner over the second party at the last election.

How small is 'small', though? Does this mean a lead of 5 per cent, 15 per cent or more? This inevitably becomes a matter of judgement because other factors might mean that the seat is not really marginal despite the small numerical majority for the winner last time around. There might, for example, be differences depending on which party holds the seat, whether the incumbent is locally popular or well known nationally or both (thus benefiting from a 'personal vote'), whether there has been a recent by-election in that particular seat, whether there are regional differences and whether it is a 'target seat' for one of the parties? If a list of marginals based on numerical majority is devised, this might not provide a list of seats most likely to change hands unless other influences are taken into account on the basis of previous knowledge and judgement. These differences in drawing up the list of marginal seats means that it is usually difficult to compare one marginal poll with another.

An added complication is the different type of marginal seat, based on which party holds the seat and which party is second. Most polls are based on two types taken together in a poll: firstly, there are Conservative–Labour marginals and, secondly, Conservative–Liberal Democrat marginals. Of course, some seats cannot be classified as easily as this if the seat is a three-way marginal, and the picture is further blurred in Scotland and Wales by the presence of a fourth party, the respective Nationalists. Classifying such seats is again a matter of some judgement, particularly if the possibility of tactical voting is present and either Labour or the Liberal Democrats could have their vote 'squeezed' by the other in an attempt to unseat the Conservative. It has to be remembered that polls taken in marginals can tell us about the state of play in the marginal seats; they are not intended to say anything about what is happening nationally.

Devising a sample for polling in marginal seats also has the same problem as for by-elections. The paucity of local data on which the sample can be based remains a real concern, in particular the accuracy of the data and the extent to which they are up to date.

Polls taken in marginal seats therefore have a clearly defined purpose: they are attempting to establish whether particular types of constituency might behave differently from the national pattern as depicted in the national polls. However, the problems involved in conducting marginal polls set out above mean that they are problematic to devise and interpret. The main question that awaits them at the end is straightforward: did the marginal polls manage to identify any variation between what was happening in the marginals and nationally, in particular whether the government was performing better in the marginal seats than in the country as a whole? In other words, were the polls conducted in the marginals a useful supplement to the national polls or did they add little that could not have been garnered from the latter?

Given the size of the samples in polls of marginals, there is more sampling error than in national polls and any deviation in the predicted share of the votes for the parties must take this into account. The main problem, however, arises from the seat projections since this extra error can mean that differing seat projections are derived as a result.

In 1987, the marginal polls overestimated the Labour vote in both the Conservative–Labour and the Conservative–Alliance marginals, the latter type of seat being less well predicted, with an average error of 3.5 per cent as opposed to an error of 2.5 per cent in the former type of seat. In addition, if *national* polls had been used to predict the number of Conservative seats on the assumption of average national swing across the country, they would have been right to within a handful of the actual result.

As a result, at the 1992 general election there was less interest in marginal polls and fewer were commissioned. This turned out to be a pity, since there is evidence that the voters in the marginal seats did act differently in 1992 from the national picture. This belief is based on the fact that the Conservatives achieved a lead over Labour of 7.6 per cent in the popular vote and yet they only had a 21-seat overall majority in the House of Commons. In addition, the Conservatives won eleven seats, whose majorities total to about 2,500 votes out of a total of nearly 33 million votes cast, suggesting that even this slender overall majority of seats could easily have been wiped out entirely if only a relatively few voters had acted differently. In contrast, at the 1959 general election the Conservatives had a smaller lead of 5.6 per cent over Labour but they ended up with a majority of 100 seats in a House of Commons with twenty-one fewer seats than in 1992. This strongly suggests that there was a discrepancy between what was happening in the marginal seats and nationally in 1992.

In the run-up to the 1992 election it was asserted that although Labour appeared to be in the lead in the polls, its vote was 'soft' and it was making little progress in the key marginals which it had to win to gain an overall majority of seats. Instead, its poll lead was based on a strong performance in the seats which it already held, but this was utterly misleading in terms of the number of seats it would actually win from the Conservatives.

Analysis of the marginal seats in the different regions in 1992 suggests that this was not the case and that Labour did better than expected, given their national vote share, largely because of its success in key marginals. Unlike in 1987, the Labour Party's strategy of investing organisational effort in the key marginal seats seems to have paid off. The party still lagged some 2.5 million votes behind the Conservatives in the popular vote but they came close to depriving the Conservatives of their overall majority of seats.

This outcome indicates that conducting polls in marginal seats will remain a good idea at future elections. If the concept of a uniform national swing is further undermined at the next general election, the marginal polls should prove to be particularly useful in telling us the story as it develops. This might happen because of tactical voting both becoming more prominent and taking place in more seats. It will still be problematic to predict the number of seats for each party, however, since the vote movements might not be in a consistent direction, meaning that the government might not actually suffer a net loss of seats.

This will certainly mean that the presentation of the results of marginal polls will need to be carefully considered. It is very easy for the media to misinterpret the story the marginal polls are telling in their search for an intelligible analysis and a summary headline. Understanding of the advantages and disadvantages of marginal polls is not in short supply amongst both the pollsters and the media, but somehow this grasp gets lost in confusion and uncertainty when the 'story' of the marginal poll is assembled for publication or broadcast.

5.4   Polls at local and European elections

Local elections are held in Britain at regular intervals, although the exact cycle varies considerably, with sometimes full local elections every four years or partial (usually one-third) council elections annually. Whilst local issues, such as the poll tax or community charge, do seem to matter to the outcome of local elections, their main interest still lies in using the outcome to estimate the standing of the main parties nationally.

This applies to the results of local elections and there are a number of problems associated with using local election results in this way. Given the varying coverage of the country as a whole, it is often difficult to estimate the current vote share of the parties nationally. In addition, in some areas, the parties do not put up candidates in every seat contested. In local elections, there is also the maverick role of independent candidates to be taken into account and the fact that, for some councils, some of the seats are multi-member, where the same party puts up more than one candidate for election. This renders it hard to calculate the vote share of each party immediately since the candidates' shares are bound to differ. Normally, either the vote of the top candidate is taken as the guide, although this risks overestimating support if that candidate is particularly popular, or, alternatively, the average vote share of all the candidates for each party is taken. This does not solve the problem, however, if one party does not put up the same number of candidates as the number of seats to be filled.

On top of all that, there are usually problems with the precise boundaries of the seats being contested in terms of aggregating the results, particularly to parliamentary level, and the usual lack of usable local socio-economic data is a further constraint. A final point concerns the probability of a very low turnout compared to general elections.

These points apply to local election results and they apply equally to polls taken in local areas. Indeed, there is little polling activity at the purely local level in the light of these problems despite the increased interest in the role of local government since the 1980s, with the activities of Conservative 'flagship' councils in Wandsworth and Westminster and the publicity attracted by Liverpool and Lambeth councils during the same period of the Thatcher governments.

More normally, local elections are used purely as barometers of the national standing of the main parties, with gains and losses in terms of local council seats being interpreted in terms of national politics. This seems reasonable if the election is dominated by national issues, such as the imposition of VAT on domestic fuel or the poll tax, for example, and the general standing of the prime minister, but local issues such as water charges, measures against crime and planning applications can still add a local edge to the overall political battle.

A particular problem at local level is the strong evidence that the various functions of the different levels of government are unclear to most voters, with city councils being assumed to carry out the functions actually within the remit of county councils in areas such as education and social services. There would not, therefore, be much point in devising a poll which included 'issue questions' which mainly produced irrelevant responses due to the incorrect attribution of local government functions.

Consequently, the media use polls only rarely in their coverage of local election campaigns. More normally, their coverage will concentrate upon 'sketches' of particular local areas or regions which draw their empirical evidence from the canvass returns of the parties and the likely impact of the results for wider political questions from interviews with candidates and officials. The use of canvass returns is of course a step backwards for the media in their election coverage, but the sheer difficulty of setting up and conducting local polls with a sufficient degree of reliability means that there is often no real choice in the matter.

Problems can also occur when planning a poll in the run-up to elections to the European Parliament, but they are different from local elections. The European constituencies involved are simply aggregations of Westminster seats, producing 'Euro-seats' with electorates of about 500,000. The major parties stand in all the seats and the Nationalists do the same in Scotland and Wales. As such, adding the results of the relevant constituencies together from the previous general election provides a basis for predicting the outcome of the European election. The size of the constituencies means that single-constituency variations are smoothed out in the process of aggregation, producing a uniform picture which makes it easier to predict which party will win in each seat.

Opinion polls specifically on European elections are nevertheless a rarity. Normal, monthly opinion polls are still carried out during European election campaigns, with the occasional addition of a few questions on European issues, but the media show little sustained interest most of the time. For example, Gallup's regular monthly survey was published in the *Daily Telegraph* on 3 June 1994, under the front-page headline, 'Labour poll rating rises to highest for 23 years.' The Labour Party had the support of 54 per cent of the voters, whilst the Conservatives were in third place, behind the Liberal Democrats, with 21 per cent. The first sentence of the report mentions that it was the final week of campaigning for the European Parliament elections but the main reason for the popularity of the Labour Party was seen as resulting from a wave of sympathy following the death of the party leader, John Smith, three weeks earlier.

In the fuller report inside the paper, no question on Europe is mentioned. Instead, the standard voting intention question is given, along with the latest appraisal of the 'feel good' factor (tapping the expectations of the respondents as to whether they believed that the financial situation of their household would change over the next twelve months) and the results of a question on economic competence. It is, however, reported that a straight projection from the overall voting intention figures would leave the Conservatives with only about twelve seats in the European Parliament out of a British mainland total of eighty-four.

One newspaper which did commission a 'Euro-poll' was, unsurprisingly, *The European*, for which MORI organised polls throughout all twelve member states of the European Union. The paper published extracts from the results over a number of weeks during the election campaign itself. Its questions were much more specifically geared towards the interests of its readership, encompassing questions on moves towards a United States of Europe and a single currency. In general, however, the British media appeared relatively uninterested in the outcome, despite occasional, although unconvincing, claims that the elections were important for more and more people.

This lack of interest was not a new development in 1994. In 1985, Butler and Jowett concluded that the elections to the European Parliament in 1984 had been 'extraordinarily quiet, depoliticised' and that the level of public interest and the amount of newspaper coverage declined as the campaign progressed. They quote a party official who said that 'the closer I got to this election, the less I knew what it was about' (1985: 131).

The campaign of 1994 was similar. The European elections held on 9 June almost crept up on the voters unannounced, despite some media attention and good reporting in the quality press. The parties reinforced this impression with some lacklustre campaigning, largely involving tactics designed to limit overall damage on the part of the government, whilst the opposition merely tried to continue their regular attacks on the government with a thin veneer of European issues covering an agenda of largely domestic issues. These tactics were mostly designed to mobilise their respective rank-and-file supporters but a turnout of 36 per cent suggests that this was not a success.

The 1994 European Parliament elections were used by the polling firms to test afresh some of the problems encountered at the 1992 general election. In particular, the pollsters took the opportunity to adjust their figures according to past reported votes for the 'don't know' group of respondents. The results suggested that these adjustments were effective in bringing the poll results close to the actual result, although there were specific problems with the vote for the Liberal Democrats and 'other' parties.

The overall implication, though, is that the problem of differential refusal can be overcome and that this might be important since the problems apparent at the 1992 general election seem to be persisting. The current adjustments based on re-allocating the 'don't knows' and weighting by reported past vote would appear to be the way forward (MRS 1994: 105–8).

5.5   Conclusion

In this chapter we have looked at the use of polls below and above national level. There are clear differences, compared with national polls, in the way in which polling data are used at by-elections and in single constituencies, and additional difficulties involved in conducting polls at local or European level. In this context, national polling seems almost straightforward, given the lack of local data on which samples can properly be based, the problems of deciding the definition of a marginal seat and the sheer lack of interest in purely local and European issues on the part of the voters.

We must be careful in particular not to ascribe too much significance to elections below national level, whatever their importance might appear to be at the time. For all the attention given to them when they actually take place, particularly by the media and leading politicians, it is hard to remember a by-election that directly changed much in terms of national government policy or personnel. Norman Lamont might well disagree with this, of course, following his dismissal as chancellor after the Newbury by-election in 1993, which resulted in a landslide victory for the Liberal Democrats.

By-election defeats for the government have become expected political events. The usual discomfiture of the government is both emphasised and enjoyed by their opponents but such reversals leave few long-term traces on the national political scene since it is justifiably assumed that the government will normally regain the lost seat at the next general election. For all their media froth and surface excitement, by-elections seem incapable of striking hard and deep into the collective psyche of those in power.

As with the other types of elections we have considered in this chapter, by-elections are very much 'second-order' elections at which national power is not at stake. This is not to say that polling data at this level of politics can be airily dismissed as being of little use. Technically, polls at by-elections have been invaluable exercises for developing polling methods of more general use. It can, nevertheless, be said that polls at below national or at European level do normally present different problems and challenges for the polling companies from those they regularly face at national level.

One of those problems has been how best to establish the nature of mass opinions on the most important issues of the day. The different ways in which those issue questions are asked and the different ways in which they are answered are the subject of the next chapter.

References

Butler, D. and P. Jowett (1985) *Party Strategies in Britain: A study of the 1984 European elections*, Basingstoke: Macmillan.

Crewe, I. and M. Harrop (eds) (1989) *Political Communications: The general election campaign of 1987*, Cambridge: Cambridge University Press.

Fishman, N. and A. Shaw (1989) 'TV87: The campaign to make tactical voting make votes count', in I. Crewe and M. Harrop (eds) *Political Communications: The general election campaign of 1987*, Cambridge: Cambridge University Press, pp. 289–303.

Market Research Society (1994) *The Opinion Polls and the 1992 General Election*, London: Market Research Society.

Norris, P. (1989) 'The emergence of polls in marginals in the 1987 election: Their role and record', in I. Crewe and M. Harrop (eds) *Political Communications: The general election campaign of 1987*, Cambridge: Cambridge University Press, pp. 223–38.

Suggested further reading

Almost by definition, there is little of general use on by-elections. The book by Pippa Norris on *British By-Elections: The volatile electorate*

(Oxford: Clarendon Press, 1990) is a good place to start, though. Robert Waller's chapter on constituency polling in the Crewe and Harrop (1989) volume cited above gives plenty of detail, encompassing 78 constituency polls in 52 different constituencies in 1987. Local and European elections are best covered in more general texts of the outcomes such as the Butler and Jowett (1985) book cited above.

6

The opinion polls and political issues

One of the key trends which has been identified in British politics since the 1970s has been the decline in the loyalty of the voters to the main two parties. It is no longer the case that electors vote for the same party simply out of habit; instead, they rely on assessing each party on largely 'instrumental' lines before deciding how to cast their ballots. The evidence for this trend has been drawn from the seemingly inexorable decline in the numbers of people who identified themselves with either of the major parties. This produced the idea that what increasingly moved the electorate much more than in the past was not blind, uncritical faith in the capacity of 'their' party to govern but the voters' changeable perception of their party's competence to govern, especially in terms of running the domestic economy. In this way, the issue of the economy became the centrepiece of a revised conventional wisdom about the key influence which ultimately decided election outcomes.

In an era of more and more 'floating voters', it seemed logical that issues in general but specifically issues of competence would indeed become more significant in the minds of an electorate which needed to be persuaded and then convinced of the merits of the respective parties. Much more than in the past, vote choices were seen as being grounded in cool, 'rational' decisions about which party would be best for the voters and their families in terms of the issues and policies which they cared about the most (Denver 1994: chapter 3).

The polls in Britain have often included questions dealing with issue importance. The potential significance of these data has increased since the 1970s, however, on the assumption that issues were bound to be more important in understanding the overall mood of the electorate in a period of 'de-alignment'. In addition, more specific questions dealing with issues could provide data of importance in assessing the relative standing of the parties, during both election campaigns and non-election periods. The main type of issue question used asks the voters to give their own opinions regarding which party is best at handling a particular issue. The respondents are normally offered a range of issues and are then asked to specify a 'best' party for each issue in turn.

The main conclusion, however, drawn from the last three general elections in Britain regarding 'issue voting' is that it does not work out in a straightforward way in practice, on the basis that the party seen by most people to have the best policies on the most important issues wins the election.

If we look at the issues identified by the voters as the ones that they consider to be the most important and then the party identified as having the best policy on those same issues, we should get a clearer picture of how the 'issue voting model' compares to empirical reality. At the 1992 general election, Sanders identified the National Health Service, unemployment and education as the three most important issues affecting the vote choice of the electorate. These were all issues on which the Labour Party had a big lead over the Conservatives, whilst the best two issues for the Conservatives were inflation and taxation, which were rated as important by only about 10 per cent of the respondents. Defence and law and order, two issues often and strongly seen as likely to favour the Conservatives, failed to register at all (Sanders 1993).

On the basis of this, then, the Conservatives should have been in electoral trouble if the issue model provides a good match to what the voters actually think and then do. However, further data demonstrate that not all of those voters who do identify one or the other main party as being the best party on the issues they feel are the most important actually then go on to *vote* for that party. For example, 60 per cent of those who cited health as one of the two most important issues believed that the Labour Party had the best policies on health, yet only 49 per cent of those same people actually then voted Labour, according to their reported vote. So, 11 per cent actually failed to carry out the 'logic' of the issue voting model. Similar figures applied to the issues of unemployment and education for Labour and the inflation issue for the Conservatives (Sanders 1993: 195).

Therefore, whatever the theoretical plausibility and elegance of the theory of issue voting, we need to add serious qualifications to its acceptance as a key causal factor in the deliberations of the electorate. Whilst there does appear to be a good fit between the party nominated as the one with the best policies *overall* and vote choice, this relationship diminishes greatly when we disaggregate the bundle of policies and consider each issue separately.

If the opinions on specific issues which comprise the issue voting model had been the major influences when the voters were making up their minds, the Labour Party should have received about 44 per cent of the vote in 1992, with the Conservatives a long way behind on 33 per cent. The fact that this was so far from the actual general election result inevitably throws considerable doubt on the validity and use of the issue voting model since there appears to be a significant number of voters to whom issues as such are not important in guiding their vote choice, even though some voters were clearly consistent along the lines suggested by the issue voting model.

What use, then, are all the data gathered on issues and attitudes that are now regularly contained in most polls carried out in Britain? Such data are still, despite the above caveat regarding voting, useful for depicting the current mood of the electorate, even if we need to treat issue data carefully overall in the way in which they are used.

For this chapter, we have selected five issues to consider in more detail and to analyse their impact on British politics in recent years based on poll evidence. Three of those issues were also considered by Teer and Spence (1973), and we have added two more.

The five issues are the European Community (EC), trade unions and industrial relations, race relations and immigration, the environment, and finally, electoral reform. We will look in greatest detail at the EC issue since this illustrates neatly the main points affecting the role of issues in determining political attitudes and political choice in general. The other issues will be dealt with more briefly, although each one is still useful in making key points about the impact and role of political issues and the different dimensions of public opinion we discussed in chapter 2.

The above choice of issues will also enable us to get beyond the overwhelming assumption that it is the economy that matters to the exclusion of everything else and that 'pocketbook voting' enables us to explain virtually any election result. This particular idea was reinforced in the United States presidential election of 1992 by the victory of Bill Clinton over George Bush and the prominence of the badge which provided the answer 'The economy, stupid!' to the unasked but implied question about the key influence in deciding the election result.

Regardless of the precise issue of interest, the general approach for testing the 'issue agenda' at a particular time is always similar. Firstly, the polls try to establish which issues are seen by the voters as being the most important. This might mean offering the respondents a list from which they are asked to rank the two or three issues most important to them. Secondly, the respondents are then asked which party in their view has the best policy on those issues which they have just identified as being the most important.

There are clear problems associated with this method: for example, should a list of issues be offered to the respondents at all? Some polls have asked their respondents to answer this as an open-ended question where they are not prompted with a list but can say whatever they believe to be the most important issue. On the other hand, what about the respondents who could not answer such a question, those most likely to have little interest in politics but who could not simply be ignored or omitted as a result? It might also make the continuation of the interview more difficult if, on this question, the respondent could not think of an answer themselves. A compromise solution is to offer a list of issues for the respondents to select from but to make it a long list (perhaps fifteen issues) which should cover the vast majority of possible answers. Even so, such a list could never be entirely complete, particularly in terms of local or regional issues rather than national issues.

Another problem of this approach to issues is the assumption that what exactly constitutes an issue will be the same for each respondent. This is an assumption which is hard to maintain if the issue is a very general one since issues such as education or taxation have a number of different aspects to them. The precise aspect which the respondent was using as the basis for their answer would not be revealed unless further questions were employed to follow up the initial response. This is usually not possible in a short survey, where the total number of questions that can be put is very restricted on grounds of time and cost. The argument for using a single question is that polls are not generally very detailed or specialised and, if such aspects need to examined in more detail, another more narrowly focused poll should be used for that purpose. A single-issue question is simply meant to establish the broad importance of an issue relative to others. It is not really ever intended that detailed questioning of the respondents' knowledge or motivation, for example, would follow on from the first general issue question.

Single questions are nevertheless useful in delineating the issue agenda because they establish a rank order of importance, at least as far as the electorate is concerned. The question then becomes whether the media and the politicians act upon that agenda or whether they attempt to follow an alternative set of issues in terms of public policy. If the parties do not agree with the definition by the public of which issues should constitute the public agenda, they can of course ignore it or try to change it. The basis of the political battle will be decided by the outcome of these decisions.

The rank order of issues is often not very surprising, with the state of the economy seeming to dominate most of the time. The specific aspect of the economy which comes out top may, however, change over time, with unemployment and inflation often jostling for priority. At the 1992 election, the top five issues of importance for the vote decision of the electors in Gallup's post-election survey were unemployment (56 per cent), the health service (41 per cent), education (23 per cent), inflation (11 per cent) and taxation (10 per cent). The percentages do not total to 100 per cent because the respondents could specify two issues as being the most important (Sanders 1993: 196).

In a non-election period, in 1981, the 'issue agenda' of very important issues chosen from a list was dominated by reducing unemployment at the top (chosen by 88 per cent), followed by maintaining law and order (86 per cent), controlling inflation (69 per cent), controlling immigration (65 per cent) and protecting people's privacy (54 per cent). Reducing taxation was ranked as thirteenth out of fourteen issues in 1981. Other issues which were included at that time but which were not prominent in 1992 were controlling the unions, improving race relations, increasing pensions and building more homes for owner–occupiers (Webb and Wybrow 1982: 64).

Sometimes issues wax and wane in public importance and we can often relate the prominence or insignificance of particular issues to events or decisions made by the parties to highlight or downplay particular themes. These decisions will be influenced in particular by the perceptions of the parties in terms of how they stand on each issue in turn and whether such an issue is likely to benefit them or their opponents electorally. The setting of the public agenda is therefore a constant struggle between the parties trying to extract the maximum electoral benefit for themselves whilst simultaneously ensuring that their opponents are not allowed to make the running on issues which threaten their own popularity in the run-up to the next election.

Some issues remain difficult to use in poll questions, however, often because of their technical and detailed nature. Poll questions are designed to be broadly applicable and there is little use for questions which can only be understood by some of the respondents or refer to issues that do not apply to most of the people questioned. Specific tax proposals are one example of this, and the lack of understanding which would apply to most respondents on this topic militates against the use of such questions in general samples of the public, although attempts to dig a little deeper than normal are often made after the annual Budget statement by the Chancellor of the Exchequer. It is more likely that taxation as an overall and general issue would be used, although sub-groups with the requisite interest and knowledge could still be asked more detailed questions.

Testing the opinions of voters on particular issues, therefore, often starts out with general topics relating to importance and perceptions of party competence and then moves on to specific aspects of those issues. We can now begin to look at our five issues in turn, beginning with the Common Market, the European Community and now most recently, the European Union (all the same issue, of course!).

6.1   The Common Market/European Community/ European Union

It is a common assertion that the whole question of Europe and the role of Britain in it stirs little excitement amongst the British voters and it certainly does not act as a source of changing electoral behaviour. During the 1992 election campaign, the question of European integration was only mentioned in passing by the parties even though the general election took place only four months after the Maastricht Treaty was agreed and only two months after it had been signed. This is not surprising in itself since both the main parties were internally divided on the whole question of how much more European integration they should support and at what pace it should be pursued.

Both main parties were uncertain exactly how to play the issue during the election campaign even though the Conservatives were able to allude to John Major's negotiating skills as part of his performance as prime minister. In the intervening period between the Maastricht Treaty being signed and the election campaign hotting up, the issue of Europe was effectively sidetracked in favour of engaging the political battle over the state of the economy and the relative competence of each of the main parties to produce economic recovery.

Poll questions asking about attitudes towards Europe have been asked since the late 1950s by both NOP and Gallup. Between 1960 and 1967, when Britain was applying to join the original six members of the European Community, Gallup included the same question on whether Britain should join the Common Market if the government decided it would be in Britain's interests.

Understandably, the main questions on the European issue during this period ask in various forms whether Britain should join and on what basis it should do so. The arguments for and against joining were all aired during the 1960s, including trade policy, the role of the Commonwealth, which groups in British society would benefit or suffer if Britain joined the Common Market and what the likely consequences would be in terms of the cost of living, employment and working conditions.

The first point to note is that, throughout the 1960s, irrespective of whether a general or more specific question was asked on the European issue, public opinion appeared to be very changeable, with a sizeable amount of 'don't knows' being recorded, sometimes amounting to more than a third of the sample. The number of the 'don't know' group dropped dramatically, however, whenever the issue of joining the Common Market hit the headlines or whenever the issue appeared more tangible and less theoretical and esoteric. For example, Gallup recorded a 'don't know' figure of only 14 per cent in February 1967, three months before Harold Wilson as prime minister announced that he wanted parliamentary approval to start negotiations to join. More normally during this decade, the 'don't know' percentage was within the range of 25–40 per cent.

There was also a clear perception that it was the Conservative Party which could handle the problem of Europe the best and that they were the party who were keenest for Britain to join. Conservative supporters were those such as businessmen who could expect to benefit the most from entry. For example, in September 1961, Gallup found that 49 per cent of the electorate believed the Conservatives were in favour of joining and only 9 per cent felt they were against entry. Only 24 per cent and 30 per cent respectively believed that Labour and the Liberals were also in favour. Once more, it is worth noting the uncertainty on this issue in terms of the 'don't know' category: 24 per cent for the Conservatives, 34 per cent for Labour and fully 52 per cent for the Liberals.

Whilst it was often true that the Conservatives were regarded as being the best party for dealing with entry to Europe, this did change when the Labour government was seen to be dealing with the issue in a concrete way. In a poll of February 1967, the Labour Party was seen by 39 per cent of voters to be the best party on the issue, contrasting with 29 per cent regarding the Conservatives as being the best. However, this apparent change reverted to the more normal pattern in October 1969, with 36 per cent believing the Conservatives to be the best party and 24 per cent choosing the Labour Party.

It is also noticeable that during the same period (the first six months of 1967), when negotiations actually started under the Labour government, there was a clear move in public opinion towards disapproving of plans for entry. There appeared to be a definite movement away from previous approval and 'don't know' to disapproval which reached 44 per cent by May 1967. Care is needed here in interpreting this because it might well have been part of a wider and more general dissatisfaction with the government and little to do with the Common Market as such. This is particularly likely since 'the government' was often specifically included in the question and the answers as a result might well have more to do with attitudes towards the government overall than the precise advantages and disadvantages of entry to the Common Market.

Nevertheless, we can see from other related poll questions that disapproval could equally have been rooted in the perception that the cost of living would increase if Britain joined. When asked about the potential disadvantages of entry, it was the fear that prices would go up that dominated all the other responses. The inevitable loss of sovereignty to the institutions of the Common Market barely registered at this time. Additionally, the dominance of the possible rise in the cost of living was not matched by any perception of advantage for Britain, with the most often cited advantage being a vague potential gain for British industry and agriculture.

In the light of the above, it might seem strange that even though many were against entry, they also believed that it would happen anyway, with percentages of more than 80 per cent believing this being recorded. This suggests that whatever their personal opinion of Common Market entry, a perception of inevitability was also strong amongst the electorate.

It is also the case that different social groups in the electorate reacted in different ways to the question of Common Market entry. Young people, men and the middle class were generally in favour, whilst the elderly, working-class groups and women were less in favour (Teer and Spence 1973: 113).

Additionally, we can track the feelings of supporters of the parties throughout the period. By 1969, all the parties were in favour of joining on the right terms but this was not reflected in the views of their supporters, with Labour supporters in particular strongly against entry. There was also a lack of enthusiasm from Conservative and Liberal voters. With the change of government in 1970, this pattern altered, with Conservatives more clearly in favour and even fewer Labour supporters thinking the same way. This provides another reminder of the apparent volatility of mass attitudes towards the Common Market, with attitudes being heavily influenced by changes in government, overall attitudes towards the government of the time and whether the topic was being discussed in the media or had assumed a concrete, as opposed to a vague and theoretical, form in the minds of the respondents.

During this period as well, there was little indication that the issue of Common Market entry as a whole would sway many votes.

After the negotiations for entry were concluded, Gallup asked whether, if there was a general election on the issue of the Common Market and the respondent disagreed with 'their' party's policy on the issue, they would still vote for 'their' party or not. Most (48 per cent) stated that they would still vote for their usual party, whilst only 14 per cent would vote for another party. Additionally, 22 per cent would not vote, suggesting that an election purely on the issue of the Common Market would not stir a sizeable minority to turn out to vote at all. Perhaps predictably, 17 per cent replied 'don't know' to this question.

Public opinion on the Common Market issue in the period from the late 1950s to actual entry in 1973 can therefore be summarised succinctly: the Common Market was not an issue that stirred much interest amongst the mass public. In general, the electorate displayed little knowledge or interest in the associated issues, in particular how exactly it would affect Britain, themselves and their families. The perceptions of the advantages and disadvantages were swamped by the single fear of price rises and this was seen as a key influence in moving mass opinion against entry. This was particularly strong amongst Labour supporters. The overall focus on the issue of Common Market entry was therefore almost entirely on the short term and the specific rather than the long term and the esoteric.

Of course, the question of the loss of sovereignty to supranational institutions is hard to communicate since it appears to touch so few people directly and personally and, as such, it is not surprising that so few poll respondents were able to answer within such a frame of reference. This means that for information about the terms of the debate, ordinary people are much more dependent on the way in which the issue is 'framed' in the media and what politicians and commentators say about what is good or bad about a particular issue.

So far, I have covered the period up until Britain's entry; but have things changed since then, given that Britain has had to face up to new problems and new challenges emanating from Common Market membership? The early years of British membership of the European Community were dominated by the question of renegotiating the terms of entry and then the referendum held in 1975 to decide on the acceptability of those new terms of membership. Gallup polls taken in 1974 suggested that mass opinion was that

Table 6.1   Attitudes to British membership of the European Community

	Good thing	Bad thing	Neither good nor bad	Don't know
1972	40	21	23	16
1976	43	30	19	9
1977	35	38	20	8
1978	25	48	20	7
1979	23	55	16	7
1980	24	52	18	7
1981	24	52	21	4
1982	25	46	22	7
1983	39	34	22	7
1984	30	40	24	6
1985	32	39	21	7
1986	28	39	25	8
1987	36	35	21	9
1988	36	36	18	9
1989	51	19	23	8
1990	56	13	21	10
1991	49	22	20	9
1992	49	22	20	10
1993	41	29	19	10
March 1994	40	23	28	8
April 1994	42	21	26	11
June 1994	49	19	22	10

Source: Gallup Political and Economic Index, appropriate years.

Britain should stay in (59 per cent were in favour). This was confirmed throughout 1975 with a similar figure for retaining British membership. The main reason for this view appeared to be a general feeling that Britain could not stand alone, whilst the main disadvantage was still perceived to be the threat of rising prices.

Gallup has asked a general question on Britain's membership of the European Community regularly since entry, asking respondents whether they believe that British membership is a good thing, a bad thing or neither good nor bad (see table 6.1). Where the question was asked more than once in any one year, the percentages have been averaged, except for the last three entries, those for 1994 in the run-up to the elections to the European Parliament in June.

The figures in table 6.1 suggest that there is instability in attitudes towards the European Community and that the issue as a whole is one of low salience to voters. The 'swings' between the categories of the question suggest that much depends on the current debate within the European Community and how that is seen to affect Britain, as defined by the government and other leading politicians. This conclusion can be supported by answers to another question, which asked whether the respondents would be sorry, indifferent or relieved if they were told that the European Community was being scrapped. Often, in response to this question, between 40 and 50 per cent of the sample would be relieved, whilst about one-third would be indifferent.

In view of the above, we can look more easily at the attitudes of the British people towards the European Community by considering perception questions and attitude questions, in particular the extent of party divisions, the pace of integration and the potential loss of sovereignty to the institutions of the European Union.

6.2   Perceptions and attitudes towards the European Community

One common conclusion regarding the impact of the EC issue on British politics has been that it interests few of the electorate consistently but that it has the potential to cause great unrest within the two main parties, particularly over the future pace and direction of integration. Looking at events since the 1992 general election, this seems eminently reasonable. Appearing united on the EC issue has been the exception rather than the norm for the Conservative Party recently and this appearance feeds through into mass perceptions as well.

Whenever Gallup has asked whether the parties appear united or divided on the European Community, the vast majority of the respondents reply that they are divided, reaching 89 per cent in January 1993. Only 9 per cent perceived the Conservatives to be united on the EC issue. The Labour Party was also regarded as being disunited, although not to the same extent: 54 per cent perceiving them to be disunited although far more (24 per cent as against 6 per cent for the Conservatives) did not know whether they were divided or not. This is probably the result of the focus for action on the EC issue being most strongly on the actions and decisions of the government rather than of the opposition.

On the face of it, this should be worrying for the Conservative Party because conventional wisdom has it that a divided party will be an electorally unsuccessful party and calls for loyalty to the leader are regularly heard within the ranks of the Conservative Party. This makes the EC issue potentially damaging for the Conservatives as a whole; however, the lack of interest in Europe demonstrated by the electorate means that this potential loss of votes might well not materialise since the issue remains a distant one which does not touch the day-to-day concerns of most people.

It seems more likely that for the EC issue to affect the Conservatives electorally there will need to be a direct, emotive issue which the British electorate can relate to and which they care about strongly. Gallup has tracked mass opinion as these issues have arisen, particularly the question of sovereignty over matters which directly affect Britain and its interests and the desire for further integration and the costs involved for Britain.

There is always a problem in separating out support for European integration and general support for the government of the day and the prime minister. Under Mrs Thatcher, whose views on Europe were clearly and repeatedly expressed, it would have been hard not to be aware of these views. This means that any question about 'giving up' sovereignty risks being biased because of the language used by the leading politicians of the day. Of course, this language cannot be ignored in framing the question but care still has to be taken that there may be an implicit bias which pushes the respondents sub-consciously away from really considering all the alternatives that are offered. This is another example of the 'prestige problem' we mentioned earlier, where the views of the government or prime minister are stated in the question. Unfortunately, this is likely to produce responses which are then related to views of the prime minister in general rather than any truly independent assessment of the specific issue itself. This can of course be either positive or negative but it makes it difficult to work out just how important the issue is and which proposed course of action has the most public support. In terms of Mrs Thatcher specifically, it is very likely that 'batting for Britain' and 'getting our money back from Europe' struck a chord with many people; however, the 'framing' of the question will be critical here and responses must be interpreted carefully as a result.

The main move towards greater European integration began in the mid-1980s with the signing of the Single European Act, which aimed at transforming the European Community into a single market by removing many of the barriers to trade and the free movement of people around the continent of Europe. The attitude of the British government in favour of this was rooted in the belief that it would benefit British industry. The undertow of the removal of these barriers could equally be regarded as highly political, at least in the long term, as part of a move towards greater overall integration which went far beyond simply freeing trade and removing barriers to greater economic co-operation within the Community.

Questions of sovereignty have therefore arisen more and more since the 1980s, although the signs had been there for some time before that, for example in the establishment of the European Monetary System in the late 1970s. It has become impossible for any British government to ignore the fact that in the last few years the aim of 'Project Europe' has become more and more to do with various mechanisms of integration, which make it likely that Britain will be able to take fewer and fewer decisions on its own within the evolving structures of the European Union.

Gallup has tried to trace the individual aspects of these changes as they have become prominent and we will consider some of them now in terms of the perceptions of the ordinary voter. There are of course perfectly legitimate differences in opinion regarding the degree of European integration and the speed with which this process should take place. Gallup has on several occasions asked a general question which attempts to assess which of the main options are favoured by the British public. The first option offers the possibility of a fully integrated Europe with major decisions being taken by a European government; the second option offers more integration than now but with Britain continuing to take decisions that mainly affect Britain; the third option is to leave the situation as it is now, with Britain retaining a veto over major policy changes it does not like, and the final option is for Britain to withdraw from the European Union.

The two 'extreme' options are not supported (complete integration or withdrawal) and the more 'moderate' options receive the most support, with the second option backing integration but only so far being the most popular. For example, in a Gallup poll of

January 1993, complete integration was favoured by 9 per cent, more integration but with decisions mainly in British hands 44 per cent, Britain retaining a veto received the support of 23 per cent and withdrawal was backed by 17 per cent. Seven per cent said 'don't know'. In a previous poll in November 1990, the corresponding figures were 13, 56, 19, 8 and 4 per cent, respectively.

The problem with this question is that the type and nature of decisions that Britain alone should deal with are inevitably undefined by not being mentioned. Of course, this might well change over time and so if the purpose of asking the question is to compare over time, the question must be general for comparisons of the responses to be carried out. There must, however, be some suspicion that the use of the word Britain in the question implicitly pushes people towards the reasonable option of some integration but simultaneously some control over important decisions.

At this level of generality, though, what does such an answer tell us? At what point should the British government dig its heels in and refuse more integration? We saw earlier that, in the past, there had been a high degree of acceptance of European integration as inevitable and a clear perception that Britain might well get left behind if it refused to follow the course charted by the other EU member states. There is therefore considerable ambivalence towards Britain in Europe on the part of the voters, which makes the issue as a whole difficult for the parties to take on board or indeed the polling companies to assess in any detail.

Some issues that might make things particularly difficult for the government to 'sell' to the electorate might be related to the loss of the pound sterling in favour of a common European currency. If offered the choice between a single European currency and the pound, nearly two-thirds would still want to retain the pound, as Gallup discovered in a poll taken in July 1991. However, the ambivalence re-appears when the same respondents were asked whether Britain should go along with the other EU states if they *all* move towards the introduction of a single currency. The majority (54 per cent) stated that Britain should go along with it. The main reason for this, as revealed by a later question to the same sample, appeared to be the fear that if Britain attempted to stand alone on this issue, then British firms and financial institutions would suffer, a view that echoes the main argument before Britain joined the Community in the first place.

Another related topic recently was the need for a referendum before Britain joined a single currency at some point in the future or more immediately before Britain accepted the terms of the Maastricht Treaty. This issue received publicity because of the Danish, French and Irish referenda on the terms of the Maastricht Treaty backed up by the call of Mrs Thatcher for Britain to hold one as well. Most people (69 per cent in June 1992) wanted a referendum on the issue of the Maastricht Treaty; however, when John Major firmly ruled this out, little damage appeared to have been inflicted on his government.

The most sensitive issue regarding the European Union for the future will probably be the pace of further integration. The British people might not be particularly in favour, on the basis of the results cited above, but as long as they are not strongly against, and the issue of the European Union remains largely one of marginal interest to most of the voters, the issue might still be dealt with effectively by the government of the day.

It is of course problematic to design a neutral question on the topic of the pace of European integration because the use of phrases such as 'speeding up' or 'slowing down' have several aspects to them which are never spelt out in the question itself, such as at what cost, for what reason and for what gain? These are all important contextual factors which make it hard to separate out answers to such questions into their component parts and to come to clear conclusions about the thinking that lies behind such responses. This is not the aim of such a question, it can be argued, and general questions by definition will only produce general answers.

Gallup has asked a general question on the movement towards the unification of Europe in the 1970s as well as more recently in July 1992. There appears to be considerable stability in the responses, with the most popular choice being 'continuing as at present' followed by 'slowing down', although that category has grown in support since 1977. In July 1992, the two most popular categories were 'continue as at present' and 'slow down'. This could have been predicted from the other question, cited earlier, regarding the type of integration. Even in 1992, 11 per cent of the sample were unable to give an answer to the question of the pace of European integration.

We have seen therefore that there is marked ambivalence in the attitude of the majority of the British people towards European integration and the question of Europe in all its manifestations. The ultimate test of the importance of Europe as an issue for the parties will be 'Will it win or cost us votes at the next election?' Conventional wisdom would suggest that this will not actually happen since the issue does not move enough people to be concerned or interested on a daily basis in a way that affects their lives immediately or on a consistent basis.

If we recall the dimensions of public opinion set out in chapter 2, the issue of EU membership and European integration is not an issue of salience or stability for the electorate; nor are attitudes on the issue intensely held by voters. For the most part, it is a latent issue of erratic import and significance. The voters are very much the spectators on this issue, whilst the parties are the actors, attempting to control their own internal divisions on the issue rather than worrying over the potential loss of electoral support.

One way of demonstrating this conclusion is a simple and direct question regarding the voter's own perception as to whether the European issue will affect the way they vote. Gallup data suggest that usually two-thirds say it will *not* affect the way they vote. Another test is to explicitly ask the voters to rank the importance of the European issue with another competing issue. The most obvious issue in this regard would be the economy in general and again the result is as expected on the basis of the above. The respondents were offered the option of choosing 'a great deal of influence on their vote'. Only 10 per cent of the sample in November 1991 stated that the European Community would have such an effect, whilst 37 per cent stated that the economy would have a great deal of influence on the way they voted. Twenty per cent said that the European Community would have no influence on their vote, whilst half that figure (10 per cent) said the same about the economy.

The above results will certainly make it easier for parties in government to risk open displays of disunity and to take 'unpopular' decisions since they can be reasonably sure that public opinion on most aspects of the EU issue can be moulded and shaped at the time and as required rather than automatically act as a stumbling block which will cost the party votes.

We will now move on to our second issue in this chapter, that of attitudes to trade unions and industrial relations.

6.3   Trade unions and industrial relations

The gathering of data on attitudes towards trade unions specifically and industrial relations in general goes back a long way in Britain. Gallup have asked questions on various aspects of these topics since 1946 and they have asked the same general question on a regular basis, thus permitting comparisons of attitudes over time. This question asks: 'Generally speaking, do you think trade unions are a good thing or a bad thing?' More specifically, questions have also been asked which relate to particular issues of the time such as the Conservative government's Industrial Relations Act of the early 1970s. This means that it is possible either to use a broad and long-term perspective of attitudes towards the trade unions or specific issues can be investigated but only for a short period. These latter issues cover such matters as the closed shop, the need for a secret ballot before calling a strike and profit sharing by the workers employed by a firm.

It is now widely accepted that one of the main changes instituted by the Thatcher governments of the 1980s was to introduce a series of Acts designed to curb the powers of the trade unions in a variety of ways. As a result, the 1980s have inevitably become the focus of any examination of the importance of trade unions and the way in which this particular issue overall was important for partisan politics. This decade tends now to overshadow equally important periods such as the actions of the Heath government between 1970 and 1974 in terms of reforming the roles and powers of the unions. The relationship between the unions and the Labour Party also became a key bone of contention between the parties and this is reflected in the questions asked by Gallup throughout the 1980s. More generally, a long-standing concern has been the role of unions in politics as opposed to fighting for their members' interests in terms of wages and conditions and how representative the union leaders are of the overall union membership. Perceptions of the relations between the parties and the unions have also been examined and we will consider this evidence as well.

We can divide this section of the chapter into two parts: firstly, the general question about unions cited above; and secondly, more specific questions relating to unions and politics and the overall power of the unions in British society as perceived by the sample respondents.

Table 6.2 **Attitudes to trade unions, 1952–94**

	Good thing	Bad thing	Don't know
1952	69	12	19
1954	71	12	17
1955	67	18	15
1960	56	17	27
1965	57	25	18
1969	63	18	19
1972	55	30	16
1973	57	24	19
1974 (February)	62	25	14
1974 (August)	54	27	19
1975	43	41	16
1976	60	25	14
1977	53	33	14
1978	57	31	12
1979	44	44	12
1980	53	36	11
1981	56	28	16
1982	53	37	10
1983	63	25	12
1984	57	31	12
1985	69	22	9
1986	67	22	12
1987	71	17	12
1988	68	21	11
1989	68	24	8
1990	67	21	12
1991	70	17	12
1992	62	26	13
1993	71	18	12
1994	64	21	15

Source. Gallup Political and Economic Index, appropriate years.

6.3.1 The general question

Gallup has asked its general question about whether unions are a good or bad thing regularly since December 1952. This is obviously very broad but it does still provide an overall indication of attitudes which gives an insight into the public mood. The value of such a question is that it enables us to track any changes over time and to try and account for those changes.

We can see from the Gallup data that unions have consistently been regarded as a good thing, with something like 60–70 per cent of

most of the samples agreeing with this. The highest proportion perceiving unions as being a good thing occurred in August 1954 but
also in August 1987 and very recently in September 1993 (71 per
cent). The lowest percentage agreeing with the view that unions are
a good thing occurred in July 1975, with 43 per cent, and in January
1979, with 44 per cent. The latter date was the month of the so-
called 'Winter of Discontent'. The percentage claiming to have no
view on whether unions are a good or a bad thing has usually been
between 10 and 20 per cent, with a low of 9 per cent in March 1985
and a high of 27 per cent in September 1960 (see table 6.2).

It appears therefore that a general acceptance of unions as good
things survived relatively intact the legislative changes wrought by
the Thatcher governments throughout the 1980s. Of course, we
cannot tell from a single question what people were using as the
basis for such an opinion but it does suggest that the general value
of unions is regarded in a separate way from the more specific
functions and relationships of unions which we mentioned earlier.
One of those relationships is obviously the link between the unions
and the Labour Party.

6.3.2   Specific questions

A question regularly asked by Gallup has attempted to investigate
this relationship between the unions and the Labour Party. This
question has asked whether the links that exist are regarded as
being a good or a bad thing. This question was first asked in
August 1956 and the data over time indicate that the links have
usually been regarded as being a bad thing. The gap between the
percentages saying good or bad has sometimes not been very large
(for example, in 1966 it was 37 per cent saying good and 38 per
cent saying bad, and in September 1993 it was 41 per cent for both
categories). Nevertheless, the *general* perception over time has
been that the links are seen as being a bad thing.

This can be supported by examining another issue raised by
Gallup, which questions the relationship in terms of union say in
the affairs of the party. Again, this question has been asked on a
regular basis and, again, the general results indicate that there is a
widespread perception that the unions have too much say in the
running of the Labour Party. This option has often been chosen by
roughly half of most of the samples over time, with the next largest

category being those who respond that the amount of say given to the unions is about right.

A similar question has then been put in terms of the Labour Party: whether it is good or bad for the *party* to have such a close relationship with the unions. This, however, often shows that the links are good for the Labour Party, as in September 1993, when 48 per cent said that it was a good thing for the party that such a relationship existed. Again, we cannot say what exactly underlies this view but it presumably relates to financial help and support provided for the party by the unions.

The above suggests that this issue should be investigated in more depth in an attempt to tease out the underlying attitudes towards trade unions and the actual sources of those attitudes.

Throughout the 1980s, the issue of trade union reform had a high priority on the agenda of the Thatcher governments. The hostility towards the unions was widely noticed by the British public and this comes through clearly in responses to polling questions on this topic. For example, a regular Gallup question asks whether the Conservative Party is seen as being hostile to the trade unions. In the mid-1970s, this was seen as being marginally true but when the Conservative Party had been elected to power, the perception changed and the party was widely seen as being hostile, particularly in the early 1980s. This overall perception does not seem to have reduced the general value of unions as being good things, as mentioned earlier, but such appraisal is seen as being conditional on particular events and actions by the government of the day.

It is therefore not straightforward to draw the conclusion that unions are unpopular and that the Labour Party must loosen the link between themselves and the unions. The link is not *necessarily* unpopular but might well depend on perceptions of its exact nature rather than the overall relationship seen in broad and unspecific terms.

The evidence would suggest, however, that unions are regarded most positively when they engage in narrow functions clearly related to the interests of their members, such as working for better wages and conditions. Engaging in 'political' activities is not widely supported over time. Gallup asked a specific question on this throughout most of the 1970s and the percentage of respondents who believed that trade unions should not be concerned with political matters ranged between 54 per cent and 65 per cent in the years 1971–8.

It remains the case, however, that the significance of trade unions reached its peak in the 1980s, when they were thrust into the limelight by the actions of the Thatcher governments. One of the main claims of the government was that the union leaderships were not representative of the views of their members. The polling data collected by Gallup suggest that this view was widely shared by the general public. This question was initially asked in 1975 but it has been repeated on occasions ever since. For each of the samples, more respondents stated that they believed the union leaders to be unrepresentative of their members rather than representative. The difference between the two percentages has varied from a maximum of 58 per cent in January 1979 to a minimum of 18 per cent in both August 1976 and September 1993. The range of those who answered 'don't know' to this question was a maximum of 26 per cent in both 1991 and 1993 to a minimum of 15 per cent in two polls taken in 1985.

In the five years between 1988 and 1993, Gallup has asked a supplementary question to this, which attempts to add a dynamic element by asking whether the union leaders are becoming *more* representative of the views of their ordinary members. The results suggest that about one-quarter 'don't know', about a quarter think they are becoming more representative, about another quarter think they are becoming less representative and the rest (often the largest group) believe that the situation has not changed.

Whilst 'futurology' is clearly a dangerous activity to indulge in, perceptions of the future influence of trade unions have also been included in Gallup polls. Even though the answers to these questions are inevitably vague, they do nevertheless provide some idea of perceptions of recent change and beliefs as to whether this might continue in the future. The relevant question put since 1988 asks the respondents to speculate whether unions will be more powerful, less powerful or have much the same power as today in ten years time. The two main options chosen by the respondents are less powerful or much the same as today. The smallest category is 'more powerful', often vying with the 'don't know' category in terms of the number of respondents choosing it.

It seems reasonable to assume that the events of the 1980s must have had some impact on the perception of the respondents even if their basic attitudes towards trade unions have not changed much. We would need to dig rather deeper than the questions we have cited to get at the roots of these attitudes and why and under what circumstances they might change or display continuity. From the question we have considered above, we cannot draw any firm conclusions other than to point out that whilst the trade union link is often portrayed as being an 'albatross' for the Labour Party electorally, this might well depend on the specific context in which the issues are 'framed' rather than simply assuming that the link almost by definition will be a vote loser for the party.

On the basis of the evidence we have cited above, trade unions can be unpopular and they can appear to be perceived by the electorate as being too powerful in terms of their influence on the running of the Labour Party. The evidence is too mixed, however, and the question asked too broad and general to reach firmer and more definitive conclusions about whether the link is something which should be reformed or broken altogether for reasons of electoral popularity.

The evidence, again drawn from Gallup data, suggests that the issue of the links between the unions and the Labour Party is electorally largely a neutral one. When asked whether the connection between the two made the respondents more or less likely to vote Labour or whether it made no difference to their intentions, nearly 60 per cent between late summer 1991 and late summer 1993 said that it would make no difference. Obviously, this is a highly subjective response but it does suggest that attitudes to trade unions are but one factor amongst others in the general perceptions that voters possess of the parties.

On their own, these attitudes might be significant but as with most of these ideas, they are not set in concrete and the context of the questioning can be critical in guiding the responses in a particular direction. Certainly, unions, in terms of particular aspects of their activities, do appear to be consistently unpopular but whether that by itself would make much difference to the way that people actually voted is very much open to doubt.

We can conclude this section of the chapter by saying that there has been a good deal of stability in the attitudes of voters towards trade unions in general, a stability which survived the legislative changes affecting the roles and powers of the unions throughout the 1980s. Opinions on issues of unions and industrial relations can be intensely held and their salience will usually be strong for those most directly involved in union activity. For the voters, however, it would be necessary to explore their attitudes towards trade unions in rather more detail by means of more shaded and differentiated questions tapping the separate aspects of the topic before we could conclude anything about the issue's direct impact on voting behaviour. On the basis of the evidence cited above, it appears likely that the overall picture would be mixed and highly conditioned by the form and content of the questions put to the respondents.

We can now move on to look at our third issue, that of race relations and immigration.

6.4   Race relations and immigration

Formulating neutral questions on the topic of race and immigration is always difficult. This is because there has long been evidence that strong social norms are at work when this theme is examined, which means that the 'true' feelings of respondents are not properly revealed. There is often a strong sense of the 'right' answer which is then given rather than an accurate response in line with the actual attitude of the people questioned. This problem is not of course solely confined to the question of immigration and race but it does mean that we need to be cautious when interpreting answers to questions on this particular topic. Nevertheless, we can examine attitudes to race and immigration over time by once more considering the data which Gallup has collected. There are a number of discrete aspects of race relations and immigration which we can look at separately, some relating to specific events and actions, others to more general ideas about race and its consequences for society as a whole.

Gallup began asking about the topic of race in 1958 and the main focus of enquiry then was disturbances between whites and blacks. The questions also touched on how many coloured people the respondents knew, whether they would object to coloured children being in the same class as their own children and whether coloured people from the Commonwealth should be allowed to compete for jobs in Britain on equal terms with people born in the United Kingdom. This last theme is undoubtedly a key test of a respondent's 'liberalism' towards immigrants since it has a concrete aspect, along with housing, which puts glib answers to such questions under pressure. Unsurprisingly, there has always been a substantial minority who do not believe that immigrants should be allowed equal access to the labour market.

Other aspects of the topic of immigration relate to further immigration to the United Kingdom, with an overwhelming majority of the respondents approving tighter controls on immigration regardless of its exact restrictions, usually via the imposition of quota controls fixed by the British government.

The importance of immigration as a social problem has waxed and waned in importance over much of the post-war period. For example, in December 1968 it was named by 69 per cent of respondents as being a 'very serious' social problem. In June 1976, the corresponding figure was 71 per cent. By April 1982, the figure was 28 per cent. The prominence of the issue of race and immigration appears to depend on a number of related issues and its impact is equally likely to be inconsistent and erratic.

Two particular periods stand out in this regard, when issues of race appeared to be especially salient and of direct political importance. The first period was in 1968, after Enoch Powell's infamous 'rivers of blood' speech. According to Gallup, fully 96 per cent of one poll taken in April 1968 had heard or read about that speech. The vast majority agreed with the sentiments of the speech (74 per cent). At the same time, similar percentages of the sample agreed that restrictions had to be imposed on immigration and that current controls were not strict enough. At the same time, the Labour government was piloting a race relations Bill through Parliament which made it an offence to discriminate against people on grounds of race or colour. The respondents appeared to be very divided on the provisions, with 47 per cent saying that it should not be an offence to turn down a suitable applicant for a job on racial grounds.

The second main period of racial tension took place in the mid-1970s with the rise in support for the National Front in key British cities on the back of disturbances in Notting Hill and the arrival of Asians from Uganda. In 1977 Gallup tested people's attitudes towards the future shape of the United Kingdom. Most of the sample (38 per cent) saw Britain in the future as being a multiracial society with tensions, followed by 22 per cent who saw Britain as a society where different groups live separately but with tension.

The actual importance of immigration as an election issue was also erratic in its appearance between January 1978 and March

1979. Its importance as an issue which the politicians ought to concentrate upon peaked at 48 per cent in early 1978 before reaching a low of 24 per cent just before the 1979 general election got under way. Moïe important issues were unemployment, the cost of living and prices and, on occasions, law and order.

The image of being tough on immigration has often been widely associated with the Conservative Party, particularly when questions have focused upon immigration controls. Thus when Edward Heath sacked Powell from his Shadow Cabinet after the 'rivers of blood' speech, most of the respondents disapproved (69 per cent). It appeared that most people agreed with Powell's ideas, although this percentage did appear to be changeable, from a peak of 64 per cent in June 1969 to 48 per cent only six months later in January 1970.

The issue of immigration does appear to come and go without any regular pattern to its appearance or disappearance. The main problem for the political parties is to 'control' the issue and not to allow fringe or extremist parties to wrest control from them by setting the agenda on the issue. Appearing to be tough on immigrants may be one way of achieving this but the issue retains an unpredictable nature sufficient to make both government and shadow spokespersons nervous.

One useful way of getting more detail on racial attitudes is to sub-divide any sample into a variety of social characteristics, such as gender, age, social class and region. In a poll conducted in October and November 1993, Gallup asked a series of questions on the topic of race and then broke the results down into the constituent categories of the above variables. The results are instructive. For example, when asked whether controls on the number of immigrants are too strict, not strict enough or about right, nearly two-thirds (63 per cent) of the total sample said that they were not strict enough. However, if we compare the different groups that comprise the sample, a number of differences do emerge. There is little difference on gender grounds but there is, in contrast, a difference on grounds of age, with the oldest group (those more than 65 years old) clearly more in favour of stricter restrictions, particularly in comparison with those of the youngest age group (those aged between 16 and 24). There is also a class difference, with skilled and unskilled workers being more in favour of stricter controls on immigration than the AB group of professionals and managers. There were only minor differences on this question in terms of region of residence within Britain.

These differences on age and social class grounds are also clear when another question was put to the respondents, namely, whether immigrants should be admitted to council house lists on the same conditions as people born in Britain. Once more, fewer younger people recognise this as a problem compared to the oldest group within the sample and there is greater agreement within the social classes C2 and DE (skilled and unskilled workers) that this should *not* happen.

On a more general question, such as whether the respondent would object if there were coloured children in the same class as their own children at school, the sample shows greater overall agreement, with the overwhelming majority stating that they would *not* object to this. Once again, it is the elderly who are not so keen as the other age groups to go along with such a proposal.

There were similar responses across all the social groups when the question of whether feelings between white and coloured people were getting better, getting worse or remaining the same. There was evidence of a consistent pessimism, with all social groups believing that things were getting worse. Even the youngest group was not markedly out of line in the answers to this particular question.

What does this tell us about the importance of race as an issue in British politics? It suggests that this is a very sensitive and emotive issue that needs to be handled with care. Its impact is erratic and inconsistent but it can be potentially explosive in particular contexts and circumstances.

One reason for the dislike of immigrants could be a lack of acquaintance with them. This was especially the case in the early Gallup polls but is seen as less of a problem now that there are more immigrants settled in this country and they have become part of everyday life for more people. One indicator of this would be the change in perception regarding mixed marriages. In 1968, the majority polled believed that marriages between whites and non-whites were wrong. By 1993, this figure had dropped to only 15 per cent, with 77 per cent agreeing that it was acceptable. This question was initially asked in the context of mixed marriages also between Catholics and Protestants and between Jews and non-Jews. There appears to have been a general growth in more liberal attitudes regarding all these three types of relationship.

What, then, of the future? The 1993 poll also asked whether the respondents' own feelings towards coloured people had become more favourable, less favourable or had remained the same. For about two-thirds of each of the social groups mentioned above, they claimed that their feelings towards coloured people had remained the same, and there were only minor differences when the separate categories were examined on the basis of gender, age, class and region. The group with the most favourable feelings were the youngest group, aged 16–24. Very few people claimed that they did not know on this question: 4 per cent overall for the whole sample and only 2 per cent each for the groups comprising those aged 25–34 and 35–44, respectively.

Attitudes to immigrants and race relations can certainly be intensely held and they can often also be highly salient and stable for individuals. The main difficulty for pollsters is to persuade respondents to admit their 'true' feelings on the issue given the strong social norm of denying 'racist' views. The central problem for the political parties is to retain control of immigration as an issue and not to allow fringe groups or parties to fan the flames of racial prejudice and fear.

We can now move on to consider the fourth issue in this chapter, that of the environment.

6.5   The environment

The issue of the environment and its protection is a very new one in terms of overt public concern. Worries about the state of the environment first came to prominence on the public agenda from the late 1970s onwards. The end of the 1980s saw the Green Party win 15 per cent of the votes at the 1989 election to the European Parliament, although they won no seats. Since then, the party has imploded over the direction of policy and the party's tactics. Nevertheless, the importance of environmental protection can still be measured by the issue being forced on to the political agenda without having a party championing its interests in Parliament.

The main problem in examining environmental concerns as political issues is the difficulty in designing questions which will provide differentiated responses. If the aim is to give some indication of how some people will respond or behave, the design of the question must make the respondents in any poll choose in a concrete way. In other words, it is very easy for respondents to simply agree that the environment is of major importance to them and their family, that it has been getting worse recently and that the government should do more to deal with environmental problems. Answers to such questions are of course useful for tracking changes in the priorities which people give to different issues. There is, however, a huge gap between giving environmental issues a high priority and doing something effective about them, particularly if that involves more spending via raising taxes, which would almost certainly be the case for most proposals.

The best way to test for the 'true' concern over the question of environmental protection is to force a choice on the respondents. Even this might not 'work' in delineating those who are genuinely in favour of putting the environment first since the reality of paying more tax or more for fuel, for example, is still not 'real' in terms of less money for the respondent at the end of the month. So even if a choice is explicitly needed to answer a question between the environment and spending, the choice is still theoretical and is likely to produce answers in line with the perception of social norms on the topic. For example, in September 1993, when asked if the government should do more to tackle environmental concerns even if it costs the respondents and everyone else more money 80 per cent of the sample agreed that this should be done. It would indeed be interesting to compare the relevant percentage if that was actually seen to take place.

The polling data on environmental issues are therefore interesting for what it does *not* tell us as much for what it does. This relates clearly to our previous discussion about 'trade-off' questions and the need to force a choice on the respondents in as concrete a way as possible, whilst being aware that the choice is purely a question and does not require any action or reaction in reality.

There is also some evidence that the stability of responses to questions on the environment is low compared to other issues of importance. This can be tested by looking at the ranking given to the question of the environment when the respondents are asked about what they believe to be the most important problem facing Britain today. We would need to cover a longer period here to give the full picture in terms of the other issues involved but much of the evidence suggests that the question of the environment has the potential to be rated very highly but that its ranking is not consistent and it can rise and fall very quickly in terms of its importance on the political agenda. For example, in a Gallup poll of June 1992, the environment was ranked eighth out of a list of ten issues, a list topped by a wide margin by concern over unemployment and economic conditions in general. Only 2 per cent of the sample thought the environment was the most important problem at that time. This can change, however, when the issue of the environment receives more publicity and is debated more vigorously, as in 1989, when the Green Party made the issue a 'live' one for all the parties to confront.

The main parties, however, have the problem of not alienating key sections of their electorates by talking about the environment and, by doing so, neglecting other issues which their supporters believe to be more important for them personally, often the state of the economy. This situation is not helped by the degree of uncertainty about what exactly the policies of the various parties are on the question of the environment. In late 1988, Gallup asked which party's view on the environment came closest to the views of the respondent. The largest category of responses was 'don't know or none' at 36 per cent. This can breed a cynicism about the reasons why the major parties in particular talk about the environment: it is less to do with a genuine concern about the future of the planet and much more to do with a desire to win or retain votes by appearing concerned.

In addition to a lack of clarity in the policies of the parties to deal with environmental questions, there is little evidence that votes can be won pursuing a particular policy on the question of environmental protection. In a poll conducted in October 1989, the sample was split 50:50 between those who were and those who were not concerned enough about the environment to consider voting for another party at a general election.

Gallup has asked a number of detailed questions on the environment which have painted a picture of growing concern about the state of the environment. These questions have dealt with many different aspects of the environment such as the purity of drinking water, noise, air pollution, the disposal of industrial and chemical waste, nuclear waste and the extinction of some plants and animal species. Most of the responses have shown over time a growing concern with these questions but the central problem identified earlier remains: how do we get the respondents to give an answer that truly reflects their concern with the question of the environment in such a way that their behaviour and actions might subsequently be predictable from their responses? This is of course a central dilemma of all opinion polling: the questions are questions with no inevitable link to decisions and actions in the future.

We can establish easily from polling data that many people are concerned about the environment but how far they would go to put things right cannot be inferred from such data since the concrete responses to give us firmer evidence are often missing. This means that politicians only tend to address this particular issue when it hits the headlines with the latest oil tanker spillage or natural disaster affecting wildlife, for example. At other times, there are many platitudes but not much real action, particularly action that forces real choice in all seriousness on real voters.

The breadth of concern relating to environmental issues has certainly grown in recent years but its depth remains unclear and uncertain, particularly when the logic of action demands sacrifices in terms of changing consumer patterns, such as restricting the use of cars. Where the problem is most visible, for example in terms of industrial pollution, the concern is the greatest but understanding and support for action lag some way behind.

The problem is often not one of a lack of public awareness, which has certainly increased in recent years. It is much more one of a lack of emphasis by the political parties, a classic case of 'short-termism' on an issue whose very long-term nature lies at its very core.

Environmental issues were hardly mentioned during the 1992 election campaign. Cynics might conclude this was because it was in the parties' own interests not to talk about the issue since a more interested and informed public would possibly demand more action. This would inevitably cost money and would split the parties on the precise action to be taken as a result. There is little doubt that the cost of paying for a more environmentally active Britain would be a central and unavoidable concern. In a political arena dominated by the desirability of tax cuts rather than tax rises, the meaning of being 'green' would indeed be exposed by a ruthless appraisal of the real choices being offered to the voters.

'Green issues' can sometimes appear to be of major importance on the political agenda. The problem is that they lack direct salience and stability for enough people although it is undeniable that views on the environment can be intensely held, stable and highly salient for those directly involved in debating and promoting them to a wider audience. This is not, however, the case for the wider electorate, whose interest in the topic of the environment rises and falls according to the prominence of green issues in the glare of media publicity.

The government and parties react to this latency of opinion on the environment to declare the issue an important one on occasion but they then let it slip from view when the hard choices for serious action are put forward. The long-term nature of environmental questions means that they are not well suited to the cycle of electoral politics whose time horizons rarely extend beyond the next election in four years time. Certainly, knowledge about the environment and threats to the future of the planet are much better and more widely known than twenty years ago, but the link to the change in behaviour that is needed to tackle the identified problems in a serious and effective manner has not yet been sufficiently nor effectively enough established.

We now want to complete this chapter with a consideration of another issue which illustrates well some of the questions relating to issues and their role in structuring political choice in Britain, the issue of electoral reform.

6.6   Electoral reform

A variety of questions on the different aspects of electoral reform have been put to ordinary voters since the 1950s but the first real bout of sustained interest occurred in the mid-1970s amidst wider worries about 'governability', the breakdown of the post-war consensus and the actions of an 'overloaded state' in Britain. Interest in the issue of electoral reform has also tended to wax and wane according to changes and political developments in other areas, such as whether Britain needs constitutional change or whether voters would change their minds and vote for another party if party policies on the issue of electoral reform were altered.

The latter focus of interest rose to prominence most recently in 1991 in terms of whether Liberal Democrat voters would switch to backing the Labour Party if the latter changed its view and backed some form of proportional representation (PR), which they would then implement after coming to office. The Electoral Reform Society was also prominent in lobbying for its favoured change to the single transferable vote system of election and the whole issue became enmeshed in wider concerns about whether the Labour Party could win the next election if it did not do a deal with the Liberal Democrats, the central plank of which would involve a change in the method of electing representatives to Parliament.

A majority of Labour voters, according to a question contained in the Harris/ITN exit poll of 1992, appeared to be willing to support a change to PR if that was the price to be paid in a hung Parliament. In 1992, 58 per cent of Labour voters agreed that their party should introduce PR under the circumstances of a hung Parliament, whilst 36 per cent disagreed. For Conservative voters, the corresponding figures were 33 per cent agreeing and 63 per cent disagreeing; of Liberal Democrat voters, 79 per cent agreed and 12 per cent disagreed. The figures for the whole sample were 52 per cent agreeing and 42 per cent disagreeing (ITN 1992: 27–8).

There has been much discussion and debate in the last few years about the role that electoral reform could play in producing a non-Conservative government at the next general election. This debate has been supported by various simulations and predictions of how the seats of the current Parliament would have been distributed if a different system had been in operation in 1992 (Dunleavy *et al.*, 1992, 1993). Neither side of the debate has yet managed to land a knock-out blow and, doubtless, as a result the debate will continue to flare up and then die down again as in the past.

In this section, however, we are mainly going to consider mass attitudes towards the issue of electoral reform rather than the often breathless debates going on at elite level. The evidence regarding mass attitudes on the subject of electoral reform is very mixed. The central argument underpinning analyses of mass beliefs on this issue turns on the wording of the questions used and the stability of the responses given over time.

It might appear that there is a majority for change if we consider one question or poll only but this conclusion might be based on a 'cost-free' question in which the respondents give hypothetical answers to what they perceive as hypothetical questions. If the electorate are offered a change to 'fair votes', they will tend to support that change. If they are informed that this will lead to coalition government, more uncertainty will emerge in the responses. If the question or questions imply that there are no disadvantages to any change to 'fair votes', then most people will back such a change. If the question is more balanced and suggests that one result of such a change might be several different parties forming a coalition government together, the outcome is likely to be less in favour of any change. This is unsurprising in a wider context of respondents wanting contradictory things. If a particular idea is not especially unattractive, there will be a good chance that it will receive support on the basis that most respondents want to be positive rather than negative, and to be able to say yes rather than no to questions.

The precise wording of the question on electoral reform is therefore crucial and the resonance of the question in the context of the interview as a whole will be vital in steering responses in a particular direction.

One alternative to change is of course to retain the present system. The main and often cited justification of the present electoral system in Britain is that it is likely to produce one-party and, therefore, strong and effective government. If these words are included in the question, the percentage wanting or backing change to a form of proportional representation usually declines considerably.

General questions which ask about satisfaction with the prevailing system are useful for setting out the main divisions within the electorate but more detailed questions are always needed to delve deeper into the topic. Asking such an initial question on satisfaction may also reduce the numbers of those expressing a desire for change, which follows later in the questionnaire, since general satisfaction with the system in general is likely to be high. To then appear to want to change the electoral process of a political system with which the respondent has just expressed satisfaction would appear contradictory to many respondents.

This is where the debate starts about the meaning of key words included in the questions and whether the alternatives offered to the respondents do in fact produce a balanced question or whether the alternatives on offer are in reality biased, by either omission or commission. This is particularly difficult to trace over time since different questions have been used by different polling firms and there appears to be little agreement about which one works best on general samples of the electorate.

Gallup has asked the same question on electoral reform between 1985 and 1988: 'Some people say we should change the voting system to allow smaller parties to get a fairer share of MPs. Others say that we should keep the voting system as it is to produce effective government. Which view is closest to your own?' The option of change in 1988 received the backing of 38 per cent (45 per cent in 1985), to keep it as it is won 51 per cent support (47 per cent in 1985) and 'don't know' 11 per cent (8 per cent in 1985). In contrast, the Harris/ITN polls carried out at the last two general elections, held in 1987 and 1992, contain a simpler formulation: 'Should the system of electing MPs be changed from the present "first past the post" method to a form of proportional representation?' The results showed support for the present system at 52 per cent in 1992 (49 per cent in 1987); a form of PR won 47 per cent backing in 1992 (46 per cent in 1987).

There was a drift away from supporting PR between the two elections overall, with Conservative voters hardening their attitude against it (22 per cent in favour compared to 28 per cent in favour in 1987), whilst Labour voters slightly increased their support for PR (50 per cent in favour in 1992 and 46 per cent in 1987). There was no shift in the view of Liberal Democrat voters, who were very strongly in favour at both elections (76 per cent in favour in 1992 and 75 per cent in favour in 1987).

The most common conclusion on the topic of electoral reform is that there is little stability over time in mass attitudes and that there may well be some inherent contradictions in the answers which people give to such questions. In other words, the voters want the best of both worlds and they give answers to match.

Another problem is that the results of polls on electoral reform are eagerly and quickly converted by active pressure groups into material for propaganda, so much so that it is difficult to tell which interpretation of the results of any poll is likely to be most reasonable. The use of different questions to tap public attitudes on electoral reform reflects this 'competitive' attitude amongst pressure groups, some advocating change and others opposing it. This means that it is inevitable that conclusions about the public mood on this question will be both blurred and tentative.

One main difficulty in designing questions concerning electoral reform is the inclusion of 'knowledge' elements in the question to try and overcome the likelihood of widespread ignorance surrounding the topic. MORI, in its polls, has found that between 40 and 55 per cent of respondents have either never heard of proportional representation or they do not know what it is. Only about one-quarter of most samples normally claim to know either 'a great deal' or 'a fair amount' about PR.

Whilst explanations of what the terms mean might be useful and neutral for some respondents, the danger is that key words might bias the question to less knowledgeable and interested respondents and consequently steer their answers in a particular direction. For example, the word 'effective' is often used in questions about electoral reform. This word has positive connotations and if it is attached to a particular electoral system, the risk is that a particular option will be chosen because of the positive link that is embedded in the question. In addition, there would certainly be disputes amongst analysts about whether the claim to be effective was a balanced and reasonable conclusion to draw from *any* specific system of voting procedures without including the 'cost' of such effectiveness, in other words, the particular disadvantages which all voting systems inevitably produce.

The argument against including such material in the question is the sheer length of the question which would be needed and the problems involved in retaining clarity for the respondents, particularly their ability to produce even a reasonably considered response and not utter confusion instead. The possibility of confusion being produced as a result of a complex and conditional question is very real. There is evidence from polling data on electoral reform that there is a lack of familiarity with the terms of the subject. As a result, there will always be a substantial number of 'don't know' responses to any question on the topic, as noted with the MORI data earlier. Efforts can be made to reduce this number but there is then the risk of forcing respondents to choose options which they do not understand and which they have not considered to any degree before the question was actually put to them.

In addition, there is a strong argument that attitudes on electoral reform are 'soft' and changeable depending on the options that are offered to the respondents. This is based on evidence that when respondents are unprompted as to the most important issues of the day, the question of electoral reform usually barely registers, suggesting that the significance of this issue depends heavily on its being debated and publicised in the media at the time the poll is being conducted.

The prominence of the topic of electoral reform is rarely high even in the context of related questions. For example, in the 1991 *State of the Nation* poll conducted by MORI for the Joseph Rowntree Trust, they asked how the system of government in Britain could be improved, a question which emphasised constitutional reform. Proportional representation was only specifically mentioned by 11 per cent, whilst 28 per cent responded by nominating the abolition of the 'poll tax' and 14 per cent by improving the National Health Service (Smyth 1992: 63).

The problem of a lack of salience of electoral reform for most people most of the time is therefore substantial. This applies particularly to the place of electoral reform in wider analyses of problems with the operation of the overall political system, as the MORI poll quoted above suggested. In other words, the question of electoral reform is often seen by parts of the political elite as being part of an overall critique of the way Britain is run. This does not appear to have seeped through to mass attitudes, where the question is still largely seen as a discrete and isolated aspect of various possibilities for reform.

For those in favour of electoral reform, there remains the problem that it is rarely seen by voters as being part of a wider malaise, leading to an unrepresentative Parliament, leading to bad and incompetent government which makes all problems of governance worse for ordinary people. Those who advocate electoral reform argue that if only these connections could be explained to more people, the salience question and the immediate and direct relevance of electoral reform would become much more apparent to more people. As a result, the issue would be put more firmly and consistently on the political agenda of the day.

It remains the case that no issue exists in a vacuum, and the same applies to the question of electoral reform. The difficulty in establishing its importance as an issue is the same as with the other issues we have considered in this chapter. The danger is that those without any great knowledge or interest would simply respond with an attitude which reflected their current perceptions of the overall performance of the government of the day or some more general attitude unrelated to the specific topic being examined. This holds particular dangers for one option to test opinions on

electoral reform: the national referendum, which has been suggested as an option at various times, most recently by the late
leader of the Labour Party, John Smith, who promised a referendum on the topic in 1993.

The use of a referendum looks straightforward but in fact involves many problems. Firstly, what would the actual question be?
We have already noted in chapter 3 the difficulties of designing a
question which is not biased or leading but which also does not
include steering knowledge which would probably have the same
effect. Secondly, would the referendum produce a result which
would bind the government or would that be dependent on the
percentage actually supporting the proposition? Given the sea
change which any alteration in the prevailing electoral system
would entail, this would be a crucial decision. Thirdly, who would
draw up the question and to what extent would the major parties
allow their members to campaign against one another during the
campaign preceding the referendum?

Whilst most of the Conservative Party would back no change
and the Liberal Democrats would support change to some method
of PR, the Labour Party would probably be split between a
number of different alternatives for change and those who continue to think that no change at all is necessary. This latter group
base their view on the belief that any change would effectively end
the chances of there ever being a majority Labour government in
the future.

The pressure within the Labour Party to take a position on the
topic of electoral reform began after the party's third election
defeat in a row in 1987 and ended messily with the final version of
the Plant Report, which recommended the supplementary vote in
an attempt to bind the various sections of the party together. The
decision of the late John Smith to permit a referendum on the issue
is explicable in this context of internal party division but the problems of arranging and conducting such an exercise nevertheless
remain formidable.

It seems unlikely that the issue of electoral reform will die away
completely whilst it remains of central importance for plans for
reform of the British state. Much will depend on the result of the
next general election for the context in which the debate continues
but the fundamental features of the debate do illustrate neatly the
differences between the concerns of the political elite and the

mass, between the actors and the spectators, as described in chapter 2.

The interests and knowledge of the latter diverge to a large degree from those of the former, whose views nevertheless are most frequently propagated through the media to which the mass allegedly pay attention. The agendas of the elite and the mass nevertheless appear to be different in both priorities and content in terms of electoral reform, with a lack of knowledge on the part of the ordinary voters leading to a lack of salience and stability in terms of their opinions on the issue.

6.7 Conclusion

We can now bring together the main points regarding the polls and political issues which we have illustrated in this chapter via our consideration of five different issues. The key point to be remembered is the extent to which issues have an existence independent of other attitudes, such as partisan predisposition towards a particular party or a general attitude towards the government of the day. The overall evidence would suggest that the 'issue model' of voting receives little consistent support. It appears likely that the issues of the day are closely related to other attitudes and mediated through a partisan filter comprising overall attitudes to the parties and their leaders, so much so that the idea of issue independence, while theoretically elegant, remains empirically weak. In many cases, it seems clear that attitudes on a variety of issues are consequences rather than causes of voting intentions.

The basis of the idea of issue independence founders on the twin rocks of lack of knowledge and lack of interest from ordinary voters. This applies particularly to issues which exercise the minds of the political elite but which leave the mass of ordinary voters uninterested and unmoved. This effectively reduces the issue agenda for most people to a few major economic concerns which do have a day-to-day impact on the everyday lives of the respondents in mass samples.

The dimensions of public opinion which we set out in chapter 2 – intensity, stability, salience and latency – clearly apply more to some issues than to others. They apply mostly to the concrete, tangible and direct issues that affect the perceptions of ordinary people often on the basis of personal attitudes and group identities. Given this situation, it is not surprising that more esoteric issues, such as the European Community, the environment or electoral reform, wax and wane in importance at mass level as interest in them is increased or decreased via media exposure.

It is important never to underestimate the importance of parties in setting and shaping the issue agenda of politics. Of course, this will be highly partisan as the struggle between the parties to win support for 'their' issues gathers speed, but whether this is noticed or taken on board by the ordinary voter beyond an overall and general perception of the parties and their leaders must be open to wide and sustained questioning. This seems to apply to most issues, with parties acting as frames of reference for the complexity of the real political world, a world in which small minorities sustain their own interests and in which the vast majority of voters have only a very fitful interest.

Whilst polling data on issues remain useful for producing a broad delineation of mass attitudes, the probing and testing of knowledge and the evident changeability regarding these issues tend to reveal a rather repetitive story. When it comes to political issues, we can expect changeability and inconsistency from the voters. What excites the elite in the fields of politics and the media reaches only a very limited and circumscribed mass audience and then often only in a fragmented and incomplete form. In this sense, politics in Britain is often largely a matter of control by a narrow and self-sustaining elite group whose definition of the political agenda holds sway over ordinary people. The latter's direct involvement in decision making can only be regarded as fitful, erratic and uncertain within these prevailing parameters of the British political system of the 1990s.

References

Denver, D. (1994) *Elections and Voting Behaviour in Britain*, 2nd edn, Hemel Hempstead: Harvester Wheatsheaf.

Dunleavy, P., H. Margetts and S. Weir (1992) 'How Britain would have voted under alternative electoral systems in 1992', *Parliamentary Affairs* 45: 640–55.

Dunleavy, P., H. Margetts and S. Weir (1993) 'The 1992 election and the legitimacy of British democracy', in D. Denver, P. Norris,

D. Broughton and C. Rallings (eds) *British Elections and Parties Year-book 1993*, Hemel Hempstead: Harvester Wheatsheaf, pp. 177–92.

ITN (1992) *British Voting Trends 1979–1992*, London: Independent Television News.

Sanders, D. (1993) 'Why the Conservative Party won – again', in A. King, I. Crewe, D. Denver, K. Newton, P. Norton, D. Sanders and P. Seyd, *Britain at the Polls 1992*, Chatham, NJ: Chatham House, pp. 171–222.

Smyth, G. (ed.) (1992) *Refreshing the Parts: Electoral reform and British politics*, London: Lawrence and Wishart.

Teer, F. and J. D. Spence (1973) *Political Opinion Polls*, London: Hutchinson.

Webb, N. and R. Wybrow (1982) *The Gallup Report: Your opinions in 1981*, London: Sphere.

Suggested further reading

The European Community

Butler, D. and U. Kitzinger (1976) *The 1975 Referendum*, London: Macmillan.

Eurobarometer reports of the EU Commission (reporting polls conducted twice yearly in all EU states; in Britain since 1973).

Flickinger, R. (1994) 'British political parties and public attitudes towards the European Community: Leading, following or getting out of the way?', in D. Broughton, D. M. Farrell, D. Denver and C. Rallings (eds) *British Elections and Parties Yearbook 1994*, London: Frank Cass, pp. 198–215.

George, S. (1990) *An Awkward Partner: Britain in the European Community*, Oxford: Clarendon Press.

Jowell, R. and G. Hoinville (1976) *Britain into Europe: Public opinion and the EEC, 1961–1975*, London: Croom Helm.

Trade unions

Millward, N. (1990) 'The state of the unions', in R. Jowell, S. Witherspoon, L. Brook with B. Taylor (eds) *British Social Attitudes Survey 7th Report*, Aldershot: Gower, pp. 27–50.

Taylor, R. (1993) *The Trade Union Question in British Politics: Government and unions since 1945*, Oxford: Blackwell.

Immigration and race relations

Fitzgerald, M. (1989) 'Black sheep? Race in the 1987 election campaign', in I. Crewe and M. Harrop (eds) *Political Communications: The general election campaign of 1987*, Cambridge: Cambridge University Press, pp. 275–88.

Messina, A. (1989) *Race and Party Competition in Britain*, Oxford: Clarendon Press.

Saggar, S. (1992) *Race and Politics in Britain*, Hemel Hempstead: Harvester Wheatsheaf.

Studlar, D. (1986) 'Non-white policy preferences, political participation and the political agenda in Britain', in Z. Layton-Henry and P. Rich (eds) *Race, Government and Politics in Britain*, London: Macmillan, pp. 159–86.

The environment

Environmental Politics, quarterly journal published by Frank Cass from 1992.

Witherspoon, S. (1994) 'The greening of Britain: Romance and rationality', in R. Jowell, J. Curtice, L. Brook and D. Ahrendt (eds) *British Social Attitudes 11th Report*, Aldershot: Dartmouth, pp. 107–39.

Witherspoon, S. and J. Martin (1992) 'What do we mean by green?', in R. Jowell, L. Brook, G. Prior and B. Taylor (eds) *British Social Attitudes Survey 9th Report*, Aldershot: Dartmouth, pp. 1–26.

Young, K. (1991) 'Shades of green', in R. Jowell, L. Brook, B. Taylor with G. Prior (eds) *British Social Attitudes Survey 8th Report*, Aldershot: Dartmouth, pp. 107–30.

Electoral reform

Norris, P. (1995) 'The politics of electoral reform in Britain', *International Political Science Review* 16: 65–78. Part of a special issue entitled *The Politics of Electoral Reform*, with articles on electoral reform in Israel, Italy, Japan and New Zealand as well as Britain.

Weir, S. (1992) 'Waiting for change: Public opinion and electoral reform', *Political Quarterly* 63: 197–221.

7

Conclusion

Three years on from the 1992 general election, the role and impact of polls in British politics remain matters of contention and debate. The severe and widespread criticism of polls was important at the last election as one means of putting both the achievements and the limitations of polls into perspective; however, that criticism and perspective are unlikely to provide conclusive evidence that the fundamental methods of polling practice must be changed to take account of the problems which were identified in the various post-election analyses.

Some observers claim that the polling firms should have incorporated a number of substantive changes into their methods by now. They believe that the flaws exposed at the 1992 election clearly demonstrated the need for an urgent re-appraisal of polling methods as well as the need for more experimentation with the attitudes and behaviour of a changing British electorate. Others give greater weight to the dangers of implementing changes without strong evidence of the need to do so over a longer period than three years, given the degree of overlap and interdependence between the different stages of the polling process. A seemingly small change made at one point might prove to be a major change in a subsequent step. Certainly, the options available would be altered as a result.

The problem with this latter approach for the pollsters is that the next election will be a crucial test of their overall credibility rather than just another opportunity to get things right. To adapt Oscar Wilde: to get one election wrong would be unfortunate; to get two successive elections wrong would certainly be carelessness.

There are a number of different ideas that have been put forward since the 1992 general election to improve the performance of the polls at the next election. Among these is the use of a ballot box in an interview to simulate a real election (developed by ICM) in order to overcome the tendency of some respondents to refuse to state their vote intention. Other ideas include a greater use of random sampling (ICM used a random sample for their poll on the monarchy published in *The Guardian* in January 1995) and more research on the group of 'refusers', which can reach a high proportion of those initially approached for interview in a quota sample (some estimates suggest a refusal rate of at least 35 per cent in quota polls; other estimates are even higher). These ideas have all been tested in experiments by the polling firms and the general conclusion is that they are proving helpful in reducing the pro-Labour bias apparent in the 1992 election polls.

Investigating these ideas before the next general election makes good sense for the polling firms since the reputation of the polls clearly took a battering in 1992. Gallup examined the image of the polls via a number of questions put to respondents in April and August 1992. There was a greater scepticism on the part of the British people about believing what the polls were saying than in 1988, when the question had previously been asked. There was also less belief that a sample of 1,000 people could provide a reliable picture of the current state of public opinion, less belief that the polls truly reflected public opinion and a greater feeling that respondents actually lie to interviewers. When some of these questions were repeated in August 1992, the picture had changed, though, with more people believing that the polls did reflect British public opinion (34 per cent as opposed to 26 per cent in April). The latest data, from interviews conducted in May 1994, show that this figure has increased to 53 per cent.

The main reason for thinking that the polls did not truly reflect public opinion was that 'It is impossible to measure the views of the British' followed by 'The people interviewed do not tell the truth' and then 'Public opinion poll techniques are not good enough.' These three responses were the most often cited, and in the same order, in May 1994.

There was also a change in the number of people who believed that politicians take too much notice of polls. Those who felt that politicians take too much notice dropped to 30 per cent in August 1992 from 42 per cent in April (21 per cent in 1994). There is thus some instability in these responses to the role, usage and impact of polls, which suggests that the glare of bad publicity of April 1992 has not engendered necessarily negative views to polls as a whole or at least not for very long. This can be supported by answers to another question, in which the respondents were asked what they did when they came across a poll in a newspaper or magazine. More than half (53 per cent) said that they cast an eye over it (51 per cent in 1994), whilst 27 per cent claimed to read the poll story with interest (26 per cent in 1994).

The case for banning polls during an election campaign was also tested by Gallup in a separate survey. In spite of easy assumptions that there would be strong feelings in favour of such a ban, the respondents did not come out in favour of such action. Admittedly, the number in favour of introducing such a ban was the highest for a decade in April 1992, at 41 per cent, but there was still 48 per cent against any ban and 11 per cent who did not know. This indicates that the case for imposing any ban has still to be made and thus the chances of it happening are very small.

One reason why a near majority are not in favour of banning polls could be related to the perception that they do not actually influence people at general elections. The majority of respondents felt that polls had little or no influence on voters (52 per cent) in April 1992, whilst 17 per cent thought that they have a lot of influence and 28 per cent a fair amount of influence. In contrast, the influence of the polls at by elections is even more strongly rejected, with 72 per cent believing that polls have little or no influence, as opposed to 6 per cent feeling they have a lot of influence and 16 per cent feeling they have a fair amount. Arguably, this is the wrong way around, with polls being particularly able to influence outcomes at by-elections because of the possibility of the occurrence of tactical voting.

As a whole, the respondents appear to regard the results of polls as being one piece of information amongst many others, although the perception that the poll results can influence elections and can therefore 'falsify' the election results was also widely supported in a question about the role that public opinion surveys should play.

On a mass level, therefore, the widespread and bad publicity of the 1992 general election poll results seems to have induced an immediate decline in the belief that the polls were reliable. This proved, however, to be temporary, and six months after the election, there was less scepticism compared to the immediate aftermath of the election. This suggests that public attitudes to polls are unstable and changeable, largely reacting to what has been read and seen about polls most recently in the media.

This does not, however, help the polling firms to know what to do in the future. They are all wary of criticism from those clients who felt that the polls in 1992 did not represent value for money; but this is not to dismiss *all* poll results as being worthless, a trap which some media representatives fell into very easily after the election of 1992.

Some of the polling firms have tried to investigate what went wrong in 1992, and we have dealt with many of the points earlier that have arisen from these investigations. These are all set out clearly and with detailed analyses in the Market Research Society report of July 1994. Whether these ideas will lead to changes in the specific approach to the next election is still an open question on the grounds that there might not actually be a problem, since the 1992 election could have been a unique election with a unique context. As such, a wholesale rethink of methods and approaches which worked very well in previous general elections would not be justified.

Will it be enough, though, for the polling firms to be seen to analyse and investigate at length in a non-election period and then to do nothing when the next general election approaches? In this context, we have to remember that 'politicals' form only a small part of the business of polling firms and their non-political clients were not put off by the outcome of the 1992 election polls. Business from the non-political clients remained stable for all the polling firms even after the bad publicity of March/April 1992. This had also been the case in 1970 after the previous problems experienced in the general election polls.

Political polls are of course different from other polls and surveys used in market research, most notably in the possibility of 'checking' them by comparing the poll results to the actual election result. This is not a test that other types of market research have to pass. This means that political polls hold the possibility of achieving both credit and credibility whilst simultaneously holding the danger of being seen to be 'wrong' in the light of the actual results of the election. In this way, the polling firms have to tread carefully in terms of the impression they give about their work by not providing ammunition for their critics.

We have tried to emphasise throughout this book the importance of considering polling in Britain as a complex process, one which comprises a series of inter-related stages when decisions and choices are made which affect all the subsequent decisions and choices. As such, the option of no change at all regarding polling methods is not possible to sustain if only because of the developing technology of polling and the continuing doubts over the reliability of the statistics used by the pollsters, such as those taken from the 1991 Census. Press reports at the end of 1994 suggested that the 1991 Census had failed to track down about 2 million people. The census validation survey used to follow up on those people who did not return the official census form traced about 900,000, leaving about 1 million still missing. The main group 'missing' from the census were young, male adults aged between 20 and 34.

In the wake of the 1992 general election, the idea of 'deliberative polling' has received considerable publicity. The main idea is to take a random sample of people and transport them to a single site for several days where they can deliberate on a single issue, discuss its various dimensions with one another and be briefed on it by a mixture of experts and politicians. Poll questions on the subject of the deliberations would be asked when the sample is first selected and then again after the discussions have taken place. The answers would then be compared to produce 'deliberative' opinion poll results.

The idea was first proposed in *The Independent* in September 1993 as a result of the work of James Fishkin (1991). The first test on the issue of crime was carried out in May 1994, with part of the debate being broadcast on television. The central aim of such a poll is to overcome the 'rational ignorance' problem, which suggests that the vote of an individual does not count for much in an electorate of millions and, as a result, few people will bother to invest the time or effort into finding out about the issues or personalities of an election campaign. This situation produces an ignorant electorate but a rational one.

A deliberative poll has a prescriptive function in that it can recommend with some force what the people *would* think if they were given more time and opportunity to consider the issues more thoughtfully and at greater length. The unsurprising result of the first deliberative poll in Britain was that ordinary people changed their minds as they were exposed to more information on the topic. This is all very well outside an election campaign and it does demonstrate the way in which the information which people receive moulds and changes their views over a longer period, but how would it work during an election campaign? Who would choose the topic to be debated? Who would be invited to give their views? In theory, at least, it might help to focus the minds of ordinary people on the key issues of the day over and above the simplicities of tabloid headlines, television soundbites and stage-managed photo opportunities in ways which accord rather more with the precepts of democratic idealism. It also makes explicit the link between television and politics which has been a key development since 1945, and it does hold out the possibility of providing a genuine 'plebiscitary' element to an opinion poll, which is only ever fitfully achieved through ordinary polls which act more as the 'echo chamber' of media and personal prejudices than the outcome of rational debate.

In this context, the original aims of George Gallup could be more nearly realised in a world of deliberative polling. His aim of replicating the direct democracy of a New England town meeting via representative opinion polls was grounded in the democratic idealism of freeing ordinary people from the tyranny of small cliques via a 'continuous audit' of the actions of governments. The deliberative opinion poll makes an attempt to come to terms with the central problem of opinion polling: the results are regarded as the voice of the people but this voice often articulates demonstrable ignorance and a widespread lack of attention and understanding.

Why should ordinary people be expected to respond knowledgeably to detailed questions on Britain's role in Europe, whether Tony Blair is making a good leader of the Labour Party or whether opting out would be the best solution for hospitals or schools? In terms of harsh reality, the 'don't knows' would form the majority 'opinion' on all of these questions (except perhaps the second) but the polls try very hard to minimise this group of respondents in order to sell their services to clients who want a story. To admit that most people do not have considered views on many topics of interest to the media or politicians would be to reveal a central and destructive idea that would inevitably lead to the demise of opinion polling, a concept whose aims were laudable but whose practices were inherently limited and constrained by their respondents.

Can we ever expect polls to 'liberate' ordinary people from the tyranny of small but powerful cliques in politics? It seems unlikely since ordinary people do not set the questions but simply answer them, they have no real influence on the issues on the political agenda and they react to a framework which they have not devised but which they have to accept. Anyone who attempts to stand outside this definition of modern mass politics is seen as an eccentric or someone who does not 'understand' the real world. From this perspective, polls provide a means of power which is hard to measure but which is undeniable in its consequences for framing politics in a specific way which acts as the major and accepted reference point for debates and decisions. The actual influence of ordinary people on this process, which polls simultaneously both measure and shape, is usually hard to discern.

The future for the polls lies in the greater development of more subtle and detailed questions, an extended willingness to consider the impact of the 'don't know' response and a constant insistence on qualifying for media clients the story the poll is telling, in particular by downplaying the 'horse race' aspect of the poll results. This will undoubtedly be difficult to achieve, given the predilection of much of the media for an easy story and an unqualified interpretation. However, the polling firms must attempt to do this since they will then be able to rebut the claims more easily that gauging public opinion via polls is 'about as scientific as looking at the entrails of a chicken', as Jim Sillars, the former SNP Member of Parliament, memorably put it after the 1992 general election.

The polling firms can always be confident that their work will continue to play a major role in the reporting of election campaigns because there is no empirical alternative. In addition, polling sceptics in the media are unlikely to maintain their resolve not to use poll material when an election news broadcast or a print deadline looms before them. The poll figures might appear dubious but they will always produce a story.

One problem which the polling firms will always have to face is the potential capriciousness of the voters. The number of voters who deliberately lie or mislead the interviewers is probably very small indeed – a handful in most samples; more important, however, particularly in a close race, will be the group of 'fickle hypocrites' who say one thing to an interviewer and then do the opposite at the moment of truth in the polling booth. The current experiments being carried out by the polling firms appear to be having some impact in reducing the impact of this group on the division of the party vote shares. Perhaps the British electorate is inherently self-interested in its attitudes to politics, although the comment in the *Sunday Telegraph* of 12 April 1992 that 'all democratic electorates are two-faced, the British peculiarly so' seems unduly acerbic.

Opinion polls are largely made up of opinions, but it is also clear that some of those opinions are largely made up. The task of the opinion pollsters in the future is to confront this problem squarely and not to fall prey to their own 'spiral of silence' in the face of sometimes vitriolic but often unfocused criticism. Fortunately, this seems unlikely, if only because unless a return to crystal ball gazing or bookmakers' odds is envisaged, the polls will remain central aspects of modern political reporting. The problems and challenges which we have set out in this book do not serve to invalidate that key claim.

Indeed, there is little doubt that, even given the alleged 'debacle' of the 1992 general election, the polls will be back at the next general election much as before. They remain the 'least worst' way of finding out what is happening out there in the wider political world. Politicians and the media will always be concerned with such developments and the polls permit them to both measure and interpret mass opinion as it develops and changes.

However imperfect polls may be, they will retain the status of an indispensable tool whose performance at elections is undoubtedly an important aspect of their value. Nevertheless, in a world of ever-increasing amounts of information, polls possess even greater value by providing a potentially vital source of information for ordinary people. The value of that information is firmly anchored in the fact that poll results are largely free from the machinations and manipulations of politicians and their self-interested definition of the prevailing state of public opinion. In this way, polls, at their best, can perform significant roles in a liberal democracy by acting as sources of information which clarify an often blurred and confusing political picture. For ordinary voters, untainted and genuinely independent polls are therefore vital in providing a substantial counterweight to any narrow and exclusionary interpretation of the current state of British politics.

Reference

Fishkin, J. (1991) *Democracy and Deliberation: New directions for democratic reform*, New Haven: Yale University Press.

Appendix I

Glossary of technical terms used in polling

agenda setting   a concept much used in work on the mass media. It is suggested that television, radio and the press do not simply report events but, rather, set agendas in that they select particular issues for discussion in particular ways by particular people. Through this process of selection, certain issues or points of view are excluded from debate.

attitude   a relatively stable system of beliefs concerning an object and resulting in an evaluation of that object. How attitudes are measured exactly is a critical debate, particularly if we want to predict someone's behaviour. Some argue that attitudes tell us little or nothing about behaviour and that the use of methods such as participant observation or qualitative research are better approaches to assessing the attitudes of ordinary people.

attitude scale   attitude scales consist of sets of standardised statements with which respondents are asked to either agree or disagree. Scaling assumes that an attitude will have various aspects that together will constitute the attitude being measured. The intensity or strength with which people hold the various aspects of the attitudes is measured by rating scales for each item, often by asking them how much they agree with each statement (often on a five-point scale running from 'strongly agree' to 'strongly disagree'). Attitude scales produce a single score for each individual respondent constructed out of the many items contained in the questionnaire in order that each respondent can be placed somewhere along an attitude continuum.

baseline sample the original sample on which a panel survey is based.

bias systematic error or bias is the difference between the 'true' value of a characteristic and the average value obtained by repeated investigations. Any discrepancy between the true value and the obtained value in a single investigation is the sum of two factors: bias and sampling error. This assumes that there is indeed a 'true' value. Some would argue that these values are not independent of the measuring process being used: for example, it is often argued that the gender or race of the interviewer will affect the responses given by an interviewee.

CAPI computer-assisted personal interviewing. The questions are programmed into a personal computer which the interviewer uses to put the questions. This means that the order of the questions is set by the computer software and question filtering is performed automatically. The responses are entered straight onto the computer and this saves time by cutting out the extra data entry stage after the interviews are completed. As a result, the data analysis can begin almost immediately.

case study the detailed examination of a single example of a particular phenomenon, often as a preliminary to more extensive investigation, sometimes in a comparative context. Case studies often provide a great deal of detail that is difficult to get from surveys focused at a broader level but they are difficult to generalise from.

CATI computer-assisted telephone interviewing. Similar to CAPI (see above) in terms of the interviewer entering the answers straight onto the computer and the next question being provided automatically depending on the response entered.

causal explanation when one state of affairs is said to bring about another. Causal explanations in social research are problematic because it is very difficult to set up an experimental procedure with proper control groups as in the physical sciences. This idea assumes that humans are like natural objects; however, the actions of humans are partially determined by meanings and contexts which they themselves give to their world and events within it.

causal modelling   in a complex and inter-related political world, it is often important to attempt to understand the causal connections between a number of variables simultaneously, yet it is impossible to do this under experimental conditions which would permit precise specifications for the effects of the variables upon one another. It is generally the case that poll data provide correlations rather than causation links. Causal modelling is the generic title for a set of statistical techniques that enable the researcher to specify the causal linkages among the correlations. These techniques include regression analysis and path analysis. Various assumptions have to be made in terms of a model of the linkages in advance of the testing of the model. These techniques are most commonly used on large and detailed data sets with thousands of cases.

census   a regular collection of demographic, economic and social data about all the people within the boundaries of a country. Censuses are designed to produce lots of information about such topics as industrial production, housing and occupational structures.

closed-ended question   a question for which the respondent chooses from a list of possible responses given to them by the interviewer or marked on the questionnaire.

clustering   a means of selecting those to be interviewed in two or more stages, where the first stage selects a number of geographical areas (i.e. constituencies or polling districts) and then individuals are selected from within those areas.

coding   the process of translating raw research data into a form which can be used in computer calculations. The process classifies the data into distinct categories and then each category is assigned a numerical value.

control group   a control group is matched as closely as possible on the relevant variables with an experimental group. The experimental group is then exposed to an independent variable whose effects are being investigated. The control group is not, however, exposed to this variable. Any differences which are found between the two groups are then attributed to the effects of the independent variable. In this way it is possible to separate out the effect of one variable as opposed to another.

correlation   if one variable provides information about another variable, the variables are said to be associated or correlated. A positive correlation means that the values of the two variables tend to increase or decrease together, whilst a negative correlation is where the value of one variable increases whilst the other decreases. There are a variety of sorts of correlation coefficient, but they all measure the strength of association between two or more variables. The fact that two variables are correlated does not mean that one causes the other or that they are causally related at all, since both may be caused by a third variable.

cross-sectional poll   observations of a new representative sample collected at a particular point in time. In contrast, a longitudinal poll involves the collecting of data over a series of time points, say, a period of years.

cross-tabulation   a common way of presenting data in two-way tables which relate the values of one variable to those of another. The purpose of cross-tabulating variables is to test the association the variables have with one another. It is then possible to elaborate the analysis by including further variables to see if the relationship between the first two variables is the same for the various categories of the third variable. The third variable acts as the control variable in such an analysis.

dependent variable   the phenomenon that is caused by something else; the behaviour or attitude that is to be explained, e.g. voting intention.

don't knows   a respondent who does not give a definite answer to a question. In terms of voting intention, this might, however, be three separate groups: (1) those who fail to nominate a preferred party, who are undecided how to vote; (2) those who say they will not vote; and (3) those who refuse to say how they will vote. Sometimes, however, the term is used to denote only the 'undecided' respondents.

empiricism the testing of theories by drawing upon a variety of evidence drawn from experience. Often criticised on the grounds that theory is downgraded in the process, and the inherent difficulties of the gathering of reliable data due to technical and measurement problems.

hypothesis a prediction derived from theoretical analysis that is formulated in a form which is precise enough to be subjected to testing against empirical data. The testing leads to modification of the original hypothesis often in the light of new data or even the abandonment of the hypothesis in favour of an alternative theory which better fits the data. The word 'hypothesis' is often used more loosely to mean suggestion or explanation.

hypothesis testing the development and use of statistical criteria to help in deciding on the validity of a hypothesis under uncertain conditions. Hypothesis testing is concerned with evaluating the criteria that minimise the likelihood of making wrong inferences.

independent variable the variable that is assumed to be part of the explanation or the cause of the dependent variable, e.g. social class, age, gender or educational level attained.

index the combining of a number of variables into a composite measure or indicator which is then expressed as a single score for each respondent. Index can also refer to an indicator that is not measured directly.

interaction between variables a situation where two or more independent variables interact together to influence the dependent variable. Interaction means that the effect of one of the independent variables is not the same for every category of another independent variable.

intervening variable   a situation where variable A mediates the effect of variable B on variable C.

interview   interviews may be formal, structured and standardised, or informal, with the interviewer able to follow up the responses made by the respondent. Interviews can provide either quantitative or qualitative data or both. Worries have long been expressed about the 'reality' of the interview situation and the typicality of the respondent's answers and behaviour. An interview is not a neutral relationship and responses may well be affected by perceptions of the interviewer and expectations about the 'right' or appropriate reply to certain sensitive questions on topics such as abortion or homosexuality.

model   an abstract way of presenting the links between social phenomena. Models are devices to simplify and aid understanding of the essential nature of social mechanisms. Formal models are those in which the relationships and links are expressed mathematically.

multivariate analysis   statistical techniques enabling the testing of several variables simultaneously, involving the analysis of relationships between a dependent variable and several independent variables using techniques such as regression, cluster analysis and path analysis.

non-response   when some of the sample refuse to co-operate with the interviewer by answering the questions. This has important implications for the representativeness of the sample if the non-respondents are different in some relevant way from those who do respond.

open-ended question   the respondents can answer the question in their own way, using their own words and ideas.

operationalisation   the providing of a means of measuring and quantifying a concept so that it can be tested. Scales have been devised to test for a wide range of factors, such as alienation. A main argument focuses upon the value and use of concepts that cannot be operationalised in this way.

panel attrition   the gradual loss of panel members over time so that, in later waves of interviewing of the panel study, the number of respondents included is lower than at the start. The factors that lead to attrition (unwillingness to continue to take part or inability to be contacted on repeated occasions) are not random, and so there may well be consequent problems with the subsequent representativeness and reliability of the panel.

panel survey   sometimes called a longitudinal study, this involves the collection of data from the same people at different times. Panels are used in particular for studying trends and the effects of changes over a specified time period, such as an election campaign. It may be difficult to get people to commit themselves to giving repeated interviews. Panel conditioning is a problem, as the members of the panel become unrepresentative because of the very fact that they are members of the panel. Each individual set of interviews in the series is often called a wave of interviewing.

population   all possible observations of a certain phenomenon in statistical analysis: for example, incomes of all residents of a particular country. It is usually necessary on grounds of cost and time to take a sample of the population of interest and to generalise about the incomes of all citizens from the sample.

probability   the likelihood of a particular uncertain event occurring measured on a scale from 0.0 (impossible) to 1.0 (certain). Probability is usually measured on the basis of the relative frequency with which an event has occurred in the past under certain circumstances. In the long run, for example, we would get 50 per cent heads and 50 per cent tails when tossing a coin. However, it is usually more difficult than this in social science to calculate the probability of events taking place.

probability sample   another name for a random sample.

public opinion   the collecting of the opinions of people on topics of public interest and the subsequent analyses of these by statistical techniques using a sample of the population in question.

qualitative analysis   analyses which are not quantitative but are based on other methods, such as participant observation. Such methods do not necessarily involve any measuring or counting of particular forms of behaviour. Historical analysis might not be possible on the basis of quantitative requirements.

questionnaire   a set of questions given to respondents with the aim of eliciting information relevant to the research topic under investigation.

quota sample   a type of sample in which the interviewer selects respondents himself or herself in proportion to the relative size of each sub-group within the total population. Quota samples are frequently used in market research, opinion polls and other statistical surveys because they are generally quicker and cheaper than random samples. The interviewer is free to choose any person to interview within the confines of a sub-division of the population into pre-determined sub-groups whose sizes reflect the proportion that they comprise. For example, an interviewer might be told to interview within a specific area and to obtain ten interviews comprising five with men and five with women, and of those people, three within the top social grades (A/B), four in the C1/C2 social grades and three in the D/E social grades. The overall intention is to obtain a sample that is representative of the most important sub-divisions of the population.

random sample   a sample selected by chance in which every item in the population has an equal chance of being included. This protects against bias in the selection process and also provides a basis on which to apply the statistical distribution theory that allows an estimate to be made of the probability that the conclusions drawn from the sample are correct. Interviewers are required to contact a pre-determined list of people or visit a list of pre-set addresses.

reliability   the extent to which research findings can be replicated by means of a particular research method under similar conditions. Similar results will be produced under similar circumstances if a method is reliable, within the limits of statistical or random variation. Reliability errors arise from interviewer effects, question order, transcription and data entry mistakes.

respondent a person who is interviewed for and contributes answers to an opinion poll or survey.

rogue poll a poll whose results appear to be out of line with others through a statistical chance. All samples are dependent on probabilities and the law of averages means that occasionally there will be a freak sample that falls outside the normal margins of error.

sample any part of a total group (often called the population) that can be analysed in order to make inferences about the total group without the difficulty and expense of undertaking a complete census of all the population.

sampling error sample estimates are always subject to sampling error since single samples cannot be wholly accurate representations of the population under investigation. Repetitive sampling would average out the inevitable fluctuations and thus provide a true representation. The degree of sampling error can, however, be estimated from a single sample and thus we can work out confidence levels and significance tests. Sampling errors will tend to be largest if samples are small or the population has a high degree of variability within it.

sampling frame a list of the relevant population, such as the electoral register. Selection is often performed by using a table of random numbers, although simply taking the nth name from the list is also often adequate.

secondary analysis the re-analysis of existing data sets rather than the designing of a new questionnaire and collecting of new data. The main problem is the usually different aims and preferences of the secondary analyst when compared to the aims of the original collectors of the data in terms of the questions asked and the variables and indices constructed.

social grade a schema used for classifying the population by occupation of the head of the household, widely used in opinion polling and market research.

statistical inference a process of inferring conclusions about a population from which only a sample has been drawn. It is usually too expensive and time-consuming to try and ask every member of a population the required questions and so the probability that their answers are the same as in the total population can be inferred statistically via calculations of probability and hypothesis testing.

stratified samples a sample that is selected by dividing the total population into a number of distinct sub-groups and then selecting a proportionate number of respondents from each sub-group.

survey research involving the systematic gathering of information about individuals and collectivities, using interviews and questionnaires to elicit information directly and then interpreting the resultant data by means of various statistical techniques. The purpose of conducting a survey may be descriptive or more complex causal analysis and modelling.

swing a summary measure of net change in support for two parties.

switchers those who change their stated voting intention in the repeated interviews of a panel study.

time series data that are ordered in time, typically at regular intervals, comprise a time series. Censuses and panel studies are the commonest examples of time series data.

tracking poll a series of polls, usually cross-sectional in nature, which are designed to track changes in attitudes to a particular question or theme over time.

validity the degree to which an indicator or variable actually measures the underlying concept which it is supposed to be measuring. A poll question may therefore be very reliable but simultaneously invalid because it is not asking about the right thing.

variable a term that can take a range of numerical values.

weighting   a mathematical adjustment of the survey or poll results, making the answers of some respondents 'count' for more than others' in order to correct for imperfections in the sample. For example, if the sample only contains 10 per cent of council tenants and it is known that the actual figure from the census should be 18 per cent, then the council tenant group is 'weighted up' to 18 per cent in the analyses so that the correct balance within the housing variable is actually obtained. In this way, each council tenant's response would be given a value of 18/10 when the total sample is constituted. It is possible to weight by a number of variables at the same time, although this is more complex and needs to be performed with care. All the calculations are done by computer, of course!

Appendix II

Sample questions taken from polls

Voting intention
Taken from the final polls before the 1992 general election. The main question is first, with the follow-up in parentheses to 'squeeze' an answer from the undecided respondents.

> For which party do you intend to vote in the forthcoming general election? (Which party are you most inclined to support?) (Harris)
>
> How likely is it that you will go and vote in the general election? If you vote, which party would you support? (Which party would you be most inclined to vote for?) (Gallup)
>
> In the general election tomorrow, which party will you vote for? (Which party will you be most likely to vote for?) (ICM)
>
> How do you intend to vote at the general election on 9 April? (Which party are you most inclined to support?) (MORI)
>
> What party will you vote for in the general election? (Which party would you be most inclined to support?) (NOP)

The final report to the Market Research Society, from which the above questions have been taken, concluded that the slightly different question formulations above were unlikely to have made a difference to the polls of the different organisations.
Source: Market Research Society (1994: 99).

Voting intention in a non-election period

If there were a general election tomorrow, which party would you support? (Gallup)

If there was a general election tomorrow, which party would you vote for? (ICM)

Party identification

Generally speaking, do you think of yourself as Conservative, Labour, Liberal Democrat, Nationalist or what? (If 'None'/ 'Don't know') Do you generally think of yourself as a little closer to one of the parties than the others? (If 'Yes': Which party?)

Would you call yourself very strong (PARTY), fairly strong, or not very strong?

Response categories: Very strong, Fairly strong, Not very strong, Don't know.

Party leaders

Are you satisfied or dissatisfied with Mr Major as prime minister?

Response categories: Satisfied, Dissatisfied, Don't know.

Do you think that Mr Blair is or is not proving a good leader of the Labour Party?

Response categories: Is, Is not, Don't know.

The 'feel good' factor

How do you think the financial situation of your household will change over the next twelve months?

Response categories: (1) Get a lot better; (2) Get a little better; (3) Stay the same; (4) Get a little worse; (5) Get a lot worse; (6) Don't know.

The 'feel good' factor is calculated by adding responses 1 and 2 together and then subtracting the sum of the categories 4 and 5.

Other questions

Generally speaking, do you think that Britain's membership of the Common Market is a good thing, a bad thing or neither good nor bad?

Response categories: Good thing, Bad thing, Neither good nor bad, Don't know.

On the whole, are you very satisfied, fairly satisfied, not very satisfied or not at all satisfied with the way democracy works in this country?

Response categories: Very satisfied, Fairly satisfied, Not very satisfied, Not at all satisfied, Don't know.

There used to be a lot of talk in politics about a 'class struggle'. Do you think there is a class struggle in this country or not?

Response categories: Is, Is not, Don't know.

In political matters, people talk of 'the left' and 'the right'. How would you place your views on this scale?

Response categories: Far left, Substantially left, Moderately left, Slightly left, Slightly right, Moderately right, Substantially right, Far right, Don't know.
For the above question, the extra category of 'middle of the road' was used by about 10 per cent of the respondents in Gallup polls between 1991 and 1994.

Do you agree or disagree with the following statement: 'The Conservatives these days give the impression of being very sleazy and disreputable'?

Response categories: Agree, Disagree, Don't know.

Suppose a Labour government were formed under Mr Tony Blair. Which of these three statements would come closest to your own reaction?

Response categories: Would be delighted, Would be dismayed, Wouldn't mind, Don't know.

Which, if any, of these phrases more applies to Mr Blair?
    Caring/Uncaring
    Tough/Not tough
    Can be trusted/Cannot be trusted
    Decisive/Indecisive
    Likeable as a person/Not likeable as a person
    Able to unite the nation/Not able to unite the nation

NOP poll for *The Independent* and BBC's *Newsnight*, published in *The Independent*, 20 and 27 September 1994

(To Labour and Liberal Democrat supporters)
Some people say that Labour and the Liberal Democrats should do a deal so that in some constituencies one party would stand down where the other has the best chance of beating the Conservatives. Other people say that both Labour and the Liberal Democrats should fight every seat so that voters have the widest choice. Do you think the two parties should . . . ?

Response categories: (1) Do a deal? (2) Should they both fight every seat? (3) Don't know.

(ALL RESPONDENTS)
These days, would you say there are big differences or only small differences between the policies of (a) the Labour Party and the Liberal Democrats (b) the Conservatives and the Liberal Democrats (c) Labour and the Conservatives?

Response categories: (1) Big differences; (2) Small differences; (3) Don't know.

Do you agree with the following statements?
    A vote for the Liberal Democrats is a wasted vote.

I would seriously consider voting for the Liberal Democrats if I thought they stood a chance of winning.
It is hard to know what the Liberal Democrats stand for these days.
A strong contra party is needed to fight extremism in the other parties.
Labour has made big changes for the better in recent years.
Whatever Tony Blair says, a Labour government would be run by the trade unions.
It is hard to know what Labour stands for these days.

Response categories: Agree, Disagree, Neither/Don't know.

Do you think there would be more unemployment under Labour than under the Conservatives or less unemployment or about the same?

Response categories: More, Less, About the same.

Do you think the economy would be stronger under Labour, or weaker, or about the same?

Response categories: Stronger, Weaker, About the Same.

Do you think standards of health care in the NHS would be higher or lower or about the same?

Response categories: Higher, Lower, About the same.

Do you think Britain would get a better deal from the rest of the European Community, or a worse deal or about the same?

Response categories: Better, Worse, About the same.

Specialist questions put to specialist groups of the population: University lecturers

Which party has the best education policies?

Response categories: nominated party.

Do you approve or disapprove of a four-term year?

Response categories: Approve, Disapprove, Don't know.

Do you approve or disapprove of concentrating research in a small number of universities?

Response categories: Approve, Disapprove, Don't know.

Do you think the following changes can be improved upon, whether they are all right or whether they need to be replaced by something else?
  (1) Doubling student participation in higher education.
  (2) Competitive bidding by institutions for extra students.
  (3) Ending of the distinction between polytechnics and universities.

Response categories: Improved upon, All right, Needs to be replaced, Don't know.
  Source: ICM poll for the *Times Higher Education Supplement*, published in the *THES*, 27 March 1992.

Conservative voters in 1992 who live in the seats of the nine Tory rebels who lost the party whip in late 1994

Your MP did not support the government in the Commons vote on contributions to the European Union. Do you think he/she was right or wrong?

Response categories: Right, Wrong, Don't know.

Do you think the whip should be restored to your MP?

Response categories: Restored immediately, Restored after shown some loyalty to government, Not restored at all, Don't know.

How do you rate Mr Major as prime minister?

Response categories: Satisfied, Dissatisfied, Don't know.

Would you prefer closer links between the EU (Common Market) countries?

Response categories: Closer links, Looser links, Stay as they are, Don't know.
Source: MORI poll for the *Mail on Sunday*, published 8 January 1995.

Senior Managers of City Financial Institutions

When do you think economic and monetary union for all members is likely to come about?

Response categories: By 1997, By 1999/2000, By 2005, By 2010, Don't know when, Never, Don't know.

Do you think EMU, if within the next ten years, is likely to have a direct effect on the profitability of your firm?

Response categories: Yes, No, Don't know.

Do you expect EMU to affect business opportunities for the City– or will it have no effect?

Response categories: Increase, Decline, No effect, Don't know.
Source: Harris poll reported in *The Independent*, 9 January 1995.

Appendix III

The polling experience

For anyone who has read this book and is still sceptical about whether polls actually take place, the following should be instructive. Whilst I was in the process of writing the final version of this book, I was approached to take part in a survey which involved viewing an advertisement for W.H. Smith's Do-It-All chain of DIY stores.

Initially, I refused (somewhat guiltily) to take part when approached, since I was heading home, but I allowed myself to be persuaded by the interviewer, who assured me that it would not take long and that I would probably be interested in the questions. I also saw an opportunity to test some of the ideas of this book at first hand.

We went into a specially equipped room at the local library, where a series of video machines and headphones were ready. The male interviewer noted my gender and then asked me some basic questions about my name and address, age and occupation, but not about my income (not even on a showcard). All the screens were occupied and so he made me a cup of coffee whilst we waited. A place soon became free and I sat down to view five brief television advertisements, which included the Do-It-All advertisement in the middle. The other four were vaguely familiar. They had all been on television before, I think. They were advertisements for Asda, Cadbury's Boost, Halifax Building Society (I have forgotten the last one!), presumably to sensitise me to advertisements before we got onto my view of the Do-It-All one.

I was then given a series of showcards to express my views on the advertisements. The questions asked after clarity, interest and memorability of the product being advertised. I was also asked if I had ever watched BSkyB, which was cleverly slipped into the middle of the questions. I was then asked to watch the Do-It-All advertisement again and to register my feelings by moving a lever to the left or the right or leave it in the centre. It was explained that moving to the left signified that the part of the advertisement was boring, to the right, that it was interesting and no movement meant that my feelings were neutral. The lever was linked to a computer which would map the movements of the lever as the advertisement progressed. I asked what this particular process was called and was told that it was called 'tracking'. It is more commonly known as 'people metering'.

I was asked to watch the advertisement twice, since the first run-through was to practise using the lever to register my feelings. At the end, the advertisement was shown for a third time and I was asked to point to the screen with a stick to show where I was looking when the advertisement was stopped near the end. I duly did this. I was then thanked and offered a gift of a notepad or bookmark emblazoned with the name of the polling organisation carrying out the research. I was also given a leaflet produced by the Market Research Society which explained the purpose of such research and invited me to ring a freephone number to check on the credentials of the polling firm. I duly did this and was reassured that they were a proper firm who were conducting their research under the MRS code of conduct.

Polls of various sorts and involving different approaches and techniques are taking place all the time. The fact that you have never been asked only means that you have not been in the right (wrong?) place at the appropriate time. Your chance will come, although I would not advise you to hold your breath! Taking part in a poll or survey is often interesting and most people are flattered that their opinions are being sought. If you get a chance to take part, please do so. It will probably be fun and it will give me an excuse to write another edition of this book in due course!

General bibliography

There are four main series of books which include material on various aspects of opinion polling in Britain.

The first series is the Nuffield College studies by David Butler and various collaborators for every British general election since 1951. The second is the *Britain at the Polls* series, beginning in 1974. The third is the *Political Communications* series for every general election since 1979. The fourth is the *British Elections and Parties Yearbook*, published annually from 1991 onwards.

There are, in addition, a number of useful guides to various elections published by ITN and *The Guardian*, for example, as well as *The Times Guide to the House of Commons* for all the post-war elections.

Nuffield series

D. Butler, *The British General Election of 1951*, London: Macmillan, 1952.

D. Butler, *The British General Election of 1955*, London: Macmillan, 1955.

D. Butler and R. Rose, *The British General Election of 1959*, London: Macmillan, 1960.

D. Butler and A. King, *The British General Election of 1964*, London: Macmillan, 1965.

D. Butler and A. King, *The British General Election of 1966*, London: Macmillan, 1967.

D. Butler and M. Pinto-Duschinsky, *The British General Election of 1970*, London: Macmillan, 1971.

D. Butler and D. Kavanagh, *The British General Election of February 1974*, London: Macmillan, 1975.

D. Butler and D. Kavanagh, *The British General Election of October 1974*, London: Macmillan, 1975.

D. Butler and D. Kavanagh, *The British General Election of 1979*, London: Macmillan, 1980.

D. Butler and D. Kavanagh, *The British General Election of 1983*, London: Macmillan, 1984.

D. Butler and D. Kavanagh, *The British General Election of 1987*, London: Macmillan, 1988.

D. Butler and D. Kavanagh, *The British General Election of 1992*, London: Macmillan, 1992.

Britain at the Polls series

H. Penniman (ed.) *Britain at the Polls: The parliamentary elections of 1974*, Washington, DC: American Enterprise Institute for Public Policy Research, 1975.

H. Penniman (ed.) *Britain at the Polls, 1979: A study of the general election*, Washington, DC: American Enterprise Institute for Public Policy Research, 1981.

A. Ranney (ed.) *Britain at the Polls 1983: A study of the general election*, Durham, NC: Duke University Press, 1985.

A. King, I. Crewe, P. Norton, P. Seyd, D. Denver, K. Newton and D. Sanders, *Britain at the Polls 1992*, Chatham, NJ: Chatham House, 1993.

Political Communications series

R. Worcester and M. Harrop (eds) *Political Communications: The general election campaign of 1979*, London: Allen and Unwin, 1982, especially part four (chapters 10–14) on the polls and psephology.

I. Crewe and M. Harrop (eds) *Political Communications: The general election campaign of 1983*, Cambridge: Cambridge

University Press, 1986, especially part six (chapters 20–2) on opinion polls and the media in 1983. See also the chapter by Paul Whiteley (chapter 26) on the accuracy and influence of the polls in the 1983 general election.

I. Crewe and M. Harrop (eds) *Political Communications and the British General Election of 1987*, Cambridge: Cambridge University Press, 1989, especially part seven (chapters 20–1) on opinion polls in the 1987 campaign by Pippa Norris and Robert Waller.

I. Crewe and B. Gosschalk (eds) *Political Communications and the British General Election of 1992*, Cambridge: Cambridge University Press, 1995, especially part five on the opinion polls in the campaign (chapters 14–18).

British Parties and Election Yearbook

I. Crewe, P. Norris, D. Denver and D. Broughton (eds) *British Parties and Elections Yearbook 1991*, Hemel Hempstead: Harvester Wheatsheaf, 1991.

P. Norris, I. Crewe, D. Denver and D. Broughton (eds) *British Parties and Elections Yearbook 1992*, Hemel Hempstead: Harvester Wheatsheaf, 1992, especially chapter by Moon on exit polling.

D. Denver, P. Norris, D. Broughton and C. Rallings (eds) *British Parties and Elections Yearbook 1993*, Hemel Hempstead: Harvester Wheatsheaf, 1993, especially chapter by Heath, Jowell, Curtice and Clifford on late swing at the 1992 general election.

D. Broughton, D.M. Farrell, D. Denver and C. Rallings (eds) *British Parties and Elections Yearbook 1994*, London: Frank Cass, 1994, especially chapter by Farrell, McAllister and Broughton on campaign volatility since 1964.

C. Rallings, D.M. Farrell, D. Broughton and D. Denver (eds) *British Elections and Parties Yearbook 1995*, London: Frank Cass, 1995, especially chapter by Curtice on the MRS report into the opinion polls and the 1992 general election.

Additional useful sources

Abrams, M. (1963) 'Public opinion polls and political parties', *Public Opinion Quarterly* 27: 9–18.

Abrams, M. (1964) 'Opinion polls and party propaganda', *Public Opinion Quarterly* 28: 13–19.

Crewe, I. (1990) 'Matters of opinion', *Social Studies Review* 6: 47–52.

Crewe, I. (1992) 'A nation of liars? Opinion polls and the 1992 election', *Parliamentary Affairs* 45: 475–95.

A. Heath, R. Jowell and J. Curtice (1985) *How Britain Votes*, Oxford: Pergamon.

A. Heath, J. Curtice, R. Jowell, G. Evans, J. Field and S. Witherspoon (1991) *Understanding Political Change*, Oxford: Pergamon.

A. Heath, R. Jowell and J. Curtice with B. Taylor (1994) *Labour's Last Chance*, Aldershot: Dartmouth.

International Journal of Public Opinion Research, 4:3, Autumn 1992. Public Opinion Polling: Critical Perspectives.

R. Jowell, B. Hedges, P. Lynn, G. Farrant and A. Heath (1993) 'The 1992 British election: The failure of the polls', *Public Opinion Quarterly* 57: 238–63.

E. Noelle-Neumann (1993) *The Spiral of Silence. Public Opinion – Our Social Skin*, 2nd edn, Chicago: University of Chicago Press.

Index

Note: emboldened page references indicate glossary definitions. Most references are to public opinion polling, which is therefore often omitted as a qualifier.